d

Baggy Trousers on the Camino de Santiago

To Karen

Best wishes

Paula Rooney

Paula Rooney

Fortis

First Edition 2023

ISBN-13: 978-1-913822-54-5

Acknowledgements

Thank you to everyone who bought a copy of *I hope there's a kettle in my room*. If it wasn't for the success of my first book, there simply wouldn't be a second book.

Thank you to everyone who has left lovely reviews, messaged me, and enjoyed my book. I hope you enjoy this one just as much.

Huge thanks to Phil Rowse, my other half, for his artwork that was used for the cover; it captures the Meseta perfectly. It's also particularly poignant to have a combined piece of work: his art and my words. Thank you also for buying me the Brierley Camino book for Christmas, as without this, I wouldn't have gone on the Camino.

I want to thank my publishers, Fortis Publishing; they are such an amazing team of enthusiastic, professional, and very approachable people. They offered me endless support at every stage of the book writing journey.

Thanks particularly to Ken Scott and Reinette Visser for their continued support and availability at the end of my keyboard.

Special thanks to Dan for skillfully blending my concepts of the Meseta while maintaining the visual coherence with the cover of my first book.

Thank you to Emily Ould from Emily Charlotte Editorial Services for working so hard on the edit of this book.

Thank you to Cotswold Truro for their help and advice and allowing me to come in on several occasions to try the bag on before I committed to buying it. They never pushed me to buy anything, just offered me lots of advice. My bag was a great choice and choosing a bag to carry for 500 miles is a very important decision.

Thanks to every person whom I met on my Camino: the friends that I made, and every fellow walker, the hostel owners, and all the kind people whom I met along the way.

Huge thanks to Emma for her friendship, all the laughs and for taking the photos in Santiago. Her phone was much better than mine, and I am glad to have the photos, particularly the one on the back of the book.

About the Author

Paula Rooney was born in 1965 in Harlow, Essex, then spent several years in Ipswich, Suffolk before settling in St Austell Cornwall in 2001 to raise her family.

Journaling holidays started with the first family holiday to Cornwall when she was ten, followed by a trip to Scotland and another trip to Cornwall. When she was thirteen, her dad left the family for good, taking the car with him.

Then aged sixteen, her mum took them on a holiday to a caravan park at Burnham on Sea. Paula, her sister, her brother and her brother's friend, all went by bus, as her mother didn't drive. It was a big adventure and lots of fun.

This might have ignited her passion for travel and instilled a sense of adventure. If you don't have a car, you get a bus. If you don't know where you are, look at a map.

This is Paula's second travelogue.

Her first book, *I Hope There is a Kettle in my Room,* is also available on Amazon.

Facebook: PaulaRooneyAuthor You will find lots of photos to accompany both of my books.

Instagram: PaulaRooneyAuthor

Twitter: @PaulaRooneyAuth

TikTok: PaularooneyAuthor

Dedication

This book is dedicated to Emma Jarvis.

I didn't go on the Camino to make friends, but I am very grateful for having met Emma. We were both in sync with each other and instinctively knew when we wanted to walk together and when we needed to walk solo.

We both shared the same sense of humour and all the laughs we had certainly helped balance out the pain from the blisters.

Table of Contents

Prologue

Why did I walk the Camino de Santiago? It's a very good question and I don't have a straightforward answer.

It was honestly a case of 'Why not walk 500 miles across Spain?' rather than 'Why would anyone want to walk 500 miles across Spain?' They both sound similar but are complete opposites. It's a similar question to: 'Is the glass half full or is the glass half empty?' It's simply a perspective, an opinion and a way of thinking.

Once I knew there was a set walk across Spain, I couldn't think of a reason not to do it. I am lucky to have a flexible job that could spare me for seven weeks, that I could also manage without seven weeks of money coming in, and I had a partner who supported me. I don't have young children to care for, and my mum, although she is 80, is in very good health. So, there were very few obstacles to stop me walking the Camino, or walking anywhere, or going on any trip anywhere in the world.

What drew me to the Camino was a gift in the shape of a book, along with a desire to spend some time in Spain. I have spent many holidays in coastal Spain and I liked the idea of seeing the rural side of it, experiencing its culture, away from the neon signs and the tourists.

I am not religious, so I didn't walk the pilgrimage for religious reasons but, in a spiritual sense, I felt that my life had aligned so that I could go. It was more a question of telling myself, 'No one needs me right now, my own health is good, so I should just go. Now. Before any of that changes.'

Although my physical health was fine, my mental health had been poor for about a year before starting the Camino. Perhaps I should have gone to the doctor's to ask for support, but I am stubborn and independent. I thought I could work it out on my own, like I have always done. With the Camino, there was an element of stepping away from everything, so that I could take a closer look at life, and re-evaluate it. Going on a trip also meant that I didn't have to do this thing called 'life'. I got a break from it, and I really needed a break.

My life hasn't been an easy one, with three children very close together in age and an abusive marriage. Even though the difficult times are way behind me now, the effects of trauma don't just evaporate. They hang around and affect you day-to-day. It's good to take stock of what you have been through, acknowledge what it did to you and work out how to live the rest of your life in as much harmony as you can. The Camino gives you the time to think all this through.

I had no idea if anything in me would shift, if I would feel better or worse. Would seven weeks on my own pick me up, or pull me down?

But I did have a very strong sense that I wanted to give it a try. I am eternally grateful that I was able to 'walk' the Camino. It is a 500 mile walk but it's also 500 miles of life, 500 miles of living, 500 miles of digging deep and 500 miles of joy.

It was a very special experience.

Plymouth, England to Spain

I am 57 years old, a little bit overweight, and I have an old injury from breaking my ankle on the South West coastal path. I haven't trained as much as I planned to, because I worked a lot over the summer to put some pennies in the bank. But I am going to try and walk 500 miles on the Camino de Santiago, from St Jean Pied de Port to Santiago.

I didn't know what the Camino de Santiago was until Christmas Day last year. Most people who walk the Camino de Santiago have longed to do it for many years. That wasn't me, I had to look on a map to even see where Santiago was. So, this has not been a dream of mine, it wasn't even on my radar.

For Christmas 2021, my partner, Phil, bought me a book. I had mentioned to him that, if I went on another solo trip, I might get the ferry to Santander and wander around and practise my Spanish. On Christmas morning, I opened my gift, a book called *A Pilgrim's Guide to the Camino de Santiago (Camino Francés)* by John Brierley. Over a cup of tea, chilled on the sofa, and popping Quality Street into my mouth, I had a proper look at it. I discovered that it was a 500-mile walk with maps of the Spanish villages that you had to walk through.

So, I announced to Phil that I would walk 500 miles across Spain, as suggested in the book. He was surprised, as he hadn't fully understood what he had bought me. He thought it was a useful book of maps to help me navigate Northern Spain. He also said that next year he was going to be very careful about what he bought me for Christmas.

This is a pilgrimage and I think that makes me a pilgrim. I am not a religious person. I have my own views of religion and the universe, but they don't fall into any particular box. But I do like the idea of walking for a month across the Spanish countryside and finding some inner peace. I don't know if that's going to happen, or if it's possible, but I should enjoy the actual walking. It's probably the challenge that appeals to me. Can I do this?

I am certainly going to try.

Today, I am on the Pont Aven ferry crossing from Plymouth over to Spain, and the weather is bad. I am sitting in the fiesta lounge and, as I look out of the huge window at the front of the boat, the horizon dips up and down, making my tummy heave. Soon, the heavens open and it looks like we are in a giant car wash, with water crashing on the windows. Everyone around me is drinking red wine but the thought of alcohol is making me queasy. I decide to make it back to my room, if I can swagger across the floor safely enough.

My room is so cute. I was expecting bunk beds, but it's a miniature room, with my own tiny compact bathroom, where you could probably have a wee and shower at the same time. The floor is jittering like we are moving on stony ground, which we obviously aren't, but it's better than being out in the common areas.

This is not how I pictured my trip to Santander.

I almost fall asleep even though it's only 6.15 pm. It's mentally exhausting packing your luggage and preparing for an adventure that could last seven weeks. I suddenly feel very drained. The boat is shuddering and dipping up and down and I can't settle, so I decide to go out and investigate. This room doesn't have any windows, so I can't see or hear anything.

It's not like a scene from *Titanic*. The restaurant café is much fuller now with people eating and drinking. I seem to be the only one struggling with sickness, so I go back to my room and climb into bed.

Monday 5th September

On the Ferry

I woke up a lot in the night and, at one point, almost slid out of bed.

Now, I take my packed tin of fruit and nuts to the café and make a cup of tea in my bamboo cup, with loose green tea leaves and get hot water from the machine in the canteen. I settle myself at a table. The view is much better this morning, there's a clear distinction now between the sky and the horizon. We are well on our way to Spain. One lady nearby has a piercing accent that is cutting through me so, after finishing my breakfast, I go for a stroll around the ferry.

There are huge mountains framing Santander as we sail into the port. People are sunbathing on a spit of sand and it looks like paradise.

My anxiety is a little high as I zip up my rucksack in my tiny room. This is it now, I'll get off the ferry and have to find my way to France for the beginning of the walk. Do I have everything? Can I carry this amount of stuff for 500 miles? Do I have enough? Did I forget anything?

Passport control goes well at the port and I use Google Maps to find my way to Santander bus station. I try out my Spanish at the ticket office. I was going to Bilbao but the timings weren't right so I get a ticket to San Sebastian where I will stay for the night. It's a bit closer to the start of the walk and, hopefully, I will get to St Jean at a sensible time tomorrow. Then I can get some accommodation and a hot meal before I start the walk on Wednesday morning.

For now, I am sitting in the sunshine next to the bus station, eating rice crackers and hummus that should have been my tea last night if I hadn't felt so unwell. It feels amazing to be in Spain in the sunshine, such a contrast to the weather I left behind in Cornwall. It's also very different, as I am usually in a Spanish resort with my family, not sitting outside a bus station on my own with a rucksack.

This is a solo journey, another one of my adventures. I am so lucky that I get to do a second solo trip. A lot of people don't get to do any. This feels very different to my interrailing trip. It's going to be hard work, and slightly insane.

My interrail trip was life changing for me. When your life is devoted to your children, you lose sight of who you are, especially in a tricky marriage. I loved being a mum, so when my job was finished and they all flew the nest, I went interrailing on my own for a month. It opened the world up for me, I saw places that I had only seen on the TV. I navigated myself around Europe and got home safely. Not only did I have a great time, but I felt stronger and a little more confident and, perhaps, a little bit more interesting, which I think travel does for you.

When I wrote my experiences in my journal from this trip and published it, this opened another chapter of my life. My children, family and friends read it and were proud of me. Everyone, I imagine, was already proud of me, but they now had something tangible to hang it on. People who hadn't understood how difficult my marriage was were proud of me. It has opened difficult conversations with friends, family and others who have read my book. It has been a totally unexpected, and very positive experience.

The bus trip to San Sebastian goes well with beautifully tarmacked roads, making a swift, smooth ride past lots of mountains and green hills covered in pine trees. We arrive and go down a steep slope into an underground bus station. It's better lit than Bilbao which was very creepy. I am glad

I didn't have to get off the bus there as it was almost pitch black. Someone must have forgotten to put the lights on.

I get my bag from the storage section of the bus and surface into the daylight amid all the hustle and bustle.

The hostel is in a good spot. I put my bag in the locker and go straight out to explore. San Sebastian has a vast curved beach that I am lucky to see against a beautiful sunset across the bay. I then return to the hostel, grabbing some chips on the way.

Feeling shattered after a broken sleep last night on the ferry and a busy day travelling, I go to bed. There are two snorers. People coming and going, shutting the door, turning lights on. But I fall asleep quickly which is good, because this is going to be my life now for the next seven weeks.

Tuesday 6th September

San Sebastian to Bayonne

After cleaning my teeth, I go back to the room where I can see three men sound asleep on the bunk beds, with various hairy limbs exposed.

I collect all my stuff and go to the bus station. There's a 9.29 am and 9.59 am to Bayonne, where I need to transfer to a bus for St Jean. The Flix bus office is shut, as it was last night, so I go to the only ticket window that's open. The lady there tells me that the next bus is at 12.25 pm.

My heart sinks.

I should have sorted this out last night. But it was shut then as well. She says you can buy Flix bus tickets online. Drat, I probably could have done that last night if I had known.

I pause and think about what to do. I don't want to wait too long to buy that 12.25 pm ticket in case it sells out, but I want to look for a sooner one as well. I turn my data on and download the FlixBus app. The buses that I wanted are sold out as the lady said.

So, I go back and buy a ticket for the 12.25 pm bus. Now, I have three hours to explore. I don't fancy strolling around San Sebastian with my backpack on. Huge reality check: that's exactly what I am going to do for 500 miles.

Off I go to explore, backpack and all. It's a proper holiday resort, with everything from views of boats in the harbour to pretty houses and history. I wouldn't mind coming back here for a holiday one day. I pass a small open café, tempted to stop, but I have food with me and it's better that I eat what I have, rather than buy any more.

I find a bench under the trees in the shade as it's very hot, and I get out half a tin of fruit that I stored in a little plastic pot and add a handful of nuts that I have with me. In plenty of time, I go and wait for my bus to Bayonne, as I really hope I get to St Jean Pied de Port in good time. I am so excited to get there and start this adventure.

The Start

Tuesday 4th September

Bayonne to St Jean Pied de Port

The bus from Bayonne station in France is packed full of people with backpacks, walking poles and heaps of enthusiasm. I feel part of something, maybe something crazy, or something wonderful. I don't know right now. But I love the energy of these people and I am excited to be part of it.

We all pile off the bus in St Jean Pied de Port, eager to get to the Pilgrim's Office to register. I turn into the thin cobblestoned street on a steep hill. The pretty houses with window shutters and flowers all stagger at angles down the street. I can see a view of the mountains at the bottom of the hill. The street feels intimate, old, and historic. And today is a very important day for a lot of pilgrims.

I look up and down the hill, trying to work out where to go. Luckily there are plenty of people eager to tell me that it's up the hill on the left. And there it is, the queue of walkers spilling out of the Pilgrim's Office onto the street.

This is the beginning of my seven week adventure. After three days of travelling from Cornwall, here I am in France. I feel quite proud that I have got this far. It wasn't the most straightforward of destinations.

It's my turn to enter the office and I put my backpack on the floor next to others. There are tables to the left with five friendly faces. I wait to be seen and, as it's not a big room, I can hear every conversation. I learn before I get to sit down that today is a very busy day. If you haven't booked accommodation, then you might struggle to find somewhere. Oops. I didn't book anything because I wasn't sure I would even get here today, as I was in San Sebastian yesterday and very unsure of the buses. A lady at one of the tables tells a young lad that if he doesn't find anywhere to stay, then he can come back as they have a room with no showers or facilities but at least he won't be outside. Gosh, that's a harsh way to begin this journey.

When I sit down and say that I haven't booked any accommodation, she asks if I can afford €25 as the lady in the house next door has a bed. I take her up on her offer, even though it's a bit over my imaginary budget. I can't afford €25 every night for seven weeks but, today, it will save me an awful lot of time and hassle.

I get my *credencial* and the first stamp, a list of accommodation, and a daily plan of the recommended 33 stages to get to Santiago. The *credencial* is a piece of card with spaces on it for all the stamps that I need to collect along the way to qualify for my *Compostela* certificate in Santiago.

Am I really going to walk 500 miles to Santiago? I can't be crazy as there are lots of people here, all doing the same thing.

But it is crazy.

Maybe we are all crazy, maybe we are all bored of beach holidays, or we are all having a midlife crisis? Maybe we are all naive and have no idea what we have signed up for.

I am worried about carrying my bag. It's very heavy and I struggled in San Sebastian walking around with it on. It has to come with me for all of those 500 miles. Can I honestly carry it that far? It's too late now, I am here. All I can do is try. If I fail, at least I tried.

The lady's house is literally next door. I knock and go in and she shows me up to my room. She doesn't speak English and talks very fast in French. She explains that I will be sharing my room with a man, is this OK? The room is big enough to hold two double beds on opposite walls. '*Monsieur*,' she keeps saying. I tell her that I am OK with a *Monsieur*. I shared a room with five other *monsieurs* last night in San Sebastian at the hostel, so one should be fine. Although, there are only two beds, so that feels a little weird already. But they are big old-fashioned beds with tall bits of wood at the foot of each, so we won't actually see each other when we are sleeping.

The shower and toilet are outside my room on the first floor, built into the corner of a large outdoor-indoor balcony area. The view is jaw dropping; the wooden balconies, the red roof tops from a scattering of buildings and the gorgeous, rich green mountains right there in front of me. I really am at the foot of the Pyrenees and it feels good.

I have a shower because the woman insisted and handed me a towel. She is quite a character. After a change of clothes, I hang up my washing on the airer in front of the view and go for a stroll to look for something to eat. The thin, steep street is buzzing with an amazing atmosphere and lots of happy faces. The restaurants don't seem to be open yet, but I am starving. I buy a large waffle covered in Nutella and sit on a bench outside the shop to eat it. It's not the nutrition I was going for, but it is delicious and the only thing that I could see to eat. It is very, very sweet and has made me thirsty, so I make my way back to the house. I get my bamboo cup and my little pot of green tea and go downstairs. The lady is in the hallway. I ask her if I can have some hot water to make my tea. She says, 'No.'

OK then.

A French man who is just arriving here translates. He says she is too busy and she's 89 years old, and if I want hot water there's some in the upstairs tap. That is very strange.

I make my cup of green tea with the water from the tap, as hot as I can get it, but it obviously isn't hot enough to sink all my leaves, and most float there on the surface, so it's not very pleasant. But huge respect to the 89-year-old host.

I sit on the balcony and look at the view of the mountains, trying to drink what I can of my tea. I will be climbing over mountains tomorrow, but I don't think it's these as we have to go under the arch way at the bottom of the hill. Still, I can't believe I am going up a mountain tomorrow. How tough is it going to be?

What I am most looking forward to on this trip is time on my own. I only ever feel totally at peace when I am alone. If I don't have to react to other people, I can just be me. I have lived a lot of my life walking on eggshells. My childhood with an alcoholic father was tricky. Luckily, he was away a lot of the time and my mum was a great mum, so the eggshells were only there when he was home. Then I married a man very similar to my dad, which some counselling many years ago pointed out is quite normal. We are drawn to normality, and that was my normal.

But those eggshells tear holes in your soul, and the end result is that I am hypervigilant, which means that my body is still looking for danger even when there isn't any. In fact, I might attend some more counselling when I get back and get some more help. If I had to come all this way to sit on this French lady's balcony looking at this view to realise I need more counselling, then it's been worthwhile. But I have seven weeks of adventure ahead of me, and I can't wait to see what that looks like.

The thought of spending seven weeks walking across the Spanish countryside, on my own, is something I am looking forward to. Because the strange thing is, I am not scared of strangers; I have, in the past, been scared of people close to me. I don't think I am going to feel afraid at all on this trip. I think it's going to be amazing.

My roommate arrives and he is called Eugene, from Ireland, and he's very nice. We chat for a bit on the balcony and then I decide to go and get something more to eat. I have somewhere in mind that opens at 7.00 pm.

Disappointingly, all the restaurants have huge queues outside or are not open at all. I walk around the small town before coming back to one which now says full. So, I reluctantly get something from the tiny supermarket: a sandwich, a long-life salad, and a banana for tomorrow. I really wanted a hot meal today. But it wasn't to be.

Back on the balcony, I book a night's stay in a monastery for tomorrow in Roncesvalles with the QR code that I got in the Pilgrim's Office. I pay by credit card which is good as I meant to get some money out and I only have €50 on me. I book a bed, dinner, and breakfast, everything they offered. Then I am covered and don't need to worry about food tomorrow. I have no idea what it will be, but hopefully it will be hot. I am probably going to need it after climbing over the Pyrenees.

I need to fill my water bladder as well before I pack my bag, as it needs to go in first. If I fill it up too much, it's difficult to slot inside so it has a special place which can be a tight squeeze. I try to empty it out a bit and learn very quickly that you can't empty a little bit of water out of a wobbly water bladder. I can't control it at all and water spills all over the floor. I use my towel to mop it up and hang it out to dry with my washing.

I spend some time sorting my bag out. It's bursting at the seams. When it's all over the floor, it looks like so much, but it's all essential, just a few clothes, tiny toiletries, literally the head off my electric toothbrush and some squeezed toothpaste into a little pot. I have the free hotel-sized shampoo, a small bar of soap in my knitted soap bag, a phone charger, lace up shoes ... I don't see anything that I don't need.

Eugene has gone to Mass, so I am going to get to sleep before he returns to avoid any awkwardness. Plus, I am shattered. It's been quite a day getting here after leaving England on Sunday and tomorrow I have to climb over the Pyrenees. I don't even know what that means. I can't picture it.

Day 1 Wednesday 7th September

St Jean Pied de Port to Roncesvalles
16.56 miles

I woke up naturally at 6.00 am but I kept my alarm on. I can hear people moving about in the house. I think Eugene is still asleep, it's dark and I can't hear any movement from him.

Today is such a big day. I am actually going to start my walk. But 6.30 am is very early for me. I get dressed in the dark, have a wee, and go downstairs. In the dining area, around a rectangular table big enough for about ten people, is the French lady and a guest, who is eating bread quietly. The French lady is shouting at me in French and pointing to the clock, which says 6.40 am.

She asks where my bag is in French as she doesn't speak any English. With my limited school French and her hand signals and body language, I can tell that she is annoyed. I say that it's in my room and she slams her hands down on the table and tells me to go and get it.

I freeze for a moment; it all feels very unreal. It's so early and I wasn't expecting this kind of reception at breakfast. I ask the other lady if she has brought her bag down and she says yes, and I look in the hallway and see it. The French lady carries on shouting at me and I scuttle back upstairs.

I don't think I have ever been spoken to like that by a complete stranger and it's certainly not what you expect when you pay to stay at a guest house. I feel like a naughty child who had no idea that they were misbehaving.

Eugene is awake but he is still in bed as he has only just woken. I think he heard her shouting. I put my shoes on, as I had gone down barefoot. I was going to pack after breakfast, maybe take another shower, as it was hot in the night, and definitely clean my teeth. But now, I run around collecting up all my things, grabbing damp washing off the clothes horse. I squeeze everything in my bag and any left-over stuff I put in my nylon bag with the damp clothes. I have a quick scan of the room and drag my bag downstairs into the hallway. As I sit down, my host is saying, '*No vacances, allez, Espana …*' She is one angry woman.

She asks if I want coffee or tea and I ask her for hot water. She doesn't understand, so the other lady translates, and she runs the kitchen tap to fill up a metal teapot, and hands it to me. Never in my life has anyone given me hot water from a tap to make tea. I feel like I am in a parallel universe. The lady opposite looks shocked too, but she keeps quiet and nibbles her bread.

On the table, the 'good' breakfast the other lady spoke of in the Pilgrim's Office is a baguette cut into slices with some butter and jam. I manage to eat one slice with jam even though it's way too early for me to eat. But the hot water is welcome.

Eugene arrives in the dining room along with the French man that I spoke to yesterday and she is pointing to the clock again, saying we are all like children, *les enfants*. We are pilgrims, *dormir*, up and out. Her hand gestures make up for the lack of English words.

So, at exactly 7.00 am, after breaking my walking pole trying to extend it in a panic and haste, me and Eugene are outside on the dark street, wondering what on earth happened.

The steep, dark hill is full of pilgrims, all coming out of buildings and walking down towards the archway. It's a nice feeling being part of it. You can feel the excitement, we are all eager to start our Camino. We stop and take some photos in the dark by the archway. I have my sun hat on in the dark as I didn't know what else to do with it in the rush, except to put it on my head. The photo is ridiculous but catches a moment in time. We walk out of town with some people that Eugene had dinner with last night. Lucky him getting a hot meal. I wasn't expecting this walk to be so sociable.

The first thing we do is climb a hill that doesn't want to stop. I am thrilled that we have a stunning sunrise. It was on my wish list to see a sunrise on the Pyrenees and it's been granted so I take some photos. Orange and gold streak across the black sky. I am incredibly lucky.

Me and Eugene chat as we walk, but it starts to become a little difficult. We are trying to make conversation, instead of enjoying the walk. I don't think either of us wanted to walk with another person and yet both of us are too polite to say so. We're still working out how to behave. So, after a while, Eugene says he is going to stop and sort his bag out and we part. We have sort of accidentally been thrown together but he is stopping at Orisson for the night and therefore not in any hurry, so I continue happily on my own.

This is exactly the situation I wanted to avoid from 'real life'. Working out how other people feel, interpreting their feelings and wants and then reacting to them. This takes up too much of my time, makes my brain hurt and is exactly what I wanted to get away from. So, now that I am on my own, I will try and stay on my own. This is the reason I am here, walking over the Pyrenees, to experience a sense of peace. That's not going to happen, if I ask Eugene, or anyone else how many kids they have, just for the purpose of making conversation. I don't need that conversation.

I can relax now. It has been nice to have some company. But every time I stopped to take another photo, because I do like to take a photo, I felt like I was holding him up. Now I can stop and stare at the views, and take as many photos as I want without feeling a burden.

It's been quite a climb and now I am hot and uncomfortable, plus I have my nylon bag swinging off me. So, after three miles, I sit down on a grass verge and sort myself out. I take my cardigan off, eat the banana that I had the brains to buy yesterday and find room in my rucksack for my things, so that I can put away the extra bag. I also hang my damp clothes off the back of the bag to dry.

I'm ready and what a difference it makes. It's a tough two more miles, but the scenery is beautiful, surrounded by the Pyrenees on all sides, a collection of green hills everywhere I look, and the occasional house. Sheep and cattle are so far away that they look like grains of sand.

It's a relief to get to Orisson. I had seen this albergue on the internet and tried very hard to book a bed. I thought that stopping on the Pyrenees overnight and seeing the sunrise in the morning would be very special, and it was. But I couldn't get accommodation for tonight even weeks ago so now I am quite pleased. It's very early in the day and there's not much to do here.

There's a big huddle of people in this incredibly remote café in the middle of nowhere. It's quite a contrast to the quiet walk here. It's the only stopping point between St Jean Pied de Port and Roncesvalles. I queue to get served in the café as I think it's important I try and eat something now.

I ask for soup, exactly what I need, but they say that it's not cooked yet, which is a shame. I didn't eat properly last night and soup would have been good, something warming and nutritious. Quickly, as there is a queue behind me, I order a tortilla, which I don't really want. But it's in front of me on the counter and seems the easy option.

I take it outside and sit in what must be one of the best spots on the mountain – a great outdoor seating area almost hanging off the mountain with stunning uninterrupted views. I lean my bag up on the barrier and sit down to eat my tortilla and write up my journal. The place is packed with friendly, happy faces. We are all doing the same thing and some faces I have already seen pass me, or I have spoken to.

I am still in shock over being here. Yesterday I was wandering around San Sebastian and trying to figure out buses, the day before I was on a ferry from Plymouth. Now, I am sitting in an albergue café, outdoors in the sunshine, sitting in the Pyrenees eating a Spanish tortilla.

I am not quite sure why I am here, but it certainly feels right. This could have been any path. I am not here for religious reasons, as a lot of people seem to be. I am here because it is a path with a beginning and an end. I don't have to think too much. I don't have to decide where to go next, I just have to decide how far to go. And eventually I will arrive at the end. It feels like my subconscious is pushing me, spurring me on. As if I need to do this walk. I feel that, after the success of my interrailing trip, there is so much to experience in life. Like this, sitting in the Pyrenees eating a tortilla surrounded by like-minded people.

I just hope that I am fit enough for whatever is ahead of me today. I did intend to get fitter before I came away, but I worked a lot. My job at Wheal Martyn China Clay Museum gets very busy during the school holidays, so I was needed.

I did go out walking and tested my bag when it was almost full but I didn't do enough training. I planned on losing half a stone in weight as well, but that didn't happen either. Hopefully, I can go at my own pace until I get fitter.

Eugene arrives and reminds me to get a stamp on my *credencial*. I forgot that we have to do that at least once a day. So I go and get that done, my first stamp on the route, and get on my way. I don't want to sit for too long as there's a long way to go.

When I lift my rucksack up, I notice that my sleeping bag is wet at the bottom. That's annoying, the water bladder must be leaking, drat. But there's nothing that I can do about it. It is what it is.

Off I go to Roncesvalles. I have water in the water bladder, if it's not all leaked out, two bottles and there are a couple of water fountains along the way. I am set. The road is still going up and it's long and hard work but the scenery is stunning. If I concentrate on the road, let my mind wander, and then look up I am surprised again and again by the scenery. I am constantly surrounded by huge, beautiful mountains.

I stop at the water fountain, take my bag off and sit down for a moment. My feet feel sore and a lovely lady offers me cream for my little toe. She dives into her bag and retrieves it.

The next bit of the journey is lovely and peaceful. I am on my own with very few people passing by and it's so quiet. When I thought about crossing a mountain range, I didn't think I would be walking on tarmac roads, so whilst it is climbing up, it's not uncomfortable. I am still trying to unwind from the journey yesterday and take in the fact that I am actually walking across the Pyrenees. It's not easy just starting the walk and immediately chilling. Life has been busy for the last month, and I can't just switch off.

There are sheep walking on the path, and cattle in the fields and lots of bells on the animals, ringing as the cattle move about. I keep taking photos. It's just so gorgeous and everywhere seems a better photo than the last.

I chat to a few people briefly, as I pass them, or they pass me. No one really wants to get 'stuck' with someone, we all seem to get it. Plus, why would you want to ruin this serenity with chit chat? It's nice to stop when you want to and take a photo when you want without someone else waiting for you. And we all seem to be walking at different paces.

As we keep climbing, I see a few cars up ahead, which seems strange. There are roads here and I have moved out of the way for a few cars. As I get closer, it looks like a beauty spot. How can you have a beauty spot in the middle of beauty? Two men are sitting by a parked car on chairs at a table and they give me a leaflet as I pass them. I laugh to myself, I am in the middle of the mountains and still people want to try and persuade me that I need religion in my life. It seems a bit silly to me; this is a pilgrimage and a lot of people are already doing it for religious reasons and the others probably don't want leaflets. But maybe it's a great idea for those sitting on the fence. It just seems a little intrusive up here surrounded by nature, and now I have a leaflet that I don't want.

As I get closer to the edge, I can see it is a fantastic view. There's also a religious statue up ahead on the rocks and a lot of people are clambering up to it, but I am not going to bother about the figure. This spot is lovely for a quick rest.

I take my bag off and sit down on the grass and chill for ten minutes, taking it all in. It's important to burn all these images into my soul. I have been walking for an hour and 20 minutes since leaving Orisson.

After a nice little rest, I walk on and talk with a lady called Jeanette. We chat for a while and then I walk on alone. I thought we must have reached the highest point by now, but oh no, in front of me is a climb that would be challenging on any day, and I am tired. But I have to find the strength and get on with it.

I meet a chatty, unfrazzled energetic American lady at the top who recognises me from my toenail polish which she noticed in Orisson. That makes me laugh. She is reading a book and says that we have another climb to do. It's her second time doing this walk and she is waiting for her sister who isn't walking as fast as her.

The air is a bit cooler now, a slight wind, not enough to put my cardigan back on but almost. I must be so high now. A horse casually walks towards me on the path and I carry on and get to another water fountain. I take my bag off and fill up my water bladder by tipping my bottles into it, so that I can control it and I don't have to remove it from the bag. It doesn't have a leak which is great news. I must have put my bag in a puddle without noticing. I re-fill both bottles as well.

My bag feels so heavy putting it back on. I am very tired, it's been quite a day. I feel physically drained and a bit overwhelmed. Next to the water fountain is a cattle grid. Ahh, I remember someone saying that when you get the cattle grid, you are entering Spain. There's no fanfare, just a cattle grid and a graffitied post as I step over from France to Spain.

The paths are bad now with scatterings of large stones that are making my feet hurt and I am having to concentrate with every step. Then I go through a lovely wooded area with tall pine trees on a very steep incline. The trees look like they are all sliding down the hill. This is a gorgeous section and a welcome change of scenery, plus I get out of the sun for a bit. I can still see glimpses of mountains through the trees. The ground is also fluffy from the fallen leaves, so it's nice to walk on after those rocks.

Then a steep incline. Everyone is struggling now; some are resting before the next climb which seems to be on every bend. The rocks are so difficult to walk on but I need to stay strong, every step is one closer to the hostel and a warm dinner. Then it's one climb too many as I turn a corner and decide to take a break.

It's been two hours since the last stop at the fountain and crossing into Spain. I sit down in a great spot, take my sandals off and look at my blisters. I eat my salad pot, which I am very grateful for. I have not eaten very much in the last 24 hours and I am using up a lot of energy. Thankfully, it's delicious.

I have always enjoyed walking. Apparently, I was walking at nine months old and haven't really stopped since. It's the only exercise that I do and even that is sporadic. I have tried the gym, badminton, cycling, swimming and I hate them all. Whereas walking always fits into my life. I can walk whenever I want without having to make an appointment. It doesn't cost anything, unless you buy tea along the way. You can walk as fast as you want or as slow as you want, test yourself on a hill, or don't. You can push yourself until you are physically exhausted or just go for a short stroll.

Walking has always been my 'go to' when I am sad or a bit low. I like the expression that 'you never feel worse after a walk'. I have walked for pleasure, over the Cornish cliffs and countryside, and I have stomped in anger. It seems to work in every single situation. It's a physical release. I have walked with frustration during difficult times, so hard and fast that I exhaust myself physically and mentally, have a bath and feel much better. I always sleep better after a good walk.

Jeanette and her friend Brett walk by just as I am getting up and we walk together. It's nice as it helps to pass the time. It is a tough walk and you begin to understand that everyone is struggling. It's not you being out of shape and weary.

Eventually, we get to the path that leads down to **Roncesvalles**. We have heard that this bit is bad and quite dangerous. In fact, we talk to one lady who has ordered transport to the bottom as she doesn't want to risk it, which does add a layer of 'oh dear' to the climb down. The path leads down through the pine trees. It's a steep incline and there are lots of loose stones. I am a little scared in case we fall. My walking poles help a bit to test the ground and support me.

I continue on. Jeanette is going at a slower pace and, while I feel I should stay with her, she has Brett. I also have to get this backpack off, it's very heavy now. I keep wondering what I can lose from it to make it lighter. If I eat a multivitamin and use some shower gel, perhaps it should be much lighter tomorrow.

I walk as fast and as safely as I can, because I want to get to the monastery so badly now. It's such hard work. Blisters are appearing but I don't have the energy to take off the backpack and sort them out. I am not sure what to do with them either. A little further yet still on the mountain, it's a lovely walk through a wooded area again and a mix of stony ground, then less stony, then tree roots, then stony. My feet feel like they are on fire, so hot and angry.

It's taking much longer than I thought it would to reach the bottom and, quite honestly, it's painful, mentally and physically. All my energy has evaporated now, but I know I must be close as I feel that I am almost down at ground level. Eventually, there's an old stone building with lots of little windows, and I really hope it is where I am going to be spending the night, as I am not sure how much further I can walk. I climb up some steps following a sign to the albergue and, thankfully, I am in the right place and a nice man in the hallway tells me to sit down. I happily do as he says.

The wide, impressive monastery hallway is busy with staff and pilgrims, and we all look the same: exhausted, stunned and relieved. Also, none of us can walk properly. We are not walking anything like we were when we set off bright and naively this morning from St Jean.

This monastery has over 100 beds. It seems big and modern and yet very old. I feel very secure and happy to be here.

We have to take our shoes off and put them in the boot room, which I can barely walk to. I leave my bag and join a queue until I get given a small white parcel and a bed number, not quite sure what it is, but I take it anyway. I ask for help with the Wi-Fi, as I need to pause my walking app and I need Wi-Fi to save it. I am told the dining area is the best spot to get a signal, so I go and sit down to sort the app out.

Wow, I walked 16 miles. That's the longest walk that I have ever done *and* it included climbing over mountains. What an achievement! I am so proud of myself – really proud.

It explains why my body feels so broken right now.

This building has digital buttons in the lift, it's very swish. I arrive on the third-floor loft space, with a steep pitch on the roof and about 40 beds in two neat rows. It's so well organised, and each bed has some privacy. The beds have tall sides so you can only see one other person, there is a storage locker which uses €1.00, and there's a socket for your phone. It's very thought through, particularly for a 'hostel'.

The little white package is a paper sheet and pillow slip. I see that others have laid theirs out on their beds and I copy. It's surprisingly robust and easy to put on. I suppose it makes a lot of sense. Washing these many sheets every single day would be quite a chore and expensive.

I go to the showers and realise that I haven't had a wee since the French lady's house, almost 11 hours ago. So, I go to the loo and it's an illuminous yellow colour. That's a surprise, I have drunk gallons of water today.

The showers are very modern as well, and I feel a whole lot fresher. I wash my clothes in the shower and stamp on them like I am making wine with grapes. Painfully, I walk out into the courtyard, round the back of the huge building to the washing line, and laugh with a man who is also struggling to walk.

I am so glad that I booked the pilgrim's meal. I really need some good nutritious food. I discover that we are going to eat in the restaurant. The monastery also has a hotel and we are going in there to eat. A pilgrim meal sounds very humble and basic, so I wasn't expecting a hotel restaurant.

I find myself sitting at a table with eight people. Three Americans, one from New Zealand, one Dutch, and two from Switzerland. The food is great, and I order the vegetable soup which is perfect after missing out at Orisson, and trout which is also delicious and perfectly cooked. The only vegetarian option was pasta which I don't really like. I need more than pasta today after that walk.

I don't drink any wine as I have made a promise to myself not to drink any alcohol on this trip. It's quite a challenge, as I do like a drink. The main reason is that being hydrated is very important and I need to take it seriously. I don't want to start my days dehydrated from drinking the night before. And secondly, I sometimes don't know when to stop, and I really don't want to start a walking day with a headache and be out of sorts. Or embarrass myself being a stupid drunk, which can happen. Plus, I want to prove to myself that I can go without.

I enjoy the food, but not that awkwardness that I always feel in these table situations with strangers. I really don't care where they live, how many kids they have. I don't want to share too much of my life with them either. I am more private than that. I am also very useless at just joining in a conversation about current affairs. So, predictably, I am the quiet, awkward one with very little to say. The conversation is going really well, talking about things I don't have strong opinions about, or a loud enough personality to join it. But it's exactly what I expected, so it is what it is.

Before going back to my bed, I go and get my washing off the line. It's still damp but it might dry in the room. Walking is still difficult as I have three small blisters, and I ache all over. I go to the dining area for a little bit and use the Wi-FI to put a Facebook post out, very proud of what I achieved today.

I am shattered so I go back to the dormitory. By 9.30 pm, most people are in bed. Then the snoring starts.

Day 2 Thursday 8th September

Roncesvalles to Zubiri
14.44 miles

At 6.00 am, the lights go on in this huge dormitory and everyone bursts into action, rustling their bags. Sleeping bags are being zipped, plastic clips snapping shut. Everyone seems to know what they are doing, where they are going, and why they are packing in a hurry. I wonder if they have done this before. This is my first proper morning as a pilgrim and I have not burst into action. I am not in a hurry as breakfast is at 7.00 am, and I have plenty of time. I won't have breakfast again, it just seemed like a good idea at the time. I can't eat much in the mornings and it does take up a lot of time, waiting to go and sit down and then eating. A banana is perfectly OK for breakfast in the future.

I need to see how my feet and legs are. If I get five miles done today, I will be pleased. Then I need to find somewhere to sleep tonight. I seem to be the only one not rustling and packing which is a bit unnerving. There's an urgency to everyone but they are very quiet. No one is talking, they are just packing their rucksacks.

It's 6.24 am, I had better get up and rustle my bag with them. I will remember to put deodorant and face cream on today. Over half the room has left already, and one person is still asleep, they are worse than me in the mornings. I take all my things downstairs.

My feet feel OK, I can walk properly again which is amazing. I was in agony yesterday and now I am healed. How did that happen? The blisters hurt a bit but not too bad and the main one has a Compeed on it. My feet feel normal, and I can walk properly on them. I still have my flip-flops on, as my shoes are in the boot room. I ask a member of staff if I can come back for them after breakfast but he says to take everything with me now, which doesn't make any sense.

The breakfast is where our dinner was yesterday and it's still dark as we wait outside for the doors to open. It's a good breakfast on linen dressed tables. A lady comes round and hands out food; fresh orange, hams, cheeses, a piece of cake and an apple which most people leave on the table.

After a cup of black tea, I go back to the courtyard to sort myself out and get my sleeping bag tucked on the outside of my backpack, which is a struggle but a nice lady helps me. Everyone has to be gone by 8.00 am, so it feels a bit panicked and I am one of the last to leave. I hang my washing off the bag again and off I go. My feet feel very cosy in my lace ups.

I reach a signpost that I have already seen on Facebook saying 'Santiago de Compostela 790' and I take a selfie next to it. It feels amazing to be standing by the sign, but also scary as that's a lot of kilometres to walk.

There is a lot of signage as we walk, not as big as the 790 kilometre sign but lots of shells to follow. The shell is to show you the way, and a symbol that all roads lead to Santiago. It's very comforting to know that you are walking the right way. A lot of people are carrying shells on their bags, but I personally didn't feel the need.

I journey on through a wooded area for a mile which is really soothing underfoot until I reach a pretty little village called Burguete. There's a café where some people have stopped but I have not long had breakfast so I keep moving. Up ahead, I come across steep steps and a tricky stretch of concrete winding through the woods.

A man is struggling up a hill, and slows down. He says his brother asked him last Thursday if he wanted to go for a walk and here they are. He laughs between panting. He says he hasn't really had time to prepare himself or give up the cigarettes. His brother is waiting for him patiently at the top.

The girl from Slovenia who offered me foot cream for my blisters, yesterday when I took a break, walks with me for a bit through the woods, then a man called Mateo from Italy, but we can't communicate very well and he walks on.

I get to a stream that has concrete blocks going over it and I decide to take a break. There are lots of people sitting by the stream eating food, chatting and working out whether to walk through the stream or walk on the blocks. I need a wee which is good news, as I must be hydrated again but I don't know where to go.

Sitting on one of the blocks of square stone, I eat the cake that I was given at breakfast, which is delicious, and I watch everyone. I have walked 6.84 miles which I am thrilled about and it's only 11.10 am in the morning. I might get to Zubiri, which is on the schedule and where most people are heading. I hope I find accommodation OK, it's worrying me a little.

I make my way through a very tiny village, Espinal, which is really old looking, traditional and rural, then up a very steep hill, puffing all the way before coming onto a rocky stretch that tests me and slows me right down.

People overtake me, then I overtake them. A tricky section with a diagonal raised rock formation seems to go on forever, before I amble through a forest that smells strongly of pine. Eventually, a food truck appears, like a gift on the horizon, and I go in the hedge out of sight for a wee *au naturel*, before I sit down for a drink. The food truck is busy with people; most of the chairs have been taken and I share a table with some Italian men under an umbrella out of the sun. I remember to get a stamp on my *credencial* and I order a home-made lemonade, which is really water with lemon in it but it's very refreshing.

I have been worrying all day about accommodation. It's been playing on my mind that I haven't booked anywhere. Two hundred of us left the monastery and our leaflet says there are five different accommodations in Zubiri, some with only a few beds. It's going to be tight. I don't think I can walk another five kilometres to the next town.

A bug bites me and it stings. I swipe it away and see it's left blood on my arm. How rude.

I need to start booking ahead so that I can relax on my walks. This stress is not good, constantly looking at the time and trying to estimate when I will arrive in the next town. I would definitely have stopped at either of those cafés earlier if I wasn't worried about getting a bed this evening.

I feel wet drips on my leg and realise that my water bladder is leaking. I haven't been turning it off. That must have been why my sleeping bag was wet. I force the switch across. It's not easy but it stops the dripping down my leg.

My left knee hurts on the climb down to Zubiri. At every corner, I sigh, it's just too much. There are shards of rock going diagonally across the path, all different heights and difficult to walk on. A man behind is having as much trouble as me, in fact I worry that he will fall as he seems very unstable and tired. Two ladies who look older than me whizz by chatting and the group of Italians go by, too. But my knee is painful with every step. At this moment in time, I think it's unlikely that I will get to Santiago. My body might not be able to do it. I wish I had packed the painkillers in my pocket so that I could reach them.

Nervously and slowly, I eventually reach the bottom of the stony hill. It's a huge relief to be at ground level again. I have had two days of severe downward strenuous walks.

Zubiri looks like a charming village, and very welcoming. I walk over a pretty stone bridge and I don't know where to go. There are pilgrims everywhere, some looking at their phones, some walking just ahead of me. I have a list of accommodation in my hand. The first one I pass says 'full' on the door, oh dear. At the next one, I see people going in, so I follow and get in the queue and wait for the receptionist to process people. I wait 15 minutes only to be told that the man in front of me got the last bed. I see another albergue further up the street but they are also full. The receptionist says to go to the hostel over the road, the building with a painted front. Thank goodness they have a bed. What a relief and it's only €9.00.

I can barely climb the stairs as I am in so much pain. I get to my room, a busy packed bedroom with seven bunk beds squeezed in, and I just lay on my bed, so grateful for a bottom bunk. This room has a big double window. Down below in the front garden is the social area, benches, and washing line.

I smell bad but I just need five minutes to unwind. I have walked 14 miles and I ache all over, I can barely move anything. The Wi-Fi is not good, so I leave my data on and shower and wash my clothes. When they're done, I hang them on the line in the outdoor area at the front of the building.

It's a busy hostel and I do love the hustle and bustle. There are so many smells, sweaty bodies at the entrance, my own included, then the lovely aroma of shower gel and shampoo. Smiles, conversations, rustling bags, everyone doing the same things.

The lady who booked me in told me the supermarket shuts at 5.00 pm, so I prioritise going there for some food. Unfortunately, it's shut, maybe she meant it opens at 5.00 pm, her English wasn't very good. Instead, there's a café so I decide to get some food there as I don't have the energy for anything else.

It's a difficult climb up the few steps to the door but I am not the only one who is struggling. It looks very strange, us pilgrims going sideways up and down a few steps. But we all laugh and chat to each other. The café doesn't have much to eat that I want so I end up with a lemonade and a portion of microwaved tempura veg, which is a bit soggy, and a cheese toasty thing. I head back to the hostel with a portion of cake. At least I ate something. When I arrive back at the hostel, a girl is asking about a bed but we are full now. I feel so bad for her. I was relieved that they had a bed for me, and if she has struggled like I did on those hills and stones, she is going to be just as tired. She asks if she can sleep on the floor, and I feel guilty that I have a bed. Poor girl, where will she go?

I get a cup of tea from the kitchen. I have to boil water as there's no kettle. I take the tea to my room and then sort out my things, my bag is a real mess. I put painkillers in the side pocket along with the sun cream. I think I have burnt my neck, so that will come in handy tomorrow.

By 7.00 pm, my bag is sorted. I have written in my journal and spent half an hour looking for accommodation in Pamplona. They were all sold out but I found one on the other side. It should be OK to walk slightly further tomorrow, as it looks easier than today.

I talk to Pearse from Belfast for a bit, he's very easy to chat to. He's travelling with his brother, Brendan, who lives in Galway. They might be who I met earlier on the hill. I have spoken to so many people I am getting muddled.

We learn that the Queen has died. We all feel a bit detached from it, no one really knows what to say. It seems so far away and we only have limited information, whatever comes up on our phones. It feels that it should be monumental but, here in rural Spain, it's not really affecting me.

It's 9.00 pm and it feels like the introverts are up here. We have been quietly respecting each other's space, with very little chat, and everyone outside is laughing and joking about. It's quite a contrast. I am going to try and get to sleep before they bundle back in.

Day 3 Friday 9th September

Zubiri to Cizur Menor
18.60 miles

I settled down for the night. The outdoor people came in quietly. A Spanish man was snoring quietly from 8.30 pm and so it was all peaceful.

Then I did something stupid.

Under the big window are four open compartments big enough for rucksacks. My bunk bed is to the left of the window, the other set of bunks opposite parallel with mine. My compartment is the second one in, with my bag and bits and pieces in it.

I woke up to see someone squatting in front of my stuff, opening a Velcro strap which looked and sounded like my camera case. It was pitch black, and I remembered the sign on the toilet door that said to look after your belongings. In the dark and, instinctively, without putting my brain into gear, I said, 'What are you doing?' Still in my bed, I was level with a man crouching on the floor.

'*Es mio*,' he says and shows me something, but it's dark. I touch his arm as if to say I'm sorry, and he goes to the loo. When he returns, we both take a while to get to sleep, turning about. Others must have heard as the metal bunk beds are creaking and people are moving about trying to get comfortable.

I feel terrible. I just accused a man of taking my stuff and everyone heard me, I feel so awful. But that honestly is what it looked like. I opened my eyes, saw what I saw, and I reacted.

Another man came in after this happened, got into bed and started snoring immediately. The church bells chimed at 12.00 am. Eventually, I did get to sleep but I had bad dreams about people dying on a roundabout which is a bit random.

At 5.15 am or 6.15am, depending how my phone is feeling, I wake up. It's all quiet except for the two snorers and a man who sounds like he is eating something in his sleep. The lady above me is awake and I have no idea what she's doing. It sounds like she is wrapping Christmas presents, as there's lots of rustling. I think she is packing her bag and getting dressed and I feel like I am on a boat, as the bed is swaying.

The Spanish man is still asleep. I decide to run away before he wakes up as I am mortified. I didn't really want to be the first to leave in case I wake people up. If I open the bedroom door, the light comes in from the hall and into the room. I need to be swift. I take my bag out to the landing, come back and put all my loose bits in the sleeping bag and carry everything downstairs. Three trips and I am done.

Downstairs, the light is on. There are people in the kitchen drinking coffee, eating food and sorting their bags. I clean my teeth in the downstairs toilet, put face cream and deodorant on. I collect my washing from the line, it's so dark that I need to use my phone torch.

On the way back to the front door with my arms full of washing, I see the Spanish man having a cigarette. I try to pretend he is not there and I don't have any eye contact with him. I pack my bag up and leave the hostel at 6.00 am.

I get away from the building as fast as I can. It's pitch black.

The lights are on in the café that I ate at yesterday and I think about getting breakfast to take away. But music by Queen is blasting from it, and I can't stand that band, it's a PTSD trigger, so I move swiftly on. It also seems a little surreal, as the actual Queen died yesterday. I wonder if it's a coincidence.

There are three pilgrims behind me so I move over and let them pass. They are heading to the bridge too, which I thought was the way. I pause when I reach it and put my tracker on as I forgot to do it before. They seem to be hanging back. I hope they don't want to follow me, or we will all get lost.

A man ahead seems to know where he is going, he has a very confident walk. So, I turn right once I am over the bridge and follow him. He is using his phone torch to show the way along the thin path. I try to manage without, as I didn't put my phone on charge yesterday because the bedroom was too crowded and there weren't many sockets. I don't want it to run out but there are unstable paths with lots of loose rocks, like the same kind of terrain on the climb down yesterday, so I have to put it on.

I can just see him ahead of me, a little light in the dark and the tap, tap of the walking poles. This is fun. I am enjoying this, being up so early and away from the hostel. We go alongside a huge processing plant which is very noisy before a lady overtakes me. She has a headtorch and much more energy than me. She knows what she's doing.

We come to a junction on the path and don't know what to do. The three people on the bridge have caught up now. They know where we are going – there was a sign, but we didn't see it in the dark. More people overtake me, but it's fine. I am up early which means I have all day. I manage with everyone else's light until the sun gradually comes up and illuminates the paths. By 7.10 am, I feel safe to go alone and let the others overtake me. I slow down.

There are a few little hills and I am dripping with sweat already; it's not even 8.00 am yet. I can hear a rooster calling cock-a-doodle-doo, and dogs barking in the distance, it's very peaceful. Today, I am wearing shorts and I keep catching glimpses of my legs, getting confused. I have worn my two long pairs of trousers alternately since Sunday, so it's nice to wear something different.

By now, I am hungry and I would like to eat my apple that I cut into four pieces in the kitchen before I left. But I don't want to take my bag off as it feels good right now. Yesterday it was hurting my shoulders. I only need it half an inch wrong and it's a different bag.

As I keep going, I feel myself relaxing as I walk through the pine section. I love the pine section and I can feel myself relaxing. I don't have anything to worry about today. I have a bed booked for tonight and it's such a different feeling, knowing that you have somewhere definite to stay. I was incredibly lucky yesterday and I don't want to be that close to not getting a bed again.

I remember that I have a bag of nuts in the zip on the roof of my bag and, if I try and bend my arms back as far as they can go, I can just open the zip. Out falls rice crackers, I forgot that I had those. I eat them for breakfast while walking across the Spanish countryside. This bag is so clever and I am glad I found out that I can get in the top, because now I can store food there, which will reduce the need to keep taking it off. It will make walking much more efficient and enjoyable.

There are green hills everywhere, and nice paths. I go through two little villages, hamlets really. Then I pass through a lightly wooded area where the air smells of leaves. It's fresh and lovely and I stop and take a lungful.

A little further on, two girls come out of an albergue. I recognise them from yesterday. They have their washing hanging neatly off the back of their bags. I keep going and come across another wooded area, where the smell of pine is deliciously strong again. I turn a corner and there's a café by the side of a river on the other side of a little bridge. It looks inviting and a grass verge goes down to the river. It's full of familiar faces.

My feet are very sore now though, so the first thing I do is take off my shoes and socks and leave them by my bag. I have a blister forming on the bottom of my foot. Ouch. The Compeed isn't working so I am not quite sure what to do. I talk to an American in the queue about bacon as you do, it's a popular conversation with Americans. I get my *credencial* stamped and order tea and cake, which looks tasty.

I feel really calm It's only 9.00 am and I have walked six and a half miles in three hours. I rest for almost an hour, while my feet are feeling the fresh air. There's a buzz of pilgrims coming and going in this lovely spot. I enjoy getting up early so I can relax like this. It's what I missed out on yesterday by worrying about accommodation, which was a valid worry as it turned out.

Eventually, I see the man from my dorm who came in at 12.00 am last night. Oh no, they are catching up with me. So, I put more plasters on the soles of my feet, roll on some fresh socks and slip my shoes back on. Taking the shoes and socks off this last hour has helped my feet. I end up walking with Jeanette for a while. I had been worried that she hadn't got a bed last night and she says that she did have trouble, but Brett sorted out some language issues and she managed to get somewhere to sleep.

The next section we come to is lovely, with open fields and mountains in the distance, and full of pine trees before a very steep hill with even more beautiful views. The sweat is dripping down my face, it's so hot and steep. At a small stone bridge, Puente de Arre, which crosses the water and goes into a town, there is a decision to make. It's here that I meet Mike from Manchester.

He has read up and seems to think we don't go over it. He sits down and reads his Brierley book. There are two routes into Pamplona, so there are two signposts. An elderly local Spanish couple offer us their opinion. They don't speak English, so it's all in Spanish, but I get the gist. The man thinks the scenic route is better, the lady thinks that going through town is, and they disagree in front of us which is amusing. In the end, we go for the scenic route which follows the river.

We chat easily. Mike is very good company and easy to get along with. At the next bridge, it is just as confusing. We start to go through the town but we can't see any more shells to follow, so we go back to the bridge. It turns out the sign was for the hostel. A local man tells us you can go either way, so we choose to stay by the river. At least it's something to follow. Mike is walking much faster than me by now and I am struggling to keep up. My feet are burning, all hot and uncomfortable. It's four kilometres to Pamplona but there are no shells, so I try to keep up with him or I will be lost.

After a little while, we arrive at Puente de Magdalena, an impressive, huge stone bridge that seems exceptionally old. On the other side there is an enormous wall, like a castle wall, and then a large stone archway to go through. Mike is in a hurry to get a bed at a hostel which is on a first come, first served basis. I wish I had done that now, as I would really like to stop walking. But after yesterday, I wanted some security, knowing that I had a bed booked. I really don't know what's the best thing to do. The hostel sounded good and I probably would have gotten a bed, as it's not too late in the day.

But I let him go ahead. I know where I am now, and I can slow right down. He was walking way too fast for me, but I am grateful for his company and getting me here without becoming lost. I have another five kilometres until my accommodation but, first, I want a hot meal.

Pamplona is quite unusual. Five or six-story buildings along narrow streets with lots and lots of balconies. There aren't many other pilgrims, I only see four.

A small shop catches my eye and I buy a peach and sit down on a bench to eat it. It's absolutely delicious and I enjoy watching the hustle and bustle all around me. People are shopping and walking around.

My feet are very sore now and I don't see any more eating places that I want to stop at. I realise the longer I stay here that I don't like Pamplona, it's too busy and it doesn't feel safe. Then again, I might just be tired and irritable and I should probably have a look around. I am torn between buying food and wanting to get to my accommodation. I keep moving.

Maybe I just made a huge mistake by not exploring more.

I walk straight out the other side of Pamplona to a park, hoping to find a smaller eating place that's less hectic but I don't see anything. I sit on another bench to sort my feet out and unpack my bag to search for my flip-flops, which are at the bottom. I can't walk any further in these lace ups and I can't wear the sandals as the blisters will hurt. My feet seem to be a bit of a mess right now. I feel exposed like a homeless person must feel, very vulnerable with all my belongings on show and people looking at me strangely, although that is very unfair as I have all my belongings at home and I am not homeless. These are, however, my belongings for seven weeks. It dawns on me that this isn't a normal thing to do, to walk across Spain with all your belongings in a bag.

I have another 4.5 kilometres to walk in flip-flops. They do feel better but the blisters still hurt. I don't see any Pilgrims here at all, they must have all stayed in Pamplona. I wish I had now.

Very slowly, I keep walking. It's going to take me ages. I also have blisters on my fingers from the walking poles. My battery is on 15 percent since I used it this morning as a torch, so I take a screenshot of my map to my accommodation in case it dies. This is not a great situation to be in. I also turn off my tracker and screenshot it, as it's probably draining the battery as well. I put on Google Maps and keep moving.

I go wrong a couple of times at junctions before correcting myself, then walk up another hill. There's no bench to rest on, so I try to lean on the wall to take the weight off my feet but it doesn't work, every step is painful. I am in a residential area, 19 minutes to go and this is hard. I eventually find my accommodation and it's a house. I don't remember booking a house, I don't want a house, it's far too personal. There's a 'Beware of Dog' sign, too. Oh no. I'm afraid of dogs.

The tall solid gate to the front garden is locked. I ring a bell on the post and no one answers. This is awful. After a few minutes, a young lad appears and reassures me that I am in the right place, which is both good and bad. He speaks English very well and, as it turns out, he tells me that he is in fact English and living in Spain. Bilingual, lucky lad. He gets his mum on the phone, and she says that she wasn't expecting me yet.

He shows me to my room and it's perfect. It has a single bed and a bunk bed, but I am the only one staying tonight so I have the whole room to myself. There's a big fluffy towel for my shower, and cotton sheets that are already on the bed. I also have my own toilet.

I take a very much needed shower, and decide to take the cheap blister plaster off, as it's not working. It hurts peeling it off but I have a few hours to let it air. The blister is quite a size on the ball of my foot, which is a shame. I wash my clothes and hang my washing on the chair in the front garden.

The lady returns home, and I'm pleased to find that she is lovely. I am very hungry now, as I stupidly didn't eat anything in that big town that probably had thousands of restaurants. Sometimes I really annoy myself with the decisions I make. The only food I have is a sachet of miso soup, so I make that and my host sells me some of the fresh bread that she just bought to go with it. It's sort of a meal.

I rest on my bed and it's a great relief to be off my feet. I find an apple in my bag from **Roncesvalles** and eat it. I don't like apples but it needs eating.

Here, I feel weirdly alone which is strange. Maybe I should have gone to the hostel instead. There are no familiar faces here. This morning, I was so pleased to get on the road and leave everyone behind and now I am missing them. I feel connected to people in a hostel, even if I don't talk to many of them. I wonder what I am missing there and then remember snoring, overcrowding, noise, wet shower floors, and no space. It's like I have left the herd, they are all somewhere else and I am here. I need to sort out my accommodation better – maybe book a few days in advance, or not book, as I could have gone to the Jesus and Maria place today that Mike stayed in. I honestly don't know what to do for the best.

It is good, though, having a room to myself and my own toilet. This bed is so comfy with its cotton sheets and fleecy blanket. Plus, all my stuff is laid out on the floor and I don't even have to worry if it's in anyone's way, or if it might get pinched. I can go to sleep when I want. I can get up when I want without waking others or being woken by them. I don't have to worry about the bed clothes covering my body if I slip out from under the sleeping bag. I will just appreciate what I have.

I know I am contradicting myself already. I didn't want to walk with anyone, being the independent woman I am, searching for peace, and I didn't want to clutter up my day with conversations about nothing with strangers. Yet here I am, all on my own, with the luxury of that, missing 'the people'.

I thoroughly enjoy my own company, but maybe life is more about balance. When I saw Eugene again at Orrison and he reminded me to get a stamp, that was a friendly thing to do. If no one interacts with you, what have you got? When I saw Jeanette again, that was nice, too, and she introduced me to Brett. What do I want from this trip, and what do I want from life? Because this walk so far is a parallel to my life. I spend much of it pushing people away so that I can have 'me' time, and then wanting to be with people and never being quite sure how to get the balance right.

This trip is already messing with my head and it's only day three. Have I really only done three days?

I make the decision to book accommodation for tomorrow night. I have a big hill to climb tomorrow and I do ache but not as bad as yesterday. I hope my feet are going to hold out. I walked 18 miles today.

Day 4 Saturday 10th September

Cizur Menor to Cirauqui
15.11 miles

The sun is rising as I leave at 7.10 am. To get back on the Camino, I need to find Burger King and turn left. It would be very tempting to buy a burger if it were open as I am very hungry. I am at the dual carriageway, level with the bridges and I walk along the path with the busy highway below. I am looking for the neon sign and eventually I spot it before crossing the dual carriageway over a bridge. It's just getting light but there are lots of car lights going underneath. I have no idea where to go, I am trying to remember the angle of the lady's hand when she was explaining it all to me.

A Spanish lady helps me and, when she realises I am English, she tells me how sad she is that the Queen has died. She seems more upset than me, but I haven't seen a television, or heard the radio, so I feel very detached from the news.

After a little while, I see three little dots with backpacks and walking poles in the distance and suddenly I can't help smiling. I am so happy to see pilgrims that it puts a spring in my step. I am literally bouncing along now. The first pilgrim I see says, '*Buen Camino.*' I have re-joined the flock again.

I felt lost last night in the lady's house. I was very comfortable, much more so than in a bunk bed with a paper sheet and my sleeping bag, but I had lost my people. Now, the feeling of belonging has hit me. I am not just walking a path from SJPP to Santiago, I am walking with other pilgrims, even if I don't want to talk to them. Just knowing they are walking the same way and we are all doing the same journey is a comfort.

The path cuts across farmers' fields and the sun shines on the expanse of newly cut hay and turns them gold. I take lots of photos trying to capture it. The birds are singing and it's blissfully quiet. I am sooo happy.

A man and a lady walk by. He says hello, and she just laughs with a big smile on her face. That about says it all. She is enjoying her Camino and I know just how she feels. Words can't describe it.

I walk on for three miles, full of flat, beautiful fields with mountains in the distance. I keep trying to work out which hill is the one we are going over. A clatter of walking poles behind me and the gentle chit chat is like a comfort blanket. I hadn't realised until I left the path how important the other pilgrims were to reassure me that I am going the right way. A couple from Washington walk a little way with me and tell me that they had a rest day in **Pamplona**. Funny, they had a rest day and I walked straight through it. This walk is full of contrasts.

Today, I am carrying some nuts in my pocket, as I ate very little yesterday and nothing this morning. I am looking forward to the café which is on the side of the hill and sounds perfect. I hope I can get a lemonade to refresh me.

Soon, there's a slight incline upwards and the ground is rocky. I get to the top and there are benches, where lots of people have stopped to admire the stunning scenery. I take a video on my phone as the camera just isn't catching it. Down below, I can see flat fields of hay and far away are the mountains. The scenery is so vast, you can see for miles and miles, which is very different to anything that I have experienced before. I can also see **Pamplona** behind us, and I am a tiny bit sad that I didn't see much of it.

Two girls are sitting down on a bench near me, one with bare feet and struggling with blisters. I stop and take off my bag and snack on a bit of the bread from yesterday. The girl says that we are at the top. I don't think we are, as I heard that we walk between two wind turbines and we haven't done that yet. I am feeling good; I have walked 4.22 miles so far.

A group of men appear and talk about how they are. One asks the other, 'How are your feet?' and he says, 'Could be better.' I know how he feels.

I put my sun hat on, some sun cream, take my cardigan off, and slip my backpack on. I am ready for the climb to the top, feeling quite excited.

The café at **Zariquiegui** is not as picturesque as I thought it was going to be, in fact you can't see any views, so I pop into the tiny shop and buy a peach, which is delicious, and I carry on up the hill. The climb is nowhere near as bad as I thought it was going to be. It's lovely walking through the wind turbines. Having seen them from the ground, they are huge when you are right next to them.

I am now at the top, reaching **Alto del Perdon**. The views are spectacular, spanning 360 degrees and reaching far into the distance. There's also a pilgrim landmark – a row of iron stencils of ancient pilgrims which must be ten feet tall – a cluster of them just as if they are walking now, all facing the way we are going, some with horses, some on foot. It's quite special with the scenery behind them. I love it up here, it has a great energy. I see a couple of familiar faces too. I speak to a lad from the monastery hostel and relax for a bit to absorb the energy and the views.

The path down is steep and dangerous with lots of rocks, many of them loose, ready to bring you to your knees. I take my time, and tread carefully, following many other people who are treading carefully as well. It's not as bad as the path down to Zubiri but I do have to concentrate.

I meet Bono from Croatia and we walk together for a bit. I went to Croatia in May, so we have lots to talk about. Zagreb, Borak and Vodice. He tells me that is proud of his name and laughs that Bono must have been named after him as he is older. I had no idea that the Irish singer Bono had a Croatian name. I had never given it any thought. Then I have to let him go ahead, as my feet won't walk as fast as him.

I see him sitting on a bench as we get to the village of **Uterga**, and he asks if I can help him book accommodation as we had been talking about it. I sit down on the bench next to him and explain how I found somewhere to stay by using the accommodation sheet. Get the name and then research it, and then email or ring them. He finds somewhere that he likes the look of, says thank you and I walk on.

It feels good to be able to help a fellow pilgrim out and I am enjoying this casual way we all just share our thoughts, and our experiences so far. Mike helped me get to **Pamplona** and I just helped Bono navigate room bookings. It lifts your spirits, and I am enjoying all the different cultures and broken English. I feel richer for having met Bono, culturally and as a human. And I may never see him again, but that doesn't matter either.

After a while, I see a perfect eating spot, an albergue called Camino del Perdon, with a restaurant and large terrace out the front. There are some familiar faces sitting in the chairs sheltered by a canopy. I find a seat where I take my shoes and socks off, then go inside barefoot and order a salad and cold lemonade. Every second out of my shoes helps me. I read my Brierley book as I eat outside. The food is delicious and extremely welcome as I haven't eaten well recently. The salad is fresh, tasty and hits the spot.

The group of Italians I saw before, and Mateo, walk by. They seem to be growing every time I see them, collecting more Italians along the way. At 12.40 pm, after getting a stamp, I slip my shoes back on and off I go. It's still hot and I have about 14 kilometres to go. My brain is confused with the distances because the Brierley book is in kilometres on the maps, which is what I try to follow, but my walking app tells me how far I have walked in miles.

My brain also understands miles much better than kilometres, so it's constantly confused.

By the time I reach **Obanos**, sweat is dripping down my face. The open countryside has no shelter but it's beautiful and peaceful so I take another video to capture the beauty and silence. Then onto **Puente la Reina** which seems like a mini **Pamplona** but with a better vibe. Here, there are lots of Spanish people eating food out the front of cafés along the narrow streets. The buildings are tall. I don't see anywhere that I want to get a drink so I walk to the end of the street where there is a water fountain. I decide to stop here and take my shoes off for a bit.

Before me, a lady is standing in the water fountain, shaving her legs. I laugh at her, which maybe I shouldn't do but, luckily, she laughs back. She said she is waiting for her husband to return, he has gone to get the car. I am very confused. Where is her husband? Why has he left her in a fountain shaving her legs, and why is it so important to shave them right now? She comes over and we chat. I say I am doing the Camino, I don't have time to shave my legs. Then I notice her bag has a shell on it and realise she's doing the Camino as well. She's not crazy, she is just a character. She explains in broken English that she is from Croatia and, as she didn't want to fly, her husband has driven their camper van up from Croatia. So, at the end of the day, he goes to get the camper van with an electric bike then drives back to her. So, he is doing it all twice, well three times, once with her pushing the bike, once back on the bike, then in the camper van back to her. She also tells me how he had his jacket stolen yesterday with his phone in it. She rang it and a lady answered and wouldn't give it back and they had to call the police. I enjoy chatting to her, she is fun and interesting.

I put another plaster on, only Compeed from now on, no more cheap blister plasters. The lady offers me one of hers which is kind but I have some. I put my sandals on and get going. This is a nice village and I might have liked to stay here, but I have booked further on. By now, it's

3.00 pm and so off I go again, leaving the village through an archway and over a very impressive stone bridge.

The Croatian lady said that it's 29 degrees today, which is way too hot to be climbing this steep hill. A great day for the beach but not so good for walking in the Spanish countryside. It's difficult to put one foot in front of the other, with the blisters, fatigue, and the heat. I climb seriously steep inclines up through a forest. It's a real struggle, and I am sweating so much that it's dripping into my eyes and stinging them. I lost my little flannel a while back to wipe my face, because I didn't put it back in my pocket properly. But it is a lovely walk, even if it is hard work, and it's so peaceful. I don't see anyone at all for an hour and a half which is bliss.

Eventually, though, I sit down under a tree and have a break. It's probably one of the most peaceful places I have been to, ever in my life, even more so than the Pyrenees. It's just complete silence all around. I sit for a while and lap it all up, feeling so lucky to be experiencing this. This is exactly what I was hoping for: solitude, peace and beautiful scenery. This Camino has already gone far above my expectations.

I have more steep inclines and, afterwards, I stop at a pretty little village called **Maneru**. I see an albergue, El Cantero, and stop to get a lemonade and sit outside in the shaded street, taking my shoes off. This hostel would have been perfect, it looks lovely, in a peaceful village and more importantly, it's here right now. It looks really old, full of character, and has the most amazing stone floor inside where I went in and ordered my drink. I would have really enjoyed staying here. But I have to make do with a brief stop, which I am grateful for. As I hobble on sore feet out of the village, the church bells ring 5.00 pm.

In front of me on the horizon, I can now see where I am going. It's only two kilometres away – a little village on a hilltop, and it looks picturesque. I try to walk a little faster but it's almost impossible. It's a slow walk across the countryside between these two villages.

I see a man sitting on a bench just before the village and I chat to him. He hasn't booked anywhere but doesn't seem at all stressed by it, calmly reading his book. His name is Roger and he's from Australia. I tell him where I am staying but that I have booked a bed. Higher and higher, I climb up the tiny lanes of this unique village. Everything is on a slope. I have to stop and take a sip of water, even though I am almost there.

The hostel, Albergue Maralotx, is gorgeous. Because it's on a steep hill, the left side of the building is much lower down and has another floor where the reception is. It's old and full of character. I love it. As I approach the front door, I hear someone call out, 'You made it!' and turn to recognise the girl from Slovenia I met a few days ago, which is lovely. I haven't seen her in a while and it's wonderful to have a greeting like that from a friendly face when you have struggled.

I sign in and try out my Spanish. '*Yo tengo una res-er-vas-as-acion-eees*.'

And the receptionist replies, 'Are you Paula?'

I laugh and ask if I said it right and he says, 'We just say *reserva.*' I laugh again at my very bad Spanish, but now at least I know for next time. He tells me that the pilgrim's dinner, which I decided to join in with at this hostel, is in an hour, so I have just enough time to shower. I walked 15 miles today.

Unfortunately, being the last to arrive means that I have a top bunk. I chat to three ladies, who are sitting in a row on the bottom bunk opposite me. One is from America, and one from Totnes so I say, 'Twinned with Narnia,' and she laughs. I have visited Totnes twice when I went on a retreat to Sharpham House and I loved it. The town had one small street on a hill, filled with a unique collection of independent shops.

There's a lovely reception room here at the hostel between the shower, bedroom and stairs to the balcony area, which has a stunning tiled floor. I sit on a chair and talk to a man from America while I wait for a shower to become free, who says I must come out looking like a flower – he is teasing everyone who goes in the shower. I bet I will look a whole lot better. I actually have crusty eyebrows from the sweat dripping down my face.

I buy a lemonade from the tiny bar that doubles up as the reception to go with my dinner, as it's water or red wine. Three fizzy drinks in one day, my poor teeth. As we are waiting to go in, a lady asks me if I was at that crazy French lady's house. It takes me a few minutes to remember, and we both laugh, and agree that it was a very strange breakfast. Unfortunately, I don't get time to talk to her properly as we are ushered in for dinner. We go through into the most stunning room which feels like a wine cellar; the walls are arched at the top, and there's lots of heavy stone. The floor has the same funky tiles as the other side of the building. It's a fantastic place to have dinner. What a treat.

There are two long tables in this room and another in a room under another arch. I sit with the American man, an Australian man living in Germany, a Scottish lady, a Frenchman, a Danish lady and a man from Canada, and Roger who I met on the bench, who had to have the private room as everything else was taken, as well as a man to my right from the Netherlands. We talk about how far we have been and they share their experience of a Michelin star tapas bar that they went to yesterday in Pamplona which sounds amazing. The Netherlands man says he went to a hotel yesterday to be on his own. I said I was on my own and I got a big towel. He totally understands and I tell him I didn't need to dry it either. We both laugh.

It's a perfect meal of salad, followed by chickpea stew. The owner asks if I want any more and I say, 'No thank you, only the recipe, please.'

He says yes, which I am surprised at – that request doesn't normally work. This place has such a great atmosphere, an interesting mix of people, a stunning dining room and a lovely host. A successful pilgrim's meal.

After dinner, I sit upstairs on the balcony, with a great view of the church just a few metres away and write in my journal. This whole building has such a good vibe. I am thrilled that this has been one of my hostels. The sun is just setting and I am drawn outside to look at the views. Because this is an unusual old village on a hill, there are lots of winding, thin streets and they all end at a view, so everywhere you look, you want to take another photo.

I phone my partner, Phil, because we haven't spoken since Sunday, although it feels like I have been away for three weeks. The Camino sounds strange when I relay stories back to him. The bunk beds, the people and the views, it's hard to get it all across. After we say our goodbyes, I go back inside to settle down for the evening. I stand outside my room, The bedroom door is shut and I can hear snoring.

Great.

I hesitantly open the door and the light is out. I quietly go to my bag in the corner and take off my shorts, but leave everything else on as I have to climb the ladder up to my bed. I don't know what to do about the rest of my clothes. When I am on the bottom, I usually put them on the floor under the bed. The ladder is hard work when you have tiny legs and sore feet. I hoof myself onto the top and lie still.

I am scared. I don't like it up here. I don't even have a wall to lean on and I could fall out of either side. I don't think I will sleep anyway as two people are snoring badly. One person gets something out of their bag in a wrapper and opens the package, it's probably ear plugs. They are not going to do the job. The snoring sounds like one of those drills that breaks concrete.

Well, it's a good job that I got a decent sleep last night and I don't have a heavy day tomorrow as this is going to be a long night. The bells are chiming regularly and we are a few feet away from the church so they are loud. Lovely, I do love a church bell, but not when I am trying to sleep.

I decide to put my top and bra at the bottom of my sleeping bag. Usually, I prefer to open my sleeping bag up because it feels less claustrophobic. I keep touching the sides of the mattress, to tell my brain how big it is. The room is lit slightly by an orange streetlamp and, when I look down to the floor, it seems such a long way away.

My face is also sticking to the pillow which isn't good. I didn't buy a packet of paper sheets and pillow slip this time. They were given to us before but they were obviously optional here as some people don't want them. So, I am sleeping on a plastic pillow and a plastic mattress with no sheets, which is not ideal. I can't believe that I wish I had a paper pillow slip. What has my life come to?

I carefully retrieve my top from the bottom of my sleeping bag and squeeze my pillow into it to make a pillow slip, which sort of works, can't say I am not adaptable. I try not to break my glasses that are at my feet in the sleeping bag, and attempt to drift off.

This is one strange night.

Day 5 Sunday 11th September

Cirauqui to Ayegui
12.17 miles

It's 6.30 am and I am alive, I made it, and I didn't fall out of the bed. I learnt how to turn over by putting my feet in the corner of the sleeping bag whilst hanging onto the sides with both hands. Some people left ages ago, and some are getting ready now. There's that whispery rustle, rustle, rustle and, of course, someone is still snoring. I have a headache which I need to sort out. It might be from too much sun yesterday, although I didn't have it then.

Before I leave the village, I want to have a quick look around again, as I probably won't be back. Actually I would like to come back here but not in a bunk bed. But just in case I don't, I want to have a wander now that my feet have recovered.

I am glad that I am only doing 22 kilometres today, about 13 miles, and hopefully before it gets too hot. I am the last to leave, and it made a change to all the rushing. I think I prefer this and I will slow it down at least until I am fitter and the blisters are OK.

Now, it's 7.30 am. The sun is just rising and I want to take a couple of photos in this wonderful village, which is so quiet and serene. Trying to leave, though, is a challenge, because the entire place is full of tiny lanes on different levels and I keep taking the wrong turns. A local man leans out of a window and points me in the right direction. He probably does that every morning, pointing pilgrims back onto the path. The air feels fresh again, the sun is rising, and there are lots of people leaving the town behind me, little *peregrinos* all in a row.

The next main village is **Estella**, where everyone that I have spoken to is staying. I am going on two kilometres. The paths are OK, even if they are a little stony. The Croatian lady I met before at the water fountain and her husband with the electric bike overtake me. She says hello with a big bright smile and zooms away. They are much fitter than me, or maybe they just slept better in their camper van. That must be very special, parking it up somewhere in this beautiful part of the world. But I enjoyed the hostel last night, the company, the historic building, and the village, so you can't have it all.

It's 2.7 kilometres to the next village. My head is still muddled with kilometres and miles. I will stop soon and eat my breakfast from my mysterious brown bag that I bought at the hostel. I liked the idea of a breakfast to take away as I can't eat food as soon as I wake up.

There's a thin dirt track for a while, at one point only one person wide, so I step aside and let people pass. Everyone is overtaking me today but that's OK. I have to go at my own pace and I have been walking for five days now so my body is a bit tired.

Then I fall down.

I have no idea why, it's not that stony or uneven. But there I am on the floor, landing on my right knee and breaking my fall with my right hand. It's not easy falling with sticks attached to you. I struggle to get back up with a ten kilogram backpack on. I look around, up and down the path to see if anyone saw me. There's no one around, so that's good. My knee hurts, I think I have cut it but, thankfully, my trousers are not ripped. My right arm aches though. I feel a little wobbly. I haven't eaten but it's not the first time I have walked without eating. There isn't really anywhere to stop right now and the village isn't far away. Maybe then I can stop properly.

About half a mile further on, next to some shrubbery on a dirt path is a random food stall in the middle of nowhere with no one manning it. There's a wooden handmade sign saying, '*Para Los Peregrinos*.' How cute is that? There are no prices, just a donation box. I spot some figs and take one. I had been thinking of trying a fig from a tree but wasn't sure if they were ripe. I have seen lots on the floor, squashed. I sit down on a bench to read and enjoy it and find it's delicious, juicy and sweet. I don't think I have had a fresh one before, only dried. This has come at just the right time because I am hungry, and a bit sad that I fell over, but now I am smiling. I get up and take a second fig when a man appears out of the hedge with a big crate of apples. He says, '*Manzanas, manzanas,*' and offers me one.

I take one, even though I don't like apples. I can't refuse that big smiley face. He is happy that I am happy. There are also some baguette slices, toasted with oil. I am so hungry that I take a piece. I have no idea what his kitchen looks like, whether it's clean or not. But it looks good.

'*Bueno,*' he says.

I thank him in Spanish, put some coins in the donation pot and move on. He has other customers now. What a nice man and a random little treat.

There's a perfect bench in the next village, **Lorca,** to eat my breakfast bag. It's outside Albergue de Lorca. I get out the contents of my brown bag just as the Dutch man that I sat next to at dinner last night comes out, who says he just had the most delicious gazpacho inside and highly recommends it. Apparently, a Michelin star chef had been by and asked the cook for the recipe but she said no. I missed out on the Michelin star tapas in Pamplona, so I decide to put my squashed roll and carton of orange back in the brown bag, then go inside and order the gazpacho. The lady behind the counter, who takes my order, very proudly says she made it and I tell her why I came in. She smiles.

I talk a little Spanish. I am getting braver. And she talks in Spanish, too, and I understand her.

Gazpacho, which is cold tomato soup, is not something that appeals to me, but I couldn't resist the Dutch man's enthusiasm. I sit down at a little table inside, take my bag and shoes off and the soup soon arrives. It's absolutely delicious, with so many flavours. I am now a gazpacho fan. Thank you, Mr Dutch man. I chill and enjoy it. I am not going too far today and I have accommodation booked, so I can take a breather and make the most of these stops. This is part of the Camino that I didn't even know existed, this stopping in cute Spanish villages and trying local foods, mingling with other pilgrims. And I love it. Because each time I stop and eat, surrounded by pilgrims, I feel a deeper connection to the Camino. It strengthens why I am here, even though I don't know why I am here, and I know it's the right thing to be doing.

I get back on the road, still walking slowly, but every step is one closer. I see the girl from Switzerland who was at the **Roncesvalles** pilgrim's dinner. I haven't seen her since. It's so strange that we stay in different hostels and eat in different cafés and miss each other.

I pass rows of olive bushes and come to the village of **Villatuerta**. It feels different to everything that I have seen so far. I walk through a residential area which has modern houses made with red bricks and wide roads and modern streetlamps, before I pass through the old town which is more traditional.

A man named Fraiser joins me for a bit of the walk and we talk about blisters, my new favourite subject. He says to pop the blisters, but I am not so sure. He tells me he is walking with his aunt but they are walking at different paces so he's walked on ahead.

I am exhausted as I enter **Estella**. There's a river at the beginning that reminds me of Bath. The heat is strong now as I hobble through town, and it's draining my energy levels. I see a *farmacia* and go in to get more Compeed, only to find there is a queue. After five minutes, I can't stand anymore and I have to sit on a chair until it's my turn.

Further along the street, I see a fruit shop and buy a bunch of tiny black grapes that I have seen on the grape bushes and a banana. In Spanish, I ask for a nectarine by saying, '*Comer ahora,*' and the shopkeeper understands. Result, all that Duolingo has paid off!

After dithering about where to eat, I sit down at an outside café. I must be more decisive about picking eating places. Not eating in Pamplona was a huge mistake. I need to stop weighing up the decor, the clientele, the menu and just sit on a chair and order something. Egg and chips and serrano ham arrives, which is not what I thought I had ordered but it's hot and I do fancy chips, even though I thought I had ordered a potato dish with no ham. I take my shoes off.

It's taken me five and a half hours to walk ten miles.

Estella is a busy place, a mix of old narrow streets, and balconies like they had in Pamplona. There are also big buildings, churches, roads and cars. Another town that I might have made an error not stopping at.

Using Google Maps, I see that my hostel is 27 minutes from the restaurant, up a hill. It's a struggle for sure climbing the hill. It says 30 degrees on the street thermometer, which is why I am dripping and desperate for a fizzy drink. I pass a supermarket but it's shut as it's Sunday. Which is a terrible shame as I am gasping for a cold fizzy drink.

It's fairly early when I arrive at the hostel, Albergue Municipal San Cipriano, at 3.00 pm. I walked 12 miles. The building has a huge mural on the outside while, inside, it's very spacious and attached to a sports centre. The room is spacious as well. I take a shower and see that my knee is all scabbed up like a three year old's. I share a washing machine with my new roommates, who I haven't met before. While the washing is going round, I get hot water from the bar to make tea, asking for *aqua caliente* and take it back to my bed. It refreshes me so much that I go and get another, I am really parched today. The brothers, Brendan and Pearse, that I met in the Zubiri hostel are in my room. Brendan kindly gives me an electrolytes tablet which seems to quench my thirst and I don't feel desperate for a fizzy drink anymore. He also sends me a photo of the room as mine isn't turning out right.

Brendan asks me while we are chilling on our beds why I am on the Camino. I tell him the story of my Christmas gift which amuses him. He has done the Camino many times and this is his third time on the Camino Frances. My other roommates are a German lady, who I talk to about blisters as she is treating them with brown liquid which I haven't seen done before, a Colombian man, another lady, and an American lad who I saw at the random food stall on the way here. We are all fairly quiet people and the room is spacious, so it has a nice vibe.

An hour later, my washing is dry. I put a post on Facebook and eat the roll from my breakfast bag for tea, so it was a good job that I saved it, and I get an early night.

Day 6 Monday 12th September

Ayegui to Los Arcos
13.13 miles

There was no snoring and I slept very well. I didn't even hear people coming in after I fell asleep. It was very hot during the night though, and my face kept sticking to the paper pillow slip.

Some people left at 5.30 am and then the light went on at 6.00 am.

I decide to get dressed and get going. I don't have a bed booked at the moment, so will see how I go. I am so busy eating the nectarine that I bought yesterday that I am out on the main road before I realise that I don't have my walking poles and have to go back for them. It's dark as I walk up the street. I can't see any shells or people but I think it's this way. It feels safe, walking by a road in a residential area.

I have my sandals on and my feet don't feel great. I also have a red swollen patch on my middle toe that I need to keep an eye on. The blisters are collapsing and I think that's what they are supposed to do, but you are probably supposed to rest, not walk on them every day. Where the plasters are sticking to my shoe, they are pulling on my skin and it's uncomfortable.

There's another thermometer street sign further on that says it's 6.40 am and 23 degrees. I keep going and see a Camino sign, and all is good. There's also a big sign saying, '*Fuente de Vino*'. I am a little excited to get to the fountain as it is supposed to have red wine in it.

When I get there, it's still dark and we need our phone torches to see what we are doing. It's not every day you see a fountain that pours red wine instead of water. There are a lot of giggles and excitement now. I am excited to try this and I don't even like red wine, but it's a unique experience, especially at 7.00 am in the morning. It tastes awful, a thick red wine flavour that stays with me, but I do enjoy the whole experience.

Just as I leave the fountain, it starts to rain. It becomes too heavy to ignore so, on a concrete table under the trees, I get my funky plastic poncho out of my bag and attempt to put it on. It's not easy trying to get it over the backpack, my arms aren't long enough to reach round. I am more worried about my sleeping bag, which is hanging on the outside and my passport in a slot on the back of the bag, than I am about me.

I get to a junction that I had talked to the brothers in my room about yesterday. There are two routes, one more scenic and one traditional. I don't know which way to go. I couldn't make up my mind yesterday and now I just stare at both the signs. Most people go left on the scenic route but I think I want to do the traditional. As I make up my mind, a local lady says, '*Mejor aquí.*' If a local says that it's better, then I am happy.

The rain stops and the poncho gets too warm, so I stop to take it off at another concrete bench. I get out the grapes that I bought yesterday and eat them along the way. I bite into one and crunch straight into a pip. They are tiny little black grapes but each have two pips in them. It takes me about half an hour to eat the small bunch, but I enjoy the walk as the sun rises behind me and lights up the whole sky.

I have walked for one hour and done 1.63 miles. That's not too bad with blisters and pulling ponchos on and off, making decisions about where to go and drinking red wine. By 9.00 am, I have walked four miles. The open countryside is stunning, with hay coloured fields again and blue sky. I go through a village, **Azqueta**, and pause and think about getting a drink, but it's not like the place I got soup at yesterday and there's building work going on, so I continue.

There's a steep hill near the village of **Villamayor de Monjardin**. I don't stop here either. Then we are in the open countryside with lots of rows of grape vines. I realise that I haven't thought about my feet for a while. That's a good sign, they might be healing. The sun is strong and there's no shade for long stretches of open farmland, but it's really pretty where the hay has been cut – the fields look tidy like they've all had haircuts. It's a busy little stretch with pilgrims everywhere. I can see them up in the distance, a line of little dots. But, for some reason, I pick up some speed and overtake a few people. I haven't done that in many days, so I'm optimistic that I will be OK soon.

After a while, the paths seem longer and straighter with nothing but hay-coloured fields for miles and miles. I wish I'd stayed at the last café and had a drink. I need to sit down but it's very open and there are no benches anywhere. So, I plonk myself down on the edge of the path instead, on loose hay next to a farmer's field. I don't like taking my bag off and putting it on the floor as it's hard work getting it back on, but I have to stop. I also need a wee which is great news. But I am not going here, it's way too open. I drink my juice box that I got in my brown breakfast bag yesterday. This breakfast bag has been keeping me going for ages.

The Dutch man who told me about the gazpacho catches up with me and stops to chat. He tells me he left money under his pillow at the hilltop albergue and forgot about it, but rang the owner who said he was going to the next village and met him there to give it back. He says they went out for dinner in a fantastic eating place. He seems to be having the best culinary experience on this Camino.

I sort all my plasters out. Some are curling up and some are not sticking. I use a couple of normal plasters to try and stick them down. Two men ask me if I am OK. I must look strange sitting here on the floor in the middle of nowhere. One I know from **Roncesvalles** and who I met again at the top of the hill with the iron statues, and one I have not met before. There is so much love on this walk and a sense of looking out for each other. I don't feel at all alone. I have walked eight miles, which I am quite chuffed with.

Mike stops to chat, too. He is going to a Dutch albergue in **Los Arcos** and I say I might as well, but haven't decided yet. It's quite early in the day and I don't feel stressed about accommodation today.

I get my bag on my back and start walking again.

But it's a struggle. My energy levels are very low and the last three kilometres are tough. I am sweating badly and my feet are hurting. The plaster arrangement is still not working and I can't wait to stop.

I rest on a bench when I get to the village of **Los Arcos** and look at the map in Brierley's book to see where the hostels are and google the Dutch one. It looks perfect, with a bit of outdoor space and a kitchen. So off I go through town. Like the others I've visited so far, it's old with narrow streets and has a square with a tall church tower. I might take a look later if my feet heal.

At 1.00 pm, I am at the hostel which is very early. My feet hurt so much that I can't stand in the queue and have to sit down. My feet feel like they are on fire again. I only walked 13 miles.

There's plenty of room here and I get a bed. The Dutch lady is nice and asks me not to knock my sticks over but when I get my passport out, they fall to the floor and she winces. I go up the stairs slowly, one foot at a time, and find my bed number. It's very squished but at least it's only €8.00. I shower, wash my clothes and hang them on the line in the front garden area, then make my way to the kitchen to brew a cup of tea, where I sit at the table and eat half a huge vegan cake that I bought in the village.

I feel quite chilled, it's so early and I have a lot of time to unwind and rest my feet. I decide to book a back massage and get an appointment for 5.00 pm when the physio comes to the hostel. I meant to get one before I left home, as sometimes I get a strange niggly pain between my shoulder blades, but I ran out of time, so today is good. It's not cheap, however, at €25.00.

The lady at reception said when I booked in to take all the Compeed off my feet. I go back to talk to her and she's very kind and helpful. She has a yellow bottle of the brown liquid called Betadine on her desk for us to borrow.

Since checking in, I have googled the pluses and minuses of using Compeed and I got a lot of different opinions. One comment was about draining the fluid, so at least I know that's an option now. I carefully take off all the Compeed covering my feet. One is nearly off and there's a small wound. The other three are still full of blisters, and another one is empty. The lady at reception said to wash my feet, which I have done in the shower, and get some tissue. She gives me a tiny syringe with the yellow bottle and tells me to drain the fluid out before adding the same amount of brown liquid back into the blister.

Off I go, nervously, to a quiet spot at the back of the garden out of view of anyone. I don't want to draw attention to myself, as syringing my foot is not something that I want to share with anyone. Plus, I have no idea what I am doing. With my foot resting on my leg at a difficult angle, I clean it with some wet tissue and dry it afterwards. Carefully, I insert the syringe into a blister and drain the liquid. There was a lot more liquid than I thought there would be. I squirt it onto the grass, while checking no one is watching. Slowly, I pour some yellow liquid in the lid of the bottle and collect it up with the syringe, then insert it into the blister. Oooh, it stings! I do the same thing with the other ones and now my once see-through blisters are a funny red colour – and look quite alarming.

I can now barely put any weight on them and wonder if I have done the right thing. I hobble back to the building in my flip-flops and make another cup of tea, looking at options for tomorrow on where to stay. I look at the next village, **Sansol**, which is six kilometres away, and hope I can get there. I will try and get going early before the rain that's forecast.

There are lots of familiar faces here: Mike, the lad from monastery and iron statues as well as a few faces I recognise but have not spoken to, like the Portuguese man, who forages a lot, plus the ever growing Italian group with Mateo.

At 5.00 pm, it's time for my massage. I am a bit nervous as I have never had one before. The massage bench is on the landing at the top of the stairs between all the bedrooms. My masseuse is an elderly man with white hair and a white uniform. He doesn't ask me to fill in any forms and doesn't even know my name which is quite refreshing. He also doesn't speak any English. But, somehow, I understand that I need to take off my top and bra while he gives me some privacy and a towel. I lie on the couch face down and he returns. He moves my shorts right down, exposing half my bum to anyone who walks past on the landing, which is a lot as it's very busy at the top of the stairs.

He seems to know what he is doing though and I try to relax. He massages my back, shakes my arms about, then spends more time on my back. After about half an hour, he's finished. I try to get my bra back on, which goes over my head, not like a normal bra, and he helps me untangle it and lay it flat, which is a bit weird. I pay him and say thank you.

When I walk down the stairs, I realise that my feet feel much better. I can walk down them using both feet, one after the other, not the strange crab steps I've become used to. My feet feel comfortable and I hope they are on the mend. I decide to go to the pharmacy to pick up my own supplies to look after them.

Once I get there, the lady behind the desk is very helpful and I buy my own yellow liquid, some dressing and some plaster tape. Before I put my shoes on in the morning, I will have to dress them.

Afterwards, I go to the supermarket and get a bread roll, cheese and a tomato, and visit the church which is stunning. Inside, it has a beautiful painted ceiling with solid, stone pillars and lots of gold. I walk back to the hostel, feeling so much better by being able to walk properly.

The kitchen is full of Italians, noisily making bowls of food to share out. So, I grab a plate, slice my baguette and tomato and sit outside under the tree in front of the hostel. There are chairs and tables with people chilling; it's a nice atmosphere. A woman I met earlier called Emma joins me, who is Fraiser's aunt. We chat until the heavens open. I grab my washing in off the line and we relocate into the busy, squished kitchen. I sit down with Emma, only to find when I look over that my knickers and bra are in the middle of the kitchen floor. We both laugh. It doesn't seem at all unusual, no one even flinches that my knickers are on the kitchen floor.

At 9.00 pm, it's time for bed. There's lots of rustling, noise and conversations travelling up the stairs from the kitchen. I manage to get to sleep even though all the lights are still on, people are snoring and the heat in the small bedroom is almost unbearable.

Day 7 Tuesday 13th September

Los Arcos to Viana
10.31 miles

It's 5.45 am and the French people are efficiently packing and out of the room by 6.00 am. There are already people in the kitchen cooking breakfast and talking at normal volume which I can hear from my bed. Lots of people are still sleeping, but I am awake now. My paper sheet didn't last this time, so my hands and feet have been stuck to the plastic mattress all night, but I did sleep well. I open the bedroom shutter and it's pitch black out there but feels fresher. I can feel rain is on the way.

I wash and dry my feet before dressing them, squeezing the dark brown liquid onto a small bit of gauze with some tape to hold it in place. My blisters are stinging right now but hopefully that means the red stuff is helping the wound.

At 7.00 am, I immediately take a wrong turn, and get corrected by the couple I took a photo of a few days ago. They had looked so adorable sitting on a log taking a break that I asked them if they wanted their photo taken.

The scenery is stunning, again, same as yesterday's vast fields of hay. If you were painting the scenery now, you would only need a few colours in your palette. A bright sunny hay colour, green for the olive trees, and a hint of brown. These are the images that I am taking away from the Camino.

I walk slowly and carefully and arrive in Sansol, chuffed with myself. It's a small place where lots of pilgrims stop for coffee but it's very busy and I want to keep moving. At the end of the town, I take a seat at a bus stop which is the only bench that I can see and peel my socks off. I air my feet for a bit while I get my banana out of my bag and notice people looking at me. I want to shout, 'No, I am not getting a bus! I am going to walk all the way to Santiago, if my feet allow me!'

There are lots of ways of doing the Camino, and an awful lot of people have their bags sent on ahead to the next hostel and walk with day bags. Sometimes I am envious of them, as they are usually the ones who overtake me and whizz on ahead. I have always enjoyed walking but carrying at least ten kilograms on your back does add another layer of difficulty.

I can't imagine walking without my bag though. This is a challenge, part of the whole experience, and I want to experience it 'properly' carrying my things. It's not that I want to be weighed down with my belongings, as such. But I want a true experience, and I like the fact that I have everything with me. It gives me freedom and it was this feeling of freedom that was really important to me on my interrailing trip. In a way, that was a very similar experience to this walk; I carried my rucksack all over Europe, choosing where I wanted to stay, getting off trains when I wanted to. Except that, on that trip, I was sitting on trains, looking out of the window or reading my kindle in comfort while the train took me to my next destination.

Without even knowing what the Camino was, and I am only just beginning to understand it now as I think about it, this is the next obvious extension of an interrailing trip. I am on a journey, I am walking to a destination: Santiago. It's a route that I am following but I have the freedom to stop at any village that I want to for the night. Or I can walk on if I feel fitter, which isn't today, obviously.

The freedom that comes with being self-contained and independent runs much deeper than this walk. It's my personality. I need to feel the freedom, I need to be independent. I want to carry my bag, even if it hurts. I want to be in control of my day and decide where I stop. If I sent my bag on, then I would know where I was stopping every day, the element of surprise would be gone, and I wouldn't feel the freedom. But, if it *does* get to a stage where I feel that I need to send my bag on, I will definitely consider it. But, hopefully, it won't come to that.

Conscious that it's forecast to rain, I put my socks and shoes back on and start walking. The German lady who was at Ayegui passes by, and we ask about each other's feet. She only has three blisters now which she is happy about, as she did have seven. You can tell who has blisters by the way they place their feet on the ground, cautiously but defiantly.

I walk down a crazy paving path, and arrive at **Torres del Rio**, which is a lovely Spanish village. The bells ring as I walk over the bridge. There are a few places to stop and get a drink, a hotel on the first corner and a small café, then another, which has a nice feel about it. But I keep going.

My new friend, Emma, says hello as she goes by fast on a steep incline. On a stone lying next to the path are handwritten words: 'You are stronger than you think.' I stand and stare at them for a while, appreciating the sentiment. It feels like someone wrote that just for me, the words really touch me. They have come at the right time because I am seriously flagging. I repeat it to myself, over and over, as I climb upwards – you are stronger than you think – and I feel quite emotional. Sweat drips down my face again and I am out of breath. I pass a place where there are piles of stones, some quite high, and close to them is a tree with rags, flags and memorabilia. It all takes the attention away from my feet and blisters for a minute. Plus, the deep smell of pine trees is gorgeous.

But oh, no. In front of me is a severe downward path and then a severe upward one, which reminds me of the South West coastal path. Little dots are climbing the yellow path ahead, almost at the top, lucky people.

Here goes, it will be tough but I can do it. At the top, there is a blue sign that says 7.4 kilometres to Viana, which is about five miles. That's still a long way to go but at least that hill is behind me.

Two men pass, deep in conversation, so I don't say, '*Buen Camino*,' or 'hello'. Then I feel a hand on my shoulder and, when I turn, I receive a big smile. I have spoken to this man before in a hostel, and it was nice that he acknowledged me.

Another steep incline but it looks doable. It will have to be doable.

There's a noisy generator and a food truck under the trees. People that I have walked with today and in the past are all sitting there, sharing titbits of their lives with each other. I am hungry and would like to stop. But if I do, it's going to be tough to get going again and I just want to get my shoes off for good, so I carry on.

The scenery has changed now, it's green and fertile, and we are in a sort of valley with trees and bushes all around. I am looking forward to being in a better place with my feet but I am feeling a tiny bit low today. I feel like a solo person, and a little lonely, I don't know why. I would like to have stopped at that food truck. But I didn't. Maybe that's it, I should have stopped and chatted to someone, it would have lifted me.

I can hear music but can't work out why or where it's from. There are only trees and countryside around me. As I turn a corner, I see a man sitting on a chair under a tree playing beautiful music with his guitar. I stop and listen along with some others. What a treat, it doesn't sound at all out of place, instead sort of blending into the surroundings. It's beautiful music, no singing, just the guitar. After a while, I put some pennies in his guitar case and move on. That really lifted me. Music just gets straight into your soul.

A sign further on says 3.4 kilometres to go. Another man asks me if I am OK, as I bend over watching the ants on the floor. There are a lot of ants on the paths, bigger than English ones, and they're fascinating. They seem to be taking bits of hay somewhere, it's very cute. The man looks at them as well, both of us bent over watching. He says that he saw one the other day carrying something huge and thought that his own backpack was small in comparison. It was a nice moment watching the ants.

Oh no, another hill. I slowly climb it, and a lady who sat down at the food truck overtakes me. I must be exceptionally slow today. It's really hard work on a long stretch of tarmac which seems to go on forever, but I think I am close now.

At the beginning of Viana, I find a bench. Another girl is sorting out her feet with a big bag of toiletries and medical stuff. She is resterilising them with the brown liquid, ready to continue, but she seems to be in a lot of pain.

I get my list of hostels out, knowing I need to work out where to go. I haven't decided on which hostel yet, so I have a look and pick one. Emma and Fraiser arrive at the bench, along with two men that I don't know, before leaving to get to their hostel and I chat with an Italian girl. She wants to get to **Logroño** as her friends are all there. I think it's great she has made friends but, if her feet are anything like mine, those extra ten kilometres are going to get seriously tough and she might regret it. I wish her luck and move on.

I have picked a different hostel than Emma. I like her and it would be good to chat to her again, but I prefer the look of the other hostel – an old monastery with views. It's difficult weighing up friendships and your own preferences.

As I walk through town, I go under an archway with a big plaque that says 'Viana 1219'. I slowly realise some kind of event is going on as everyone is wearing white clothes with red accessories. A red scarf or a red cardigan or red belt, even the children and toddlers. Like the other towns, Viana has very thin streets and tall buildings with balconies. The bars are overflowing and outdoor tables are all busy. It's a lovely atmosphere full of chatter, laughter and lots of kissing and handshakes. It feels like a real community thing. I am so glad I am staying here. It's perfect.

People that I know are booking into the hostel, Andres Munoz. It's an anxious wait to see if they have a bed. I have only walked ten miles today but that's more than I thought I would be able to when I was treating my blisters yesterday.

It's a stunning building, really old. There's a lovely staircase and big, wooden front doors, easily 15 feet tall. I am lucky that they have a bed for me. On the landing, and along the corridor to the toilet and showers, are windows, where immediately outside are the old ruins, stunning and historic. The view out of the bedroom window is right across the countryside to **Logroño**. The room only has three bunks and I get a bottom again.

I shower and then eat my cheese roll that I made yesterday. I can't decide whether to wash my clothes, go out to the festival or have a cup of tea. In the end, I choose to make tea and wash clothes but, knowing the weather might break, I change my mind and go out instead. First, I clean my feet. I have to drain a blister between my toes and refill with the Betadine. What is my life now? It feels weird having a little kit with a needle syringe, gauze, tape and brown liquid. But it seems to be working.

With my feet attended to, I go out and explore this historical place. My flip-flops feel comfortable, although my feet are a bit tender and I don't want to walk too far. I snap some photos and end up in a busy square with a band playing. Everyone watching is wearing white and red again, so I stick out like a sore thumb.

I decide to join in the celebrations, whatever they are, and step into the bar for a lemonade and tapas to go with it. It's so loud, even inside, with the music from outdoors that I can hardly hear the lady talking to me, so I don't feel confident enough to ask for what I want in Spanish and speak English instead. It is only €4.00 for the lemonade and tapas, so good value. Both are delicious – very Spanish at this Spanish festival on this wonderful, unexpected day in a beautiful town. The pain of the walk, the loneliness and the struggle, are in the past now. I am rewarded with another precious experience.

I find a free space on a concrete slab outside that other people are sitting on to watch the band. The music is happy and joyful, with an accordion, three tambourines and a guitar, so it's quite different to anything I have heard before. The crowd loves them, clapping between the songs. I look around at all the people, the band, the gorgeous buildings. I feel like I have stepped into another world and I am very grateful.

A pilgrim walks by and I recognise him even though he doesn't have his bag. He's also wearing a red scarf so maybe it's not him. But he stops and asks which albergue I am staying in so he obviously recognises me too, even though I don't have my walking bag with me either. He says he was going to walk to **Logroño** but likes it here and is now looking for somewhere to stay. So, I get Brierley out and show him the hostel that I am staying at.

After finishing my tapas, I go for a walk around the block and back to the first street I came to when I entered Viana, where it's still packed with people. Such narrow streets with a sea of white and red colour is so striking. I force myself to get another drink and tapas, to slow myself down. My natural instinct is to scuttle away but I must enjoy these experiences. Inside the bar, it's so packed I can't see the glass tapas counter so I just point to two and hope I like them. They turn out to be what looks like stuffed pimento on a thin slice of baguette, and fish.

I might as well lap up the experience. It's tricky, trying to chill instantly. I have struggled to get to Viana, unexpectedly ending up in a festival, and I have to quickly switch mindsets to go with the flow whilst on my own. There's a lot of internal dialogue and self-motivation. I want to enjoy and experience everything, even though I have no idea where I am with only a very short time frame. After a while though, I go back to the hostel as my feet are hurting again.

The Korean lady in my room is so funny, she is a pharmacist. She really wanted to get some supplies for her sore feet from the pharmacy, but it's shut because of the festival. She is very bubbly. I lend her my tape, which makes her happy, then lend her the orange liquid too. She checks it over, approves and uses it as well.

After washing my clothes, I use the dryer. It doesn't look like there's an outdoor area here, just a very big washing and drying room. So, I spend €2.00 and get them dried which is a luxury. In the kitchen, I try to make tea but there's no kettle and I can't turn the electric hobs on, it's far too complicated. I microwave water instead for the tea and get a KitKat from the vending machine. That's the second time on this trip. I rarely use a vending machine – I feel like a child having a treat.

Back in my room, Tiago from Spain is there, the man I met out on the street, who has ended up in the same place. There's a lady from Hungary, the Korean lady, Tiago and me, all trying to talk about feet and blisters with the aid of Google Translate. It's quite an experience, very multicultural and very Camino. The Korean lady says she has sore lips so I lend her my Carmex. She calls me a pharmacist, as I have everything that she needs.

Before I settle in for the night, I decide to have one last look round the town as it's only 6.15 pm. My feet are sore but I can hear the celebrations going on and I don't want to miss anything. I hear a brass band, so I squeeze my feet into my flip-flops again and grab my nylon bag.

The band has gone up the narrow street, the huge silver instruments visible above the crowds. It then finishes in the square and I look for something else to eat, finding a café with a pilgrim's dinner. But I don't want a three-course dinner for €17.00, so I ask for a menu. The owner says the street is being shut and they will be serving again at 9.00 pm. I think that's a little odd, but the Spanish do eat late and it is a festival.

So I decide to go back to the tapas bar that I was in earlier. It's empty and I can see the glass cabinet now. I order my third fizzy drink of the day and three random tapas. When I put it on the table it sort of looks like a meal and it's delicious. I have an egg mayo type thing with a baby egg on top, a fish dish with cheese on top that I had earlier, and a potato croquette which is huge. They are all sitting on a thin piece of bread. I love Spanish food. I just love Spain. I have always enjoyed coastal Spain, and the old towns, but now I love rural Spain.

As I leave the tapas bar, the front area that I walked through has a gate across it now which is a bit strange, so I slip out of a small door at the side instead. The street is full of people, some even hanging out of balconies, and there seem to be lots of older children hanging around. Something must be happening soon. I get to the end of the street and there is a wooden gate across where I walked through earlier to get to the hostel. It's literally through the gate and turn right after the monument.

I walk around the corner where I was exploring earlier. But I can't go that way either. There's another big wide gate and people hanging on it, looking my way. Why are they there, on the other side of the gate, and I am here?

I don't understand. I try to go through the ruins, the huge door that I went through earlier. No, that's shut too. People are at every entrance looking into the street, looking at me. And I am so confused. A lady looks across at me, concerned. She is at a hotel and safely behind one of these barriers. Every building seems to have one and people are behind them.

But I am not behind one, and everyone is looking at me. I am surrounded by young boys. I am definitely in the wrong place.

I ask the lady if she speaks English and, luckily, she is English and says that it's best to come inside the hotel as the boys are going to be climbing the monument. Maybe like parkour? I don't understand. But I feel vulnerable out here and the lady helps me get into the hotel, and I stand by her and a Spanish man. We try to work out what he's saying. There will be a loud bang, then we don't know what?

The lady is called Joan and she is staying at the hotel. I tell her that I am doing the Camino and she tells me she is as well. I say that I don't believe her because she looks far too elegant. She is wearing a pretty, colourful dress and doesn't look at all shabby like I do. She says she has treated herself to the hotel and has dinner booked for 8.00 pm.

Then, there's a lot of noise, boys run past us and then a bull races by. The bull has a bell round its neck and its feet clack on the ground, the boys shouting and running around. It's chaos. Thank goodness I am not out there anymore.

Before long, another three bulls race by. The boys climb the wall of the monument and hang there, safe from the bulls; some wave their jackets, goading them. The bulls turn at the end and whizz by again. They smell really bad. There's the noise of whips against the wall and I lean out over the gate to see the bulls running up the long street. It's quite mad. I don't agree personally with bull fighting or any animal being used for entertainment. But that aside, there's no denying the thrilling atmosphere, and it's just so random. I am witnessing real Spain, its culture and history.

After about half an hour or so of bulls running up and down the street, Joan decides to go for her dinner. I thank her again for saving me. I am now trapped in a beautiful hotel with the most amazing stone floor. There's no way I can go out on the street and, even if I left the hotel, I can't get to the hostel as the gates are still up. It seems to have gone quiet though. At 8.30 pm, it ends and everyone pours into the street again. The wooden gates open. I walk the short distance, stepping over cow pats, back to the hostel, a little dazed.

What an evening. I drain my blisters again and go to bed. That's enough excitement for today.

We all get woken by an angry man banging on a huge wooden front door downstairs in the hallway. He is ringing the bell, ring, ring, ring, and shouting in three different languages, one after the other, over and over.

'Open the door!'

He wakes the whole place up. I notice Tiago is not above me in his bunk. I wonder if he got locked out. He said he was going to enjoy the festival. But he would be outside trying to get in, not inside trying to get out. I look at my phone and it's only 12.30 am, I thought it was about 5.00 am and the man wanted to go out walking early.

I'm confused but also pleased that I can go back to sleep. After half an hour, I am still not asleep but Tiago is in the room next door, I can hear him snoring. So that's good.

Day 8 Wednesday 14th September

Viana to Logroño
6.50 miles

The ladies get up early. I overslept till 7.30 am, but I am having a calmer start to the day as I think I am only walking ten kilometres to Logroño. I take all my stuff downstairs to the kitchen to sort and make a cup of tea, which is the first time I have made tea in the morning. I attend to my feet and put on the dressings and my sandals.

This might be a turning point in this trip. I have been erratic in the mornings with getting up, eating, rushing, and worrying.

Now that I feel my feet might be better soon, I can enjoy the physical part of this journey. I have really enjoyed Viana. It's almost a shock that I have to walk today after my bizarre holiday here. Music, tapas, red and white everywhere, the bulls. All because my feet were sore. I would have been a good 20 kilometres ahead by now and missed all of this.

I look in the vending machine for an orange juice but there's only a fruit mixed with milk that makes me feel ill just thinking about it. At 8.15 am, I am on the road after a quick detour back to the hostel to get my walking poles.

I am hungry, so I eat the last of my rice crackers, some nuts in my pocket, and an apple – I can't remember where I got it from. Possibly the breakfast bag in Cirauqui or was it that random food stall with the figs?

By 8.30 am, the sun has broken through and it's so hot that I have to put my sunglasses on. It's quite different to yesterday and, luckily, the rain never did appear. After half a mile, just outside Viana, I have to stop and look at my feet. My little toe on the right is hurting, it might be a blister starting. Three people on a bench just under the trees have stopped and are putting plasters on as well. We wave at each other.

I tuck some gauze on my foot and put some under my little toe which feels a little better before cutting the apple in half with my spork, so I can eat it as I walk. I put my bag back on and see that the others have moved on.

A man comes over to me and says, '*Buen Camino,*' which is nothing unusual. He shakes my hand though, which is slightly odd, and says something in Spanish that I don't understand. He points to both his cheeks. I think he is saying to smile, so I do, and then he kisses me on my cheek. Weird. It all happens so quickly. I feel uncomfortable. Not in danger – he's an old man – but definitely uncomfortable.

Luckily, I am ready to go, my bag is on my back and all I have to do is walk away from him. But he points to my glasses and so I take them off. I don't know why I take them off. I have been in an abusive relationship so maybe it's that kicking in, just to do as I am told, to avoid any anger. I feel wary and very uncomfortable.

He says, '*Muy guapa.*' I know what this means from my Duolingo lessons. Pretty. He is very strange, the way he is looking at me.

I move away fast, a little unsettled by the experience. But I try to put it out of my mind. I am not going to dwell on it, I am going to dismiss it before my brain spends too long on it and it sticks in my memory. He was a dodgy old man, probably harmless, but he is behind me now.

After two and a half miles, I have to stop again. The tape on my little toe hasn't worked so I put a small Compeed on it.

After another six and a half miles, I am in **Logroño** which is much nicer than I thought it would be. It's only 11.00 am and I would rather walk on further but it's a ten-mile commitment, leaving Logroño. If it were three or four, or even five miles, I would go for it, as 11.00 am is very early to stop walking.

The albergue I researched doesn't open till 1.00 pm, so I find a café close to the huge, great church and have a black tea and tiny roll. A breakfast deal: €2.80. I'm definitely going to stay and give my feet one more rest day.

I spend an hour sitting at the café, looking at all the hostels online and getting dizzy. I have a first choice, it's not the one I picked and walked past on my way in. But my new favourite says that it's temporarily closed. So, I look at the others but some don't have good reviews. One I was thinking about mentions bed bugs, although that's not fair as bed bugs are temporary and probably brought in from another hostel. I write on my map, marking where a few of them are, as they are all close together.

I wander around the church, looking up as the stone ceiling is amazing. It still has a bright, gold, shiny ornate altar which is very impressive but I like the amount of stone that it has as well. It's a big, traditional church with lots of seating where you can sit and contemplate. It also has lots of paintings. It's really quite stunning.

It turns out that the hostel I wanted to go to is open, La Bilbaina. It has the most amazing staircase with beautiful tiles on the floor and steps. I am very happy, and even happier when I see the room and the view. There are five bunks beds and two bathrooms with a shower and toilet in each, which are for ten people in this room. I also have a key to the room, which feels a bit strange, I am used to open rooms. I haven't had a key to a room since I was on the ferry.

It feels very luxurious. The shower makes it seem like I am in a hotel and the toilet has a sash across the lid to show it's been cleaned. And there are cotton bedsheets, with a towel, so I don't need to use mine or my sleeping bag. This is a good room. The wooden balcony is gorgeous too. It's a real treat, actually standing in one of these balconies that I have seen in a lot of Spanish villages and towns so far, but only ever from the ground. From here, I can look right down at the street. I love it. I can see the church towers and the balconies opposite which are quite close, as we are on thin streets; below are shops and restaurants, so there's a lovely atmosphere.

This Camino just keeps giving to me. I could so easily have stayed somewhere else, just round the corner, and not experienced this.

I am sharing the room with Nessa from San Francisco, who is easy to chat to. I shower and go out to eat. There's a vegan place 12 minutes away, so I am going there. I take lots of photos on the way. I like Logroño, I would come back here for a longer break. It has open spaces with trees and seating areas and statues. And lots of flats which are all so pretty, some of them with very ornate decorations.

In Café el Sol, I choose vegan meatballs with mashed potato and tomato sauce. It doesn't look very exciting but, oh my, it's so good. The 'meatballs' are nutty and crispy on the outside which goes well with the mash and tomato sauce. Very homely. It's good to have a hot, nutritious meal after too much bread and cheese.

On the way back, I pop into the supermarket for fruit: a banana, some plums, and a fruit smoothie and fruit juice. I might have overdone that. But it will keep me going tomorrow. Plus, two cakes in a box and a big bottle of fizzy water and an ice cream. Back at the hostel, I make a cup of tea in the kitchen while a man calls down to his friends on the street below the window. They talk about the bulls yesterday, calling it a bull run which makes sense. This trip has been so much more than a walk. I wasn't expecting so many experiences and this community of people.

In the bedroom, I hog the balcony. I love a balcony, so I drag a chair onto it and spend the rest of the day there. Most people are still out and about, so I don't think anyone minds. I eat my ice cream, drink tea, eat cake and people-watch. I read Brierley too and put some photos on Facebook. I love my balcony so much that I even take a video. I can see far up the street and it's all so lovely. What a spot.

I talk with Nessa again and sort my bag out. She says she doesn't mind a top bunk as it's quieter up there and I say I need the storage under the bed. She looks at all my stuff and laughs, saying that I really do live under the bed.

After a very chilled, happy day, I bring my chair back in and go to sleep surrounded by lovely cotton sheets.

Day 9 Thursday 15th September

Logroño to Najera
18.81 miles

By 7.00 am, it's just me and Nessa left. She might stay another day as she has a problem putting weight on her leg.

The room and the bed are so comfortable that I don't really want to leave, so I am a bit behind schedule. It's still dark outside, although it never really went properly dark as the street was always lit by cafés and streetlamps. It was a bit noisy last night, but more just dull chatter from lots of restaurants and the clink of cutlery on plates.

I dress my feet and leave this lovely room at 7.30 am. I follow a pilgrim but it doesn't feel right, then see three pilgrims in the doorway of a café about to leave, so I wait. I follow, but they go back past my hostel. I have no idea how to get back on the yellow line. I keep up with them, just about, as they are younger and fitter than me. I end up on a roundabout and they pause. I ask if they know the way and they point to a Camino sign. At last, I can stop following people.

I walk with an Irish man for a short while, who says it's going to rain at 2.00 pm. Hopefully I will be at **Navarrete** by then.

I am so busy looking at all the flats and streets and shops that I lose my way. I get to another roundabout and there are no signs. A lady sees me and asks if I am doing the Camino and points me in the right direction, back to the previous roundabout, then right. There are lots of pilgrims now, so I feel safe again. I stop in the park at a bench to take my cardigan off and get my smoothie and plums out to eat. My bag feels very cumbersome today and isn't sitting well.

This long concrete path is very uninspiring. I don't feel at all fit and I should do by now. I am feeling a bit low again, wondering why I am doing this. Feeling low doesn't make any sense. I had such a great day yesterday and the day before. This walk and this lifestyle is very difficult. Even if I am enjoying myself, it's still hard. I am continually moving. Every day there are new sights, new people, a new hostel, it's all hard work. I don't know if I have any energy, that's what it is. The get up and go is gone. I couldn't walk the Pyrenees today. Maybe, it's good that the Pyrenees is first, when you are new and naive, with lots of energy and no blisters.

Then I see a couple of red squirrels. People walk past, but I stop and watch them, which puts a smile on my face. They are inquisitive and nervous and a joy to watch.

The girls with washing on their bags go by. I haven't seen them in a few days, I thought they would be way ahead by now.

I get to a park area, very wooded with pine trees and there are more red squirrels, so I decide to stop. I still have sunflower seeds in my bag, so I entice a squirrel down from the tree and it eats out of my hand which is lovely. He's so cute and such a gorgeous colour, a rich deep chestnut colour and so shiny. This little creature has no idea but he's really lifted my spirit.

My mood seems to be very fragile, happy one minute and a bit wobbly the next. I am thankful that the sight of a squirrel is enough to lift me again. This is how I have been at home over the last year. Mentally fragile. I can feel fine then drop to a low point, or feel down then something will boost me. I am not sure what's going on. Just a bit wobbly.

Near the big pond are swans, ducks, and a moorhen. I enjoy the scene, all the different species mixing on the pond. It's a lovely spot. Then, as I walk over the bridge, I see the sign which I can read in Spanish: Don't feed the animals. Oops.

As I approach **Navarrete**, I walk with Carol from Oregon. She has an ankle injury that she has never had before coming on the Camino, so she is struggling a bit, and going at the same speed as me. We part as we enter the village as she has accommodation booked.

It's so quiet here with only pilgrims making a noise, clink, clink of the walking poles through the village which is old and a bit shabby, and a bit poorer, not like Logroño or Viana.

I go into the church; the doors are open and it looks inviting. It's huge with an enormous gold altar, from the floor right up to the very tall ceiling, very blingy. I don't know where to look, as there's so much to see. There are figurines all the way up to the dome ceiling. I look at it for ages, trying to take it all in. It's such a huge contrast to the village and a surprise as you walk in. There is a team of ladies, cleaning everything and hoovering.

I need a break, physically and mentally. So, I stop at a busy café, order a salad and sit inside by the door to watch people coming and going. The salad is perfect, a very generous portion, fresh and crunchy and wholesome, with lots of sweetcorn and balsamic dressing beside a fresh, soft baguette.

About four different people see my salad, as I am sitting near the bar area. They point and say, 'One of those.' One person even comes over to have a more detailed look at it before ordering one for himself. But I don't mind, it's a good salad at a good price, so I am happy that the owner has sold a few more. I can feel my body thanking me for all the nutrition already.

Nessa arrives and says hello. She is staying in the *municipal* that opens at 1.00 pm. I haven't made a decision yet. I look through Brierley and online at the hostels. I have two that I am considering here in **Navarrete**.

Google Maps wants to take me back to where I came from and I realise I had the map up the wrong way. I don't want to go backwards, so I go over to the *municipal* and look at it, but I am not feeling it. It's only 1.00 pm and I don't really want to stay in this village. My feet don't feel too bad but it might rain in a few hours. So I make a quick decision and start walking. I don't want to spend the rest of the day here. I am going to try and get to **Nájera**. It's about 13 kilometres.

It's an open straight road, and I get to a junction with signs to **Ventosa**. I couldn't get any accommodation there, which is a shame as it looked nice. I could also walk that way, it's a slight detour but I walk on as I have quite a commitment already.

I seem to have found my mojo again, thank goodness. I am walking faster, almost at my normal speed. My backpack and my feet feel OK. Maybe having a decent lunch and a little break helped.

There's a difficult stretch of dry stones which are hard on my feet. Then a long stretch by the road and there's no shelter from the heat which is tough. I have walked three miles already though, so I am happy.

After four miles I stop at a little rustic shelter and eat a plum, just to get out of the heat for a bit to look at Brierley, and get out my sunglasses. Then I carry on, where it's really rough terrain. I go up to a viewing platform and there's a fantastic view back to **Navarrete**. The scenery here is stunning, vast and flat with mountains off into the distance. There are fields and fields of grape vines and hay coloured fields and, where the sun lands on the hay, it illuminates it. It's absolutely stunning.

I get back down from the viewing platform and continue. I am in the Rioja region of Spain and there are thousands and thousands of grape plants, I have never seen so many as I have the last few days. I have really enjoyed this section.

I have not seen anyone in ages, so it's very serene and peaceful.

My shin hurts a bit now and I am feeling really tired, my pace back to a sludge. But there is a light breeze which is lovely as it's scorching hot, with no sign of rain. My bag is fairly comfortable, my shoes nearly comfortable, and it looks like there are about two miles to go.

But I don't seem to be getting to the village quick enough, and my little toe is hurting now. My leg muscles are very sore and my feet are on fire. This last bit is a struggle.

The town is strange; new but tatty. It seems poor, with lots of kids roaming around, boys playing football in the street, but it's also eerily quiet. I see three youngish pilgrims going through the town and the girl asks me if I know the way to the *municipal.* I say I was going to ask her the same question, so we all go together. The first hostel we pass is full, but we get redirected us to another.

I am seriously struggling now, the blisters on my toes are hurting, another bit of gauze has come loose, and I am done in. But I am trying to follow them through town even if it hurts. And it does. I don't have the energy to figure this out for myself, so I just follow and hope that we find beds. One person leaves our group so we are now a three.

The town seems to keep going. But we cross a bridge and find a hostel there and I really hope they have room as I am not going to be able to walk much further. Amazingly, there's one private bedroom left with three beds which makes it €15.00 each. We are told it's a cancellation, so we are very lucky. I am very grateful as I have walked 18 miles today.

The hostel, Puerta de Najera, looks quirky and much better than I was expecting to end up in when I entered the village.

I take my bag off and sit on a chair as I can't stand any more. My two new friends look after me and hand over my *credencial* and my passport as we get booked in. They help me carry my shoes and things, as I have unpacked it all to get to my passport.

The room is perfect. Three beds and these new friends kindly let me have the single while they have the bunks, which is very kind as I was tagging on to them. We immediately share a washing machine and Meredith, goes and sorts it out. I reuse my paper sheet that I squirrelled away in my bag, and I keep the new one in its packet. There's absolutely no need to do this, they only cost €1.00, but just in case I end up without one again, then I have a reserve. I rest for a bit then shower and get a cup of tea, microwaving water, and then go to the supermarket to get some savoury biscuits, a Fanta and an Aquarius for tomorrow.

There's lots of loud music and lots of kids hanging out as I walk around outside, almost like a street party. On the way back through the hostel, I find a kettle by the washing machine but I have a fizzy drink now. I put up a Facebook post, clean my teeth and go to bed. Meredith and Nick have gone out (separately, they are not a couple, just new Camino friends).

I fall asleep about 9.00 pm and get woken at 10.00 pm by a band going past the window. I look out and everyone is wearing yellow. There's a big silver brass instrument like in Viana. Another random evening.

I get woken up again at 11.00 pm as they loudly came round the block again, then once more at 12.00 am. But I'm not upset at the noise, it's lovely seeing kids making memories and I love their enthusiasm and the music.

It's noisy all night long and into the morning, but I have slept well, being shattered, and I seem to be more tolerant of noises now.

Day 10 Friday 16th September

Najera to Santo Domingo
14 miles

Meredith left about 6.00 am. I got up at 7.30 am, and took all my stuff to the area downstairs, which makes up a reception, kitchen, and dining area, and made a cup of tea with the kettle I found yesterday.

I can't find my sunglasses, pen or passport so I rush back up to see if it's under the bed. Nick is getting ready leisurely and says he hasn't seen my passport. I unpack my entire bag again and find them both at the bottom. I must have shoved things in quickly to get downstairs.

I have no idea where I am going today except on the yellow line. So, I look at Brierley while I drink tea, eat some savoury biscuits and note down some distances. I will try to get to **Santo Domingo** which is 20 kilometres. But I am not sure how my feet are. Shall I dress them or not? Or try and walk and see what happens? I have no idea.

Yesterday I bought an Aquarius at the supermarket; everyone is drinking it, as it has electrolytes in it. Maybe it will give me an extra boost. My right baby toe is still sore so I am going to put a Compeed on it and hope for the best.

It's a much slower start and I leave at 9.00 am.

Having walked through most of the village of Najera yesterday, I am close to the edge and I can actually see a huge, red rock literally on the other side of some houses. It towers over them and looks like the houses are stuck to it. It's very unusual.

I walk out of the village and up a hill which is very still at this time of the morning. There are pilgrims ahead, little dots in the distance. I can only hear my poles in the dusty stone path. When I stop, I can hear the small tractor collecting the grapes for wine. It's incredibly peaceful.

There's a gentle climb on tarmac, past more grape vines bursting with black fruit, and I pass what look like 'nearly home trees' which are a Cornwall landmark, that are actually in Devon. I realise how far I am from home and feel a mix of sadness at being so far away but also an appreciation that I am here.

Solo travel always brings mixed emotions. I am out exploring the world while my family are getting on with theirs, working and cooking dinners, putting the bins out on a Wednesday night, in their familiar surroundings. Sometimes I feel that what I am experiencing is better than life back home. I am having an adventure in Spain and then I feel a bit guilty. Then other days, like today, I get a reminder of home and it slaps me in the face and I feel a bit homesick.

I can picture the map of Spain in my head and roughly where I am on the Camino. And even though I am here, walking it, I still can't believe it.

I do feel slightly guilty but also proud that I have made this happen. Everyone can make it happen, if they wanted to, with a few tweaks here and there. We get so stuck in the hum drum of life, we don't always think that we have other options. I have managed to make this work and feel proud that I have stepped out of my comfort zone and into the unknown. But this trip is full of emotions and contrasts.

Azofra is very misty. I desperately need a wee, *really* desperately, so I hope there's a café here. The village is quiet, and I can hear a few conversations in houses as I walk by. I am so happy to see a café, two in fact, and I choose to go to the second. I sit indoors as I have been outside all day.

I order a tortilla, but I don't buy a drink as I have loads of water with me. It is delicious, very fresh. I talk to a man from the north of England who is at the next table. It's his third time doing the Camino. He must be mad, I just can't imagine ever wanting to do this again.

I have walked four miles and have 15 kilmetres left. I get my Aquarius out of my bag so I can drink it on the way.

Now to crack on, there's a lot of open countryside and apparently a hill up ahead. Three ladies are sitting on the ground next to a road, which cuts across the countryside in front of us. There are no cars on it; there never are cars on the roads, I don't know why they build them all. We chat about footwear and clothes. I say that I am throwing all my clothes away at the end as I am bored of them and one of the ladies agrees. They are nice ladies but I walk on.

It's lovely and flat here. There are no grapes for a bit, just open fields. I can see the hill ahead. I stop and take another 360 video, to try and capture the beauty and tranquillity.

I thought if I walked alone that I would be reflecting on life. I would have all this time on my own to think. But, to be honest, I am not and you can't force it. Sometimes it doesn't feel like I think about anything. Whole days have gone by on my own but I couldn't have told you what I was thinking about. It's almost as if I am not thinking about much at all, which is possibly good. A sort of walking meditation, although it's not something that I am trying to do. I am just trying to enjoy it.

My thoughts can be full of how many kilometres I have walked and how many I have to go. Where will my bed be? Will they have a bed? Do my feet hurt? My bag is heavy. What shall I eat and where? But these thoughts can't take up a whole day, so the bits in between are me just *being*, enjoying the scenery, and taking it all in.

I should feel fitter but I don't think I am, and I don't think I have lost any weight. This does puzzle me, as I have walked a very long way.

These daily walks don't really feel any different to a walk at home, except the scenery is very different and all the colours are different. Walking is walking, you put one foot in front of the other. I can't see the huge distance that I have walked because I am on the ground. It's too difficult to process, so on the Camino, it's just walking.

The last five miles haven't had any benches to pause on, and no fountains. Luckily for me, it's overcast or this would be a struggle. Ahead, I can see a tough hill. I brace myself, it's not too steep but it goes on and on which knocks the stuffing out of me. I puff and sweat to the top as everyone overtakes me. I arrive at a horrible looking town. It's not horrible, that's unfair, it's just very modern with red brick houses, not the old historic villages. It's a very new estate.

I have walked nine miles, and I should have stopped at the seats at the top of the hill. I will need a sit down before the next leg. I see the golf club café and remember reading that it's open to pilgrims so I hobble in, have a wee and order a green tea and muffin. I stay for half an hour to rest my legs.

It's 1.15 pm and I have seven kilometres left. Hopefully I can get into the nuns' place, a hostel, that I had seen in Brierley, as that will be an experience. Feeling refreshed, I leave the café. My bag feels good, it was a bit uncomfortable the last five miles.

The next bit is breath-taking, I keep taking photos to capture it. It's the same vast vista of flat, hay coloured fields but it feels even more amazing. I walk on a very long, straight road and, once I go over the little hill, I can see Santo Domingo. I call my mum and chat for a bit. Then I get on with walking the last stretch. It doesn't matter how far I go, the last two or three miles are tough. I get to the nuns' place but there's very little signage. None of the doors are open and it doesn't feel very friendly. I can't actually talk to anyone to find out if it's open, so I go to the other hostel, Casa de la Cofradia del Santo.

It's huge and modern and right in the centre of a fairly big village, on one of these thin streets again, slotted between restaurants and shops. I am glad I have come here. The man working here takes my bag up for me, that's a first. It's so modern; there's an indoor balcony where I can see down to a seating area. The railings have large scallop shells which is a nice touch and looks great.

I get a room upstairs, which is along corridors and up more stairs to a huge room with single beds spaced nicely and no bunks, which makes me very happy. Fraiser and Emma are at the other end of the room, which is good, and a couple I spoke to yesterday. Emma is using her hot pad on her back as it's hurting a bit.

After a shower, I go to the kitchen, hoping for a kettle but, unfortunately, there isn't one. I make a green tea but it's in the microwave again. I take it into the garden with me, an enclosed outdoor area, and wash my clothes at special sinks before chilling for a bit.

After my rest, I go out and explore the village. It's got a few long, thin streets and a huge cathedral that you have to pay to get into. It's shut anyway. I walk out to the main road where there's a row of restaurants under the trees, which remind me of Spanish seaside resorts, the only thing missing is the sea. They look nice but they all have the same menu.

I go into a supermarket and buy an Orange Kas, some crisps, a cake, a tiny bunch of grapes, four plums and two flat peaches, as the big ones aren't ripe. I understand the weighing machine now. Much simpler than at home. Each fruit has a number so you go to the machine and enter it. No picture and very quick. I eat the grapes wandering around the town and decide to have gazpacho again in the restaurant next to an albergue. I don't get a spoon or bread, which is a shame as I was looking forward to a bit of bread, so drink it from its funny shaped glass instead. It's very good, possibly not as good as the last one, but delicious all the same.

Back at the hostel, I go to the lounge area just off the kitchen, a chilled space with comfy sofas. I drink my Kas and eat my crisps, then send a Facebook post out and read Brierley.

If I do the official stage tomorrow from here to **Belorado** it's 22 kilometres, about 14 miles, which is the same as today. It looks fairly flat while the next day looks really hilly. I am going to peep ahead and look at **Belorado** and its accommodation. Eight kilometres is the minimum I could do. I will look at accommodation in both and see how I feel tomorrow.

Back in the room, I feel a bit embarrassed using my sheet that I have used before. I now have two new sets in my bag – if I continue like this my rucksack will be full of paper sheets. Perhaps I will part with this one and put it in the recycling tomorrow.

I don't understand why I have to be a squirrel wherever I go. I don't need to save them, they are disposable. I am meant to throw them away. But for some reason I am finding that hard to do.

I have a bit of free time so I take my mini toothbrush, my dental floss, mini toothpaste and my tweezers to the bathroom. It's a huge hostel but the bathrooms are not crowded. I have not looked in a mirror properly in ages. Five long hairs are shouting at me from my chin. Two white and the others dark. Scary. What must I look like in the daylight? No wonder people are saying hello and moving on. Also, lots of my eyebrows have turned white. Maybe it's the sun. Or maybe I have been away for months and months and I have lost complete track of time.

I go back to my bed.

My neighbour has turned up and I say hello. He gives me a weak smile. You'd think a hello would be in order when you are sleeping next to each other. I don't even know his nationality.

I slip my shorts off and get into bed. There's not much privacy here, it's all really weird. I look around the room and think the man who checked us in has put all the oldies in this room. It's very quiet and civilised.

The people on the other side of me have arrived. They are a couple and I watch them drag two single beds together to make a double. I think that's a little odd. I have seen lots of couples on the Camino, there's a couple I know to my left, but I have not seen anyone move their beds close together.

They have already been together for days and days, and now they can't be more than three feet from each other.

I just hope they don't forget this is a room full of people and get too friendly. That's going to be really awkward if they do.

Day 11 Saturday 17th September

Santo Domingo to Belorado
14 miles

That was the worst night's sleep that I have had in ages.

At least four people were snoring. The door to the big bedroom was shut so anyone who needed a wee had to open and close it. At 6.00 am, alarms started to go off. The married couple were whispering. By 6.30 am, the rustling was in full motion, as people packed their bags and zipped up. At 6.45 am the light went on and I just wanted to go back to sleep. It was so early, how could these people be so energetic in the morning? It was pitch black out there. Why the hurry?

That could so easily have been a good sleep. But it wasn't.

My lace ups are downstairs and they need to be in the bottom of my bag. I didn't want to leave my ECCO shoes down in the boot room in case they got stolen. I am sure they wouldn't but things have been stolen – one man's jacket and someone else had an expensive pair of socks pinched.

I would like a cup of tea, but I am not even going to try tea again without a kettle. Almost everyone has gone, or are almost ready, and I have stuff all over the place and under my bed. I am not walking in the dark though. I want to see this lovely village as I leave.

A Spanish cleaner comes bounding into the bedroom with loud Spanish music attached to her waist and starts spray cleaning the plastic mattresses. I wanted to gently get ready, but no, she's not going to allow that. I shove everything in my bag and go down to the kitchen. It's obviously time to vacate the bedroom.

I reach the bottom floor and get my lace up shoes so I can pack them and the lady tells me off on the stairs for having shoes in my hands. They are not allowed upstairs but I ignore her.

They are in a real hurry here to get you out at 8.00 am. A man downstairs is dressing his feet in bandages so thick I will be surprised if he can get his feet in his shoes. Poor thing.

In the kitchen people are eating breakfast. I put hot water in the microwave. I will just have hot water, not tea, and unpack everything and repack and hopefully eat a fluffy cake that I bought yesterday. In the bottom of my nylon bag, I have a squashed plum and I can't find one of my water bottles.

Why am I always a mess? Four French people are sitting at a table eating yoghurt and slices of watermelon from plates and they are all ready and packed. They look so calm and organised, like an advert on the TV for yoghurt. Whereas me, I have all my belongings scattered over the floor and now I need to wash my nylon bag and scoop squashed plum off the table. Sigh.

Things get worse as I try to pour water into my water bladder from my little bottle. It usually works. I should do it while my bag is empty. But I keep forgetting. So, it's overspilled and I can't stop the water leakage because I can't swivel the top on and now I have water everywhere – all over the outside of my bag and on my cardigan which is on the outside. Luckily, I haven't got round to putting my sleeping bag on the outside of the bag yet, or that would be wet too. Today is a struggle.

The French have left. How did they do that? They were eating breakfast a minute ago, now the table is clear and they have gone, like they never existed. The music is getting worse and they are ringing a bell now. This is harsh.

But I have to laugh. They have put the song 'My Heart Will Go On' from *Titanic* on. Obviously to scare us away but I love Celine Dion and I have to confess that I have a CD of hers in my car, so I sing along and enjoy it, all on my own, the only one left in the dining area.

I am out on the street at 8.01 am, feeling harassed. I left a huge puddle of water and wet footprints from the dining area, and all my mess that I didn't have time to tidy away. I remembered to retrieve my poles though. I didn't want to forget them. But I didn't even get to eat a fluffy cake, instead only squishing them into my bag.

So off I go. I don't have a reservation for a bed, so who knows what's happening today?

I have a wet back but it will dry. There are about 20 pilgrims ahead of me on the road out of town. Rush hour – or 'turfed out of the hostel' hour. I go over a bridge with no water, there hasn't been water in a long time. It has stones and is lined with grass.

My nylon bag hangs off my shoulder with my breakfast in it. Three plums, two flat peaches and a juice box. It keeps slipping and annoying me. So, I drink the juice, eat the plums and put the peaches in my pocket. I don't need to be annoyed by bags slipping off my shoulders when carrying this much weight.

I wish I had accommodation booked, it's another stress, especially when the internet said most were booked in the next town.

Maybe I should get up earlier so that I am not stressed in the morning, but it wasn't a great sleep, so I am tired. Mind you, I have never gotten up early my whole life, so I need to be realistic about that. I used to work at Fortnum and Mason in London and my bus went from the bottom of the road, a 15 minute walk or 10 minute run, at 7.20 am. I used to get out of bed at 6:50 am, jump into my clothes and run to the end of the road, and almost always caught the bus to Redbridge where I then got tubes into London to get paid a ridiculously minuscule amount of money for the bother. But it was an interesting job. I got to meet lots of famous people and some royalty. So, no, mornings are not my thing.

I did throw the paper sheet in the recycling though, that's a result, but I kept the pillow slip. I now have two full sets and one extra pillow slip. I have to admit that I am a bit strange.

There are open fields and beautiful countryside ahead of me and I am following a busy road. By now, I really need a wee. I keep looking at the bushes but it's so open here that it wouldn't be very private. I shouldn't have drunk that juice.

I see Jeannette. I haven't seen her in days. I would like to chat but I can't stop. I have to race on before I wet myself.

I see the café, it's at the end of another long road but at least I can see it. I go up the steps and it's a small truck-stop thing but, thankfully, they have toilets. The ladies toilet is busy so I go into the men's, even though the place is full and I was probably seen. I just can't wait another second.

I was going to get a drink here, especially as I have used the loo, but there are 15 people in the queue. Instead, I drink water and eat a fluffy cake under the trees in a nice seating area. This is **Granon**. I have walked four miles. I take some photos of the fantastic mural on the wall, which has a backpacker, a signpost saying Santiago 564 kilometres, and a hill. These murals really boost my mood and enhance the whole Camino experience. Afterwards, I walk through the village.

I can't take my eyes off the scenery, it's breath-taking again. It's almost perfect; the sun is landing on the hay fields, illuminating them to a pale, shiny gold colour. The hills are gentle and smooth, while the hay fields look like they have been hoovered, like a huge sand coloured carpet. It's gorgeous. I do hope my photos come out and capture it. Suddenly I feel a bit emotional. I just wasn't expecting to enjoy the scenery so much. Especially when I have already seen so much of it. But I had no idea that it was going to be so beautiful.

The next village is by the road and very noisy. The village after **Redecilla del Camino** has shells to follow and a proper yellow path. I walk past fields of dying sunflowers. I bet they looked stunning a couple of months ago. There are fields of them, but now they are all dead with their brown heads pointing to the ground.

The next village seems poor, **Castildelgado**. The rendering is falling off the houses, with some houses even falling down. I sit down for a bit, my legs aching. It's two kilometres to the next village, then 3.4 to the next. I will try and get something to eat at one of those.

I meet a lady from El Salvador. She started today and is using the agency where they sort your bags and book hotels. She has some health issues, so it's the only way she can do the Camino, plus her mum is happier that she is being supported. She knows when her last day will be, which I find strange as I have no idea.

We stop under some chestnut trees at **Viloria de la Rioja**. There are a few people stopping here, so it's quite busy on the benches. A man from Canada who landscaped his own garden as training for this, marching up and down carrying things, says it has paid off and he doesn't have any blisters so far.

One man I hear behind me says, 'It's all downhill now, except for the ups.' That makes me chuckle.

I keep moving, my backpack is really hurting. I am hot and bothered and my legs ache. I was hoping for a café in the next village but there isn't one. It's a farming hamlet with a handful of houses but, luckily, a bench at least. It's now five kilometres to **Belorado**.

My legs are a little rested now so off I go. I eat my peach, at least I have that. The path is next to a busy road with juggernauts whooshing by noisily. It reaches out in front and I feel like I am on a treadmill getting nowhere. Like an optical illusion with the scenery not changing. It's just too vast. I pull my straps on my bag even tighter around my waist to help take load off my shoulders. So tight that I squash my internal organs. I do a kind of one, two, three pattern with my sticks to get in some kind of rhythm to pass the time and the distance. It works for a bit and I get into a kind of trance, to stop all the internal dialogue with pains from my legs and back. I talk to people from last night's hostel as they pass, including a lady from England called Karen who is walking with her son, but he has gone on ahead to look for accommodation.

I see a hostel to my right at the very edge of a village which looks good. I don't know what to do. I would rather be in town but they might all be booked. It looks nice, painted orange, and has small trees and seats out the front. It feels Mediterranean, so I decide to go in. I walk up a little incline towards the entrance and hear my name.

'Paula, good idea!' It's Emma. She has already been into town to find everything booked, so she has come back here. That was lucky of me to stop.

I see reception and ask if they have a bed. The room is perfect, with six bunks in a packed room, but it's OK. There are real sheets too, which is an unexpected bonus. I have walked 14 miles today.

I love the first 15 minutes when I get to my bed and I know I don't have to walk any further. I lie on the bed and stretch my legs on the bottom of the top bunk. It hurts a little but the stretching is supposed to help and I just relax, wiggle my feet, breathe out and enjoy being horizontal. When I am ready, I go for my shower. I can't walk properly, so it's slow progress. I wash my clothes in the bathroom sink and see I am next to the same lady that I washed clothes with yesterday. It's a strange life that I am leading.

There are some nice outdoor seats so, after hanging up my washing, I bring all my books and paperwork out to a table, get my green tea and ask a man for *aqua caliente* from the coffee machine. I am very happy with a cup of tea and another squashy cake.

Emma joins me and we try to work out the next stage. She goes back to her room and I buy an ice cream. I spend over an hour at a table trying to find accommodation. A man on the next table says that everywhere is full. I try and try but get in a pickle with which hostels I have researched, getting nowhere. I try to ring a hostel but my phone won't work so I email a few and get a reservation. It's not as far as I was hoping to go but accommodation seems to be a bit difficult at the moment.

I go and see Emma and she finds the same place to get a reservation. She points out that it's a hotel as well. So maybe I booked a hotel but I did ask for a bed which normally means you want the albergue. Eventually, I get confirmation that it's €15.00 so it is a bed.

Afterwards, Emma and I go to the bar for dinner. They have a set menu, three courses, and there's a vegan choice. I have salad and a vegan lasagne, possibly with real cheese, not quite sure. Not everyone in Spain fully understands the vegan requirements. Emma sticks to a burger that she has had before, and knows is vegan, although strangely, it is just a burger, no bun.

I am pleased that I have somewhere for tomorrow and I need to book the next day too.

Later on, I send my Facebook post out and go to bed. But when I hear something, I open my eyes and a man is on his knees, completely level with my pillow. He looks startled when I look at him, but then he smiles. He is plugging in his phone, there's a bundle of leads just by my bed. This dormitory living is very odd.

Day 12 Sunday 18th September

Belorado to Villafranca de Montes de Orca
8.50 miles

I slept really well. It was really quiet and I drifted off before the light went out and slept right through to 7.00 am.

I am walking with Emma today which is a new experience. So far, I have just done my own thing, so it's different to have a conversation about what time to leave. I normally leave when I am ready.

I notice my towel is still hanging on the line as we leave, so I grab it. Emma attaches it to my bag and off we go into town and see some lovely murals on the side of the buildings, really well painted. It would have been good to stay in the actual village, but I also enjoyed it where I was.

Meredith joins us and we catch up. She was going to have some 'me' time at her hostel but ended up cooking with some others in the albergue last night and really enjoyed it. Then we notice my towel is gone, so we say goodbye hastily to Meredith and start to walk back for it. A shower will be a struggle without it, it's a struggle as it is with it being so tiny.

I tell Emma to wait on a bench and I will go back. I feel bad putting her out, but she comes with me as she feels bad that she didn't tie it on properly. At one of the murals Emma takes a closer look to see who the artist is, so I walk on ahead to go back for my lost towel then I hear her shout my name. I turn around to see she is folded over laughing.

'Is it on my bag?' I ask and she is laughing so much, but manages to say yes. Such a relief, as I would have gone all the way back to the hostel and still not found it. So off we go again, laughing.

The scenery is similar to yesterday. I have not seen a grape vine in a couple of days now. We chatter away, learning about each other's lives. We pass people that Emma knows. She is much more social than me.

We reach a tiny town but there's nothing here, then we are almost at **Villafranca Montes de Oca**. Emma goes down a small, uneven path by the side of the road. It's quite busy with pilgrims; half seem to have gone on the road and the other half on the little track. It's soft and slippery and very uneven. I don't like the look of it, knowing I might fall on the slope as it looks really difficult and there's nothing to hold onto. It freaks me out a bit, so I decide to get on the tarmac. But there's a crash barrier between me and the tarmac. I can't climb over, I am too small, so I decide to go under.

I lie on my tummy to try and crawl under, but the backpack won't go under the barrier. I look left and see traffic coming on the wrong side of the road, well it's the proper side of the road but I forgot. Whooo, dangerous. I look at Emma. She is ahead of me, over the dodgy bit of track, safe, and she is laughing at me lying on the ground. I must look ridiculous lying on my tummy trying to get under the barrier.

I decide that, even if I do get through and don't get squashed by the traffic whizzing by, that I will never be able to get to my feet with this bag on. So, I will have to go the way Emma went.

Two kind people help me and offer to take my bag, but I am ok with the bag, I pause and look at the small incline. It's only two or three steps, although definitely scary and I don't want to slip. I manage with their help. It's a tight path and I keep catching my bag on trees but we do it and get to the town, **Villafranca**. We pass two cafés but don't stop, as we are almost at our accommodation now.

The accommodation is in a hotel but the albergue is out the back. San Anton Abad. The reception is lovely with granite walls and plush furniture, definitely a hotel reception.

I speak Spanish and find it's becoming more natural, mind you, it is the same conversation. '*Tengo una reserva*,' I say and the receptionist continues to talk to me in Spanish. Thankfully, I understand, which is progress.

Another member of staff walks us out to the albergue. It's stunning, past a little café which I will come back to later, up a slope and over a small bridge into the albergue. The staff member puts me on the top bunk, but I ask for the bottom and he reluctantly agrees.

I have my ten minutes stretching and then take a shower before heading to the café to buy a bowl of chips. I get hot water for a cup of tea and sit in the outdoor area under an umbrella in this lovely courtyard. The chips aren't great, covered in salt, so I have to wipe some off. A few chips weren't cooked properly either so I didn't eat them all. But it did satisfy my need for chips, I have not had them at all on this trip.

A lady joins me on my table who doesn't have accommodation for tonight. She is just passing through, not staying here, so isn't sure what to do next. San Juan is booked and so are the following couple of small villages. I don't know why she doesn't just stop here. Maybe they are all booked up.

The food here is a little expensive so I pop over to the supermarket since it shuts at 2.00 pm. I must book accommodation when I get back. I see the three ladies that I met sitting on the side of the road ages ago. They are going to stay at this hotel, but in the hotel part. They have to walk further and be transported back as they are on a package and everything is organised.

It's so strange being rested and showered, then seeing pilgrims looking stressed, sweaty and carrying huge bags. It seems so silly unless you are doing it, then it's OK and normal. Also, if you don't have a huge bag, no one will recognise you as a pilgrim.

Back at the hotel, I eat an ice cream that I got in the supermarket under a tree by the washing line, which has a great view across the countryside, then take my shopping back to the dorm and collect my paperwork, Brierley, accommodation list, and my cup for tea and hot water from the café. I sit down in an enclosed outdoor space which is probably part of the hotel with seats, flowers and statues. No one else is here. I do some research for half an hour, drink tea and eat a strange triangle cake thing. All the luxuries of the hotel without the prices.

If I can walk as far as **Atapuerca** then there's a hostel that opens at 1.00 pm but it only has 30 beds. It's a gamble but if I get there early enough I should be OK, and then book two nights in Burgos. I like the look of the cathedral, it seems amazing. Even if I get there at teatime, I still have the next day to look around. I will have been walking for two weeks by then, almost 200 miles, so a rest day is a good idea.

When I looked for accommodation in Burgos, I was going to book a hotel as a treat, but I couldn't justify the price and, while I would love a room to myself, I would miss the noise and people, it's a huge contradiction. Maybe this trip isn't about the hotels, it's about the Camino, the walk, the people, the hustle and bustle, not lonely hotel rooms.

There's a constant flow of pilgrims arriving here, some so early like me that we watch everyone arrive. I only walked eight miles today. It's the first time I feel I might want to read a book on my kindle app. It's hours till bedtime and I don't want to walk around the village. My route is planned for the next few days, but I don't want to interrupt this experience with a novel that I can't even remember. I don't want to leave this world and enter a fictional one, not today. I am not sure what to do.

I decide to ring Phil from under a tree. As we chat, I step on something and realise it's a walnut. I am sitting under a walnut tree! This makes me smile. It's another first. After a nice chat, I say my goodbyes and go back indoors to cook my microwave meal. Jeanette is in the kitchen along with a girl from New Zealand, plus lots of new faces. It's a lovely atmosphere; people chilling on their beds, some eating in the café, lots of us are sitting outside on chairs in the sun, which is now a comfortable temperature. I am really enjoying being a part of something.

I still wonder how I ended up here. How many of my friends back home would do this, sleeping in dormitories and walking every day? No one comes to mind. Most of them looked a bit puzzled when I tried to explain what I was going to do. But what a unique experience, meeting other people who are as crazy as you and then discovering it's not so crazy anymore, it's the new normal. That doesn't happen often in life.

There are so many accents here: French, American, Canadian and Italian. Lots of people are reading Brierley, some are playing games with dice. It's also a relatively cheap way to travel, not excluding your lack of earnings while you are travelling, but I have a low paid job anyway, so the loss is not as much as some people, which probably goes in my favour. My trip is for six or seven weeks, so where else can you travel and spend about €10.00 a night on accommodation? Even when I went interrailing, it was twice that and more. But this trip isn't just about the money, it's about experiencing hostels like this, the villages, the people along the way, the community. It's been a good decision.

My microwave risotto meal is so bad that I have to throw it away. I picked out a couple of strands of mushroom and took a few mouthfuls, but it was about as bad as a risotto could ever be. I get my orange Kas and a fluffy cake instead and sit out in the sun. A random man helps Emma with her back as she is struggling again today, doing her sexy wiggle to release the pain. She is funny. Then I decide to pack my bag to get ready for an early morning start.

I get into bed at 7.30 pm after speaking to my daughter, Ciara, for a bit. The Wi-Fi is so bad that we don't get to talk for long. A lot of us are resting in our beds or asleep now.

The church bells ring at 8.00 pm and I go and get my phone which is on charge by the door but I can't get the adapter out. It is fixed firmly in the socket. A bunch of Italians come in noisily and, after hurting my fingers for five minutes, I ask one of the lads to help. He tries, struggling too, and turns the light on, which I won't be popular for. He talks to me in Italian and I have no idea what he is saying. I feel embarrassed. Eventually, he puts the phone charger back in and gets the whole thing out which I am grateful for.

He talks to his friends in Italian and laughs, I think at my expense, but at least I have my adapter.

Day 13 Monday 19th September

Villafranca de Montes de Oca to Aterpuerca
12 miles

It was a night of squealing doors. Ours squealed when someone left the room and when they came back, which was often.

I had a nightmare about being held at gunpoint and being trapped in a car – no idea where that came from. I have been awake since the first person left at roughly 4.30 am. At 5.30 am I get myself ready in the common areas as people are still sleeping and I share the rest of my juice with Jeanette in the kitchen. Before leaving, I do a torch sweep under our beds, only to find Emma's bank card. At 6.15 am, me and Emma, find our poles in the dark which is amusing and a bit noisy; the big bucket is full and we have trouble untangling ours. Usually, mine are the last two left.

It's pitch-black outside and we head straight up a hill at the back of the hotel. Emma has a headtorch, thank goodness. By 7.30 am, it's light enough to turn the torch off. There is nothing on this path except nature: wide, red clay dirt tracks, lined with trees. It's very peaceful and lovely watching the sun come up. We walk past some totem poles and random painted wood things.

We find a quirky and colourful albergue in **San Juan de Ortega** and go in to order drinks and use the toilet. We sit outside on a bench in a little patio area and I have a tortilla and Aquarius. I take my shoes and socks off. We feed some sparrows the hard, stale bread that comes with a tortilla. They are very tame, dropping down onto the wooden table.

The next village is called **Ages** and we see the three women I saw yesterday, stopping to have a chat. The village after this is **Atapuerca**. There's a big plaque as you enter the village, with an old man's face on it. Not an old man, but a man from a long time ago. I have heard that this is an important village but haven't read up on it yet. The information on the plaque is in Spanish.

At 11.30 am, we are at the albergue, Peregrino Atapuerca. Considering the time, we are probably a bit keen, but really wanted to get a bed. We are third and fourth in queue, so we manage to get one each. The lady working there allows us to rest in the garden till 1.00 pm. People keep arriving and, by 12.45 pm, there are 12 of us. The queue is organised and people are respectful of who got here first. I have no idea if it makes any difference, as all the hostels give out beds in a different manner.

We walk into our room and are allowed to pick a bed. We both pick the two single beds by the window and smile, so excited to have a single and not a bunk. There are squeals of delight from the room over the corridor as it seems they are just as happy with their room and the single beds. We also have cotton sheets, a tiny individual table and sockets for our phones, happy days.

We have an Irish lady whose name sounds like Gronya but I am sure it's not spelt like that. If she stopped talking, I might ask her how to spell it, but she doesn't stop. She is a lovely lady, very chatty and funny. Every sentence is like a stand-up comedy show and I can't help laughing. There's also a South Korean lady who barely speaks a word of English and is travelling alone. A very brave thing to do to travel with no English.

I walk to the little shop in the village and buy an ice cream, cheese, bread, tomato and a peach before returning to the hostel to search the kitchen and actually find a kettle. What a result! Immediately, I make a cup of tea. I decide to have a day off from washing clothes and think I'll just put everything through a machine in Burgos tomorrow. I am looking forward to a mini break. We did well getting this far. It's only 18 kilometres now into Burgos.

The hostel is filling up. It's just two single storey prefab buildings in a pretty, spacious garden.

The Italians take over the kitchen again, a current theme, with red wine opened and food cooking which smells delicious. I have half a baguette to look forward to. I chill in my room for a bit as there are lots of flies outside, making it difficult to relax – plus, my bed is very comfy.

It's the Queen's funeral today and, so far, I am detached from it, without any news and limited Wi-Fi. To be honest, I am not that affected by it, she was 96 years old and had a great life and was healthy until the end. What more could anyone want? I feel for her family, it's a huge loss on a personal level, the matriarch of the family. She was a mum, a grandma, great grandma, aunt. It's also a big change to our country but I am not sure how it will affect me yet.

I am distracted with more personal things today. I have a friend the same age as the Queen and she is 97 today and it's also my brother's birthday, but in July 2020 he took his own life. It would have been his 56th birthday. I feel for my mum right now watching the Queen's funeral on the day of her son's birthday. We didn't have a funeral for Stuart but we did scatter his ashes somewhere he enjoyed going.

Suicide is difficult to process, to comprehend that someone feels so bad, without any hope that they don't want to be here anymore. Stuart was one of four men we knew that took their own lives within six months during the pandemic. It's all very difficult to process. As a mum, you want to keep your children safe. It's all you do while they are growing up, don't climb too high, mind the roads, don't go near the water, etc. So, for them to take their own life is difficult.

My own mental health has been very poor this year. I fell into a dark hole and struggled. I didn't do well. I cried a lot, especially in the car while I was on my own which wasn't safe. I bought a tent and slept in it, instead of going home. I slept in my car outside work instead of going home and all it did was make me feel even more isolated and more miserable. I just wanted to be on my own for some reason, everything was a struggle. I didn't want to continue. I was fed up with struggling, but I couldn't do that to the people who care about me. I didn't want to commit suicide. I just didn't want to struggle anymore.

So, I got glimpses of what it's like to want to end it. I didn't get that low. I was functioning but I was skimming dangerously close to it. I had no interest in anything, I didn't grow any vegetables, no interest in sewing, or seeing friends. I was just low.

Luckily, we had a trip to Croatia booked, but I wasn't even looking forward to that. So many things could have gone wrong, with Covid still being about, that I couldn't assume I was going and therefore I couldn't look forward to it. But it was a lovely two weeks in a beautiful country and it came just at the right time.

I didn't miraculously spring back to being me, it's a challenge some days to stay out of that pit. I still hover at the entrance and look down into it, but I feel stronger mentally now, not 100% but who is at the moment? Life is simply a struggle for a lot of people right now for many different reasons. But I can count my blessings, I see the good and I am here on this trip. I don't have to struggle here, life is simple. It's a new routine away from the old one. A time to reset the buttons. I don't have to work, worry about money, getting to work, hoping my old car starts, worrying about my minimum wage, zero hour job where I probably spend a big proportion of my wages, just financing the car to get to work to earn the money to pay for the car.

I have cut back on worrying here.

I worry so much about things that are out of my control. My son, Liam, drove from Brighton to Cornwall recently and I didn't worry, as I am detached a bit. I didn't know exactly what day he was travelling since I was busy walking. At home, I would have been on tenterhooks imagining his car crashing. Does that mean I don't care about him out here? Or is it healthier not to worry about things you can't change?

Here, I worry about me, not all my kids. I worry about the blisters, whether I will have a bed tonight – still worries, but in a much smaller world. Maybe I can take some of this home with me.

I make my cheese and tomato baguette and eat it in the garden but the flies are quite intense so I go back inside, make a third cup of tea, and go to my bed.

Gronya is in the room. She is full of stories and so entertaining. Saying 'fecking' a lot. She tells us about a pair of trousers at another hostel. She went to get her washing in and all that were left were a huge pair of men's beige shorts. She laughs as she still has the zip on legs to the pair the larger man took. She is the width of a pencil and the story is very funny. It's her delivery of it that's funny.

She also tells me a bit about this village. There's an archaeological dig a couple of miles away and she wanted to go and visit but she can't, so she is a little disappointed. Apparently, at this site, they have found the oldest human remains in Europe, going back 1.5 million years. There is a museum in Burgos that she will go to instead where the bones and finds are kept. I also chat to Penny and Nick in the garden for a bit. They are from Hereford. They are lovely and easy to talk to and tell me they are enjoying the Camino and all the experiences.

More food is being cooked and eaten. If they bought all those ingredients in that tiny little shop, they did well. I should eat better tomorrow in Burgos.

Day 14 Tuesday 20th September

Atapuerca to Burgos
13.40 miles

Cotton sheets make so much difference. I slept really well and got up at 6.44 am. I have heard a lot of people leave already. A man coughed in our room, I forgot he was on the bunk bed above Gronya. We were just women chilling yesterday.

I meet Gronya in the bathroom and she says she loves my colourful toenails. She goes to the loo and doesn't stop talking from behind the door. Then she leaves in a breeze of laughter. The lady at the sink next to me says she is priceless.

Emma is still sleeping, and we have to be out by 8.00 am. I sort my bag out and I am about to wake her at 7.30 am when she wakes up by herself.

We leave just as it's getting light and walk out of the tiny village up a gentle incline. We are greeted by stones, lots and lots of little ones that are annoying to walk on. It would have been very difficult in the dark. The sun is rising behind us and strong on our backs, then we get to the top of the hill and I can see how high up we are.

We reach a bit that doesn't look right, severe rocks that don't look passable, but there doesn't seem to be another option. A girl comes by with an app on her phone that says the path is right. I downloaded the app on my phone back in England and couldn't work it out, so I deleted it. We struggle across the rocks but, thankfully, they don't go on for too long.

When we get to the other side of the hill there is a lovely vista of Burgos. It doesn't look ten miles away but it's difficult to judge. It has to be.

It's not a bad path, down a nice gentle slope, not too stony. We go past another field of dry sunflowers and we hear the dry seeds rattling with the wind. I touch one and they are bone dry. Then it's open countryside again.

We walk with a man from Seattle for a while, then a man from Australia. Once we get to **Orbaneja** I need to take the weight of my feet. There's a café but it's not open yet. We sit on a bench and I take my shoes and socks off to air my feet as we check the map for the detour past the river. This seems a better option than following the main road into the city.

Afterwards, we get to what we think is the detour and find just one tiny, painted yellow arrow pointing to the left, but everyone else is going straight on. Emma looks on the app and left is the right way. We keep the river to our right and follow it.

The river reminds us of England, not with organised pine trees but English trees, all random and different with mud under our feet which is soft after all those stones. Then we come across more stones and our feet get tired. There aren't any cafés here, so we can't stop. We trail long paths past an airport, where the tarmac is a bit better and faster to walk on before we reach a concrete path.

Eventually, we see the top of the cathedral and know we are nearly there. We continue along the paved path. Burgos has a nice feel to it, very clean and bright. Then we go through a big archway which feels like a very important way to enter. We walk past the cathedral, it's huge and ornate and I can't wait to go in and have a look. Our hostel, Catedral de Burgos, is the next street from the cathedral, such a great spot.

We walked 13.4 miles without a break. I did eat a smoothie and banana but Emma didn't eat anything.

In the hostel, we are in separate rooms as we booked separately. Both of them are women only which is nice.

Women definitely don't seem to snore as much as men. The room has cotton sheets and a throw, all modern and clean. I shower and meet Emma afterwards and we head to a vegan eatery, Gaia, which we had planned already, taking advantage of city life and the food offerings.

The food is amazing, a set four course menu with a choice of five dishes for each course. The cold soup to start is so good that I want the recipe. The potato dish is fantastic and I wonder how you can get so much flavour into potatoes. The dumplings, although unusual, were also delicious and so is the pudding. A great meal. I want to get the recipes and make everything when I get home. Emma wants to know where she can buy them.

I return to my room and stretch a bit more. I still couldn't walk upstairs properly on the way back to the hostel and had to use the lift instead. For the evening, I make tea as usual in the microwave and do all my paperwork, journal, three words, and note down my mileage. Emma pops in on her way to the pharmacy to say Nessa is in her room which is nice.

I make a second cup of tea and chat with a lady who's also staying in my room. She is on the way to buy walking poles in the outdoor shop and I ask her to look at the prices of headtorches for me.

Despite my sore feet, I decide to go and get a new lead for my camera. It's not charging so I haven't been using it. There should be an electrical shop here. Google takes me on the back roads to a shop. The shopkeeper and I manage to communicate – his English is as good as my Spanish – but he says the lead is broken and to go to '*La teinda a lado*' (shop next door), which I understand.

I go in, saying, '*necesito,*' and point to the lead. Another lovely man finds me the right things and it's only €12.70 for the lead and adapter with two pins. I am really happy as I've missed my camera. As I walk back, everything is coming alive now. It's after 5.00 pm. I go to a small supermarket and get an avocado, fizzy water, biscuits, and two bananas ready for the day after tomorrow.

The girl in my room has been here since Friday with an injury which is sad. She is going to get a bus tomorrow to help her get going. She's been in The Museum of Human Evolution and says it's worth €4.00, so I will go tomorrow.

I message Emma at 7.30 pm to see if she is asleep and she suggests we go down to the bar. I meet her at her room and hand her a single plum. She laughs. We have the same sense of humour. It's been lovely spending time with her but tomorrow we go our separate ways, so it'll be nice to go for a drink. I hope we stay in touch and catch up again further along the path but I am looking forward to spending time on my own as well. A bit more 'me' time. I think Emma is too.

Day 15 Wednesday 21st September

Rest day in Burgos

Today feels different. After two weeks of walking every day, I am not. I am still snuggled in heavy cotton sheets and a warm throw.

Of course, I woke at 6.30 am and couldn't get back to sleep but I am quite pleased because I don't want to throw my routine out. I need to be on the road at 7.00 am tomorrow morning. But I can chill and relax in the comfy bed and check my emails. The museum opens at 10.00 am, and breakfast is between 7.00 am and 10.00 am. For €3.50 it's not going to be posh but better than the banana I normally eat. And there's no rushing today.

Last night, before I went to sleep, I converted my walking app data into a visual image in another app called Relive. It's 1.13 minutes long and maps me going across the Pyrenees with photos at different stages. I love it, it's such a perfect memory.

Breakfast is basic but definitely worth the money. I have mint tea, four slices of toast, margarine as I hate butter, jam, some little wrapped cakes, and three orange juices. They might not have made any profit today. I haven't had toast since England and I have missed it. I took a couple of margarines for my baguettes too, as I have been having them dry.

Outside, it's chilly and my legs are cold in shorts. Delivery drivers are everywhere. I have noticed they get all their deliveries done before it gets busy. It feels weird being on the same path that I came in on yesterday. I am actually going back on myself and I was in so much pain yesterday. Today my legs are great but yesterday every footstep was painful. Luckily, my body has reset overnight, which is amazing. There's another man washing the paths with a huge hose. Where do they get all their water from? It seems such a waste.

I am half an hour early to The Museum of Human Evolution. I need to find a spot to sit down. You need sunglasses in the sunshine and a coat in the shade. I take a selfie next to a huge green pilgrim and find a bench to sit and wait.

Inside, it's a very spacious museum, with lots of glass and height. The exhibits are in huge boxes which are very dark and difficult to walk around in. I can barely see the floor. A lady frightens the life out of me, sitting in a corner. There are bone fragments displayed in glass cabinets, all lit up in the darkness.

Some of the bone fragments are from human remains 400,000 years ago which is quite mind blowing. The way they have displayed each fragment with such respect and care, illuminating them in the dark with lights, shows how important it is. Even though my brain can't compute that much history, I can appreciate that I am looking at something very special. I leave the exhibition and go and sit on a comfy sofa and watch a film about the museum and the archaeologists and it really cements home what a find this dig has been. And they are still digging, finding new fragments. To think that, if I wasn't walking the Camino, I would never be here – that in itself is difficult to get my head around.

I finish my visit and try to digest the fact I have seen such incredibly old human remains. What would those people think now, with their bones on show in a huge modern museum? I can't even get my head round what life looked like that many years ago. I just can't do it.

I pop into the supermarket as I am quite hungry, even after the big breakfast. I buy a baguette, veggie ham and a tomato, and make a lovely baguette back at the hostel with the avocado from yesterday. The bread is fresh for a change which makes the whole lunch extra tasty. I drink a cup of tea and head back out to the cathedral.

It's not what I expected. It's not one big, open space but lots and lots of little chapels around the edge, all different sizes and they all have tall, ornate gates. It reminds me of an indoor shopping precinct, which is a strange way of describing it but that's what comes to mind, with chapels instead of shops. I get the audio on my phone from the QR code. I have seen so many churches on this trip in all the villages and, here, there are loads of saints coming through my ear that they are all lost on me. Too many names I can't remember or care who they all are. I just like looking at cathedrals, churches and the stonework, the stained windows, the tall ceilings.

I do love the height of the cathedral. It's making my neck hurt looking up at the solid stone. One of my favourite parts is the three stone carvings, floor to ceiling, and so detailed with scenes and lots of figurines. Such intricate stonework. I could stand and stare at it all day. There are little bits eroding as well, reminding you how old it is.

There isn't anywhere to get any solitude, which is something that I enjoy in a church. This is an exhibition now, not a place to relax. It's full of tourists, everyone listening to audio on their phones, trying to get the best photo, which is difficult as it's just too big to photograph. It's the detail that will stay with me, the attention to detail on every surface, in all the chapels. Such vast amazing talent and skill to create these ornate pieces.

I love the central dome, it's beautiful. Even though it's high up, I can still see the eight petaled flower shape at the top and the pale stone against the gold is beautiful.

I walk around again to try and take it all in and see Gronya. She has just been to the museum as well and is blown away with the cathedral. She says she is wobbling from it all, it's so much to see. Then I see Nessa, she is staying at the same place as Emma tonight, but Emma's probably there by now as she started walking about 8.00 am.

I decide two laps is enough and look for a way out, arriving in the cloister. Around the square cloister are wide corridors full of beautiful ceilings, stained glass and tombs. I am dizzy with it all, like Gronya, and I have taken about 300 photos.

Eventually, after two and a half hours, I go back to the hostel for a cup of tea. There's a new lady in the Canadian's bed, sound asleep, which is weird. I don't normally see the change of people. I collect all my clothes up and take them to the washing machine and treat them to a wash. It feels strange using a washing machine. After another tea, I put them all in the dryer as there's no outdoor space here, a bit costly but it's what I have to do. I meet Jenelle at the washing machine, who is travelling with her dad which is so sweet.

I get my bag ready for tomorrow. I would like to be on the road by 7.00 am, so I will have to use my phone for a torch. The lady who went in search of headtorches and poles said they had one at €40.00 which is a bit much. I will also layer up in case it's as cold as it was this morning.

I collect my washing, what a treat, a black sack full of clean clothes that smell divine and are soft and fluffy. It's a new phase tomorrow starting off with clean clothes. I have also been thinking about Burger King ever since I saw an advert by the museum. Once you get a Vegan Royale lodged in your head, there's no shaking it, so off I go. There are hundreds of eating places but it's cheap, easy and yummy.

This Burger King is a bit odd, with filthy tables which haven't been cleaned and full of rubbish with drinks on trays. But there's an old wall with a round stained-glass window leading downstairs. It feels like part of the cathedral with the same stone and such a huge contrast to the rest of Burger King as a whole. I have to go round the back in a dark corner to get my food. I test a chip as I always do before I take them away but they are cold. Oh dear, I am not eating cold chips.

I say, '*Mas caleinte.*' The server looks at me blankly, so I say it again. He says something in Spanish which probably means tough or go away. I say, '*Frio,*' and stand my ground. He gives in and puts three fingers up, I am assuming that's how long it's going to be to make fresh ones. I get super hot chips and the burger is just what I need. On the way back, I visit a tiny assorted shop and get a headtorch for €7.00, including batteries, so now I don't have to worry about the dark mornings.

I have really enjoyed Burgos. I didn't physically need a rest day but it's been lovely to explore this lovely city without being stressed. Now I am ready to get back into the countryside. This place is full of smells of restaurants and perfume. Tomorrow, I want fresh air.

Day 16 Thursday 22nd September

Burgos to Hornillos del Camino
15.83 miles

I am struggling to get going today. My bed is so comfy that I would rather stay here. Today I am hoping to look at a monastery which is only 1.4 kilometres away.

It's a 13-mile walk today, and I told the hostel that I would arrive about 3.00 pm, which should take four or five hours. Walking out of the hostel, I feel like I have forgotten something. I have mentally slipped off the Camino and I need to get back on it.

The monastery doesn't look like it's open yet and I don't want a tour but it's still nice to see it. As I walk past the university of Burgos, and get to the edge of town, the countryside appears.

My bag is not comfortable, so I stop at a bench in a park and try to sort it out. I have walked 4.5 miles and it's 10.07 am. I walk on a long path where a man overtakes me before I overtake a lady talking on her phone. Then there's a 90 degree bend to the right – that's the way the sign is pointing and the man with long legs went that way. But it doesn't feel right. At the end of a long path, there is a decision to make and no signposts. I walk a little both ways, but I can't decide. I look on Google Maps but that doesn't really help. I am going to have to take my bag off to look in Brierley for clues. It says to go under a railway track which is one of my two options.

I see the lady I overtook before approaching, so I get out my peach and plum to eat. If I keep myself busy, maybe I can follow her. But she stops and asks in Spanish if I need help. I say, no, I am OK. She starts waving her arms around, I think she is lost too. We both get our phones out and compare. She keeps saying, '*No lo sé.*' I think we have to go under the bridge and so does she, so we walk awkwardly together, as neither of us speak much of each other's language.

We get to another bridge, stopping to look at our phones again. Luckily, a local man is walking his dog. She can obviously speak to him and he points us in the right direction. We head that way. She is waving her arms around again, drawing circles, saying we have just been round in a big circle. We have gone a couple of miles out of the way, I think. I have no idea where the other man is, he must be back in Burgos.

I wish her, '*Buen Camino*,' and walk on again. I arrive at the outskirts of **Tardajos**, very tired. It doesn't look very inviting. But if it has a bench and a toilet, I will be happy. I see a café and cross a main road to reach it. I dump my bag down while I get in the queue for a drink. I can barely stand as my feet and legs hurt so much.

I get a small cake thing and lemon Aquarius and sit down. Two Irish men have sat at the table with my bag but I still sit down. I don't speak because I don't want them to know that I am English. I don't feel like talking at the moment. I have walked 9.29 miles with not a single town, just open countryside, and some of that was the wrong way.

I have 2.4 kilometres until the next village, **Rabe de las Calzadas**, 2.6 kilometres till **Fuente de Praotorre**, and 5.4 kilometres till my destination, so quite a few miles. It's 12.15 pm. After leaving the village, the views improve, similar to how they were the other day, with vast, open, flat hay coloured countryside.

My legs ache. Where's this new fitness? Surely it's going to kick in soon? I feel as tired today as I did on day one. I see a bench and sit down but it's metal and nearly burns me, so I switch to the one under a tree in this quiet village, **Rabe de las Calzadas**.

When I leave the village, a few Camino bikes go by but there are no people. There are lots of signs, so I know that I am going the right way. According to Brierley, I am now in the Meseta. There has been talk about this mysterious Meseta. It's open countryside, probably similar to what I have already seen, but even more vast and empty. Some people I have spoken to have said they are dreading it, and some people are looking forward to it. But either way, it should be an experience. I am looking forward to it, as I wanted some 'me' time and I think this is going to be it. Brierley says there's not much shade or water opportunities, so I need to be prepared.

I stop at a rock and sit down. It's quiet, not a sound except for the birds. I take it all in as it's such a privilege to be here. I mustn't get distracted with pain and the time schedule, I need to enjoy this. I take a video to remember it, and then spend a few minutes more taking it in, all 360 degrees of it.

I get going again. There's a pilgrim collecting litter in a bag using a litter stick. He has a poster on his bag but I can't get close enough to read it. Good for him, you wouldn't think there would be much litter out here. I haven't seen much on the ground but he has a bag full. I have seen socks and bits of clothes trampled into the floor that must fall off people's bags as they try to dry them. It always makes me sad, we need every single item of clothing. It's all precious.

The path in front of me goes on and on and on. Another man overtakes me and disappears into the distance. I plod on, one foot in front of the other. I know I will get there. I always do.

The flies are driving me crazy though. I have a hat and sunglasses on but they are hanging off my hat and walking across my glasses. I even ate one and spat it out at one point. They are all over my face, so very, very annoying. It's difficult to wave them away while holding sticks.

After about 20 minutes, I stop and shout, 'Go away!', waving my arms around furiously. Then I look around.

Luckily, no one else is around to see me lose it for a moment.

I get to the brow of the hill and it's stunning, truly stunning, with the village down below nestled in the vastness. The yellow track weaving through the farmer fields of hay. It's difficult to stay irritated for too long.

I arrive at the village **Hornillos del Camino**. I am shattered but I got here. I stop at the first bench and take the weight off my feet, getting Brierley out. The hostel, Alfar de Hornillos, is literally ten feet away.

I book in and they offer me dinner for €12.00 but I am not sure. It's paella, but the receptionist tells me they can do a vegetarian version which is good. I am too tired to think by now. I have walked nearly 16 miles.

After a quick tour of the house and garden, I am taken to my room. I ask if it's a bottom bunk and the lady says no. I pull a sad face. I have been very lucky with bunks. But today it's the top.

I look at my bunk. I just wanted to lie down, that's all I want to do after a tough day. But, first, I have to climb. I simply can't climb up that ladder right now though, my feet are too tender, so I sit on a chair. One lady is on her bed and the other is asleep. I hate bunk beds; they are for children, not adults.

I stretch my legs out in front of me and suddenly feel tears coming. I absolutely hate being on the top bunk. I just wanted to lie down for a moment. It's such a simple request. I feel incredibly sad and emotional but try to stop the tears before I completely lose it and embarrass myself in this dormitory.

The lady returns. I avoid eye contact so she can't see I am upset and she takes me to a bottom bunk in another room. I am so grateful. I say, '*Muchas muchas gracias.*'

I collapse on the bed with relief and stretch my legs. The bunks are not tall, there's not much space at all between the top and the bottom, so I can't put my leg up high but I do manage a stretch. It's so painful but I am happy. Now, I can just chill for a moment, stop thinking and unwind.

The bathroom has two showers with curtains and a normal toilet. Do I leave the door open so someone else can shower? What if someone comes in to use the loo and I want to get out of the shower? Oh well, I just get on with it.

After dressing, I hang my washing out at the end of the garden that backs onto open countryside. I see a grey tabby cat who looks about ten weeks old, so small and tiny, but very feisty. I pick it up for a bit before it wants to get down. The flies are bad here, so I go inside and sit on the sofa to do my paperwork. Before long, Phil rings for a catch up. A lady sits down next to me on the sofa with her book trying to plan her journey. And others, possibly Croatian, are at the table trying to book accommodation. I am going to wing it. It's too stressful trying to email, and wait for responses, possibly more stressful than not having a reservation.

When I get hungry, I order dinner, thinking the paella sounds good. Me and Emma were talking about it the other day. And the lady did give me a bottom bunk, so I will support her rather than going to the shop for a horrible microwave meal or more baguettes.

There are 12 of us for dinner, in a lovely indoor-outdoor area with a huge, gorgeous Camino painting on the wall. But dinner is not so good. I am NOT doing any more pilgrim meals. Vegetarian paella isn't even a thing. Paella is supposed to have fish and meat, so a vegetarian version is never going to be the same. I get a salad for the second course, which is put out with the first course on large plates for us to share but it's just lettuce, onion and a bit of tomato with a dressing.

Everyone loves the pudding, except me and one other lady. It's my nightmare: a bowl of white stuff. I put my spoon in, lick the back, and wince. It's like yoghurt. I never eat yoghurt and it's simply confirmed why. Even if the meal had been amazing, the flies are horrendous. I have never, ever seen so many flies, ever.

With the right food and no flies, it would be a lovely setting. I do love the painting of the Camino, it's beautiful. Half the table is French, with Germans, Danish, Russian and me. I hardly say a thing. I am very tired and bored of the 'Where do you come from?' and 'Where are you going?' questions. But the cat is cute, such a character, and keeps trying to get on everyone's laps.

I get up from the table as soon as everyone has finished. I don't think I have ever in my life left a table first and it's quite liberating. But I was bored, there is not one familiar face here. I must be so far behind now, which doesn't matter, but I can't be bothered to chat to people. I grab my washing in from the line which isn't quite dry but I will hang it off my bed. I am very, very, grateful for the lower bunk but, when I get to my room, a man in the bunk next to me has taken a siesta and is snoring badly, while another man smells really bad. I haven't met any smelly people yet, except when you first arrive at an albergue in the afternoon heat, but everyone showers and it's all good again. I hope he showers or I will need to spray impulse on my pillow. I knew it would come in handy.

I realise the foul smell isn't the man after all but the awful smelling towel hanging at the end of his bed. These micro towels can smell rancid if they are not kept clean and dried properly. This is going to be a tough night. Ten of us squished into this room, a smelly man – or towel – above me, and a snorer three feet away.

I plan on leaving early in the morning. Apparently, it was three degrees this morning and I don't have a coat but I do have a funny plastic poncho. At least there are no flies upstairs. This bed is such a contrast to Burgos, back to paper sheets, my sleeping bag and a hard pillow. I was a bit spoilt for two nights.

It's now 12.57 am and I can't sleep. I must have slept for a bit but it's been very broken. The man next to me, who had the siesta earlier, is the absolute worst snorer I have ever heard – and I have heard some bad snoring over the last few weeks. He's lying on his back, solid, and has not moved position at all since he went to sleep. Before his head hit the pillow, he spent about fifteen minutes sorting and packing his bag with his torch, so many plastic bags, rustling away. And his light kept shining at me.

I don't know how anyone is sleeping through the noise. Even if I was in the other room, I would hear him, or over the street, it's so bad. I don't know what to do. I can hear two others snoring but they are nothing compared to him.

I can't lie here till 6.00 am, that's five hours away. I have tried putting my fingers in my ears but that's not working. I don't think I have the nerves to go downstairs and sleep on the sofa. I have moved about so much that I am lying on the plastic mattress now. My paper sheet is all crumpled.

He wakes up and looks at his phone, his face illuminated. Then he moves onto his side and instantly falls asleep. Less noise this time, normal snoring. Not the pneumatic drill level of noise.

I try very hard to get to sleep but it's impossible. My pillow is like a lump of rock and one end is plastic now.

It's 2.05 am, only four hours to go. The man above me gets down to go to the toilet, falling off the last step with a bump. When he comes back, he walks towards me in his pants and I think for a moment he has forgotten where the ladder is, or that he was on the top bunk. How awkward would that be if he tried to get in with me by accident? Luckily, he was just getting a drink from under his pillow and stands by my bed drinking it, in his tiny pants, which are right there, it's a bit unnerving. Then, thankfully, he gets back onto the top bunk.

The snorer has changed position again and is relatively quieter so I am going to try and sleep again.

Day 17 Friday 23rd September

Hornillos to Itero de la Vega

19.17 miles

At 5.39 am, I wake to the hustle and bustle of bags being moved and packed, which means I must have slept. I try to rest for a bit more.

At 6.23 am, Mr Snorer has his little light on and is faffing around. I might as well get up now. It's pitch-black and it's going to be cold out there. I am shattered.

Now I am trapped, as a pair of naked legs and pants come down the ladder. There's not much room and he is standing where my bag is. I don't want to stand next to him till he has some clothes on and not even then. The snorer is rolling up his sleeping bag now and the weight of him is making the metal bunk bed creak. I was going to roll mine up downstairs. It seems everyone is awake now.

Oh my God! Another set of underpants. The man above Mr Snorer is at the side of my bed now. Gosh, I feel sick. I am going to get dressed in my bed, my clothes are on the end, and get out of here.

I am out on the thin street at 6.45 am, and so glad that last night is behind me. I am wearing shorts over my trousers, really rocking the fashion, but I literally put my clothes on in any order just to get out, including two cardigans and my new headtorch, which makes me feel like I am going down a mine. I am also wearing the socks that gave me blisters ages ago. I shrunk them in the wash and dryer a little so I think they fit better now. If they don't feel right, I can swap them for my other pair. They are not quite dry yet.

A German lady I meet says it's 11 degrees out so that's good. I was preparing myself for three and I don't need my poncho on which I am grateful for. I don't need any light yet while I am in the street. There are two albergues and I can see people through the windows, eating and getting ready.

I don't really know the way to go, I think it's straight out of the village. There's no one in front of me as I am one of the earliest today.

As I leave the village, I do need my torch. I can't believe I am walking in the dark across the Spanish countryside. I know the German girl is five minutes ahead but I can't see her. And about a quarter of a mile back is a tiny headtorch.

Gradually, the stars disappear along with the darkness and the sky turns pale grey as the sun tries to come out. It is so peaceful, a very special time of the day. It's the reward for getting up early. There are more people coming now, still peaceful but I can hear gentle chit chat behind me. I am loving the Meseta, the vastness again. It must feel similar to walking across a desert, it's the same colour and same endlessness, but on paths. I eat a banana and get a good pace going. Now, the sky is a gorgeous, soft pink.

I thought the peaceful village of **San Bol** was the next village but it's off to the left and I can't see it. It sounded like somewhere I wanted to visit, but I am not taking any diversions. I stay on the path. There's a hill ahead, and I fly up it. For the first time, at last, I feel fit and really chuffed. It's an important milestone, I have been waiting for ages for the fitness to kick in. I feel so happy, I knew I couldn't walk 200 miles and not feel fitter but it just wasn't happening.

I can hear music which is a bit of a surprise. I am literally in the middle of nowhere. Gentle music, it might be a church? But I can't see anything, just fields. A couple of lads in front of me keep stopping and looking around, they must hear it as well. After five miles, I stop and sort my bag out. It's 8.48 am, that's good, and I can still hear little bits of music on and off.

I think I can see where it's coming from, a building up on the right. As I get closer, I see it's an albergue and might have a café. The signs say Sidre which is what Fraiser told Emma about. Brilliant. I am absolutely going to stop. The A board says it's an oasis and that about captures it. Right in the middle of the countryside. The music is what I call hippy dippy, spiritual, whale music. And I am not being negative, I have a CD like this. It's a unique place.

They have soya milk and tea bags. Wow. I also get a bit of vegan cake and sit outside with the amazing view. I have a really good cup of tea in a huge glass. It's very comforting. I have missed a good cup of tea.

I take my shoes and socks off to air my feet.

This albergue is very special, it's in the middle of nowhere and has a great energy about it. I enjoy my tea and chill, which is very easy to do with the scenery in front of me and the music.

It's 9.20 am and I have walked 9.19 miles.

That was delicious, real tea as close as I could get to English and how I drink it at home. I feel so happy, a gentle glow of happiness in my soul. This place is gorgeous, and I feel fortunate to have stopped here. An absolute treat. I re-join the path with a fluffiness. Lots of people walk past the entrance. Silly people.

Hontanas village is in a dip, so you go down to it. A bit like the Eden Project, hidden. It's a tiny village with just one slim road going through the middle. It feels very old, very Spanish and it's picturesque.

I pop in the church. It has a seating area with candles, so you can chill and light a candle for someone, if you want. There's a tower to climb, so I leave my bag at the bottom and climb but I can't see out. Not sure what that was all about.

The village is tiny, so I am soon at the other end. After walking for a little bit, a man in a hedge gives me a handful of blackberries that he has just picked, which is very kind. He continues picking more as I walk on eating them. He could be there all day. A lady with a notice on her back saying 'free haircuts' goes by. I stop at Arco San Anton where there is a very basic albergue by huge, impressive old monument ruins.

Castrojeriz is up ahead. I walk to it along a tree lined road. I can see another monument at the top of a big incline and discover the village is wrapped around the base of the conical shaped hill, as if someone drew it.

I look for somewhere to eat. I have a wee at the first place I find but they only offer pizzas and I want a salad. I feel tired and it doesn't look like I am going to find anything unless I wander round the lower streets, so I carry on. Thankfully, I spot a café in one of the last streets. The ladies from the albergue yesterday, the Russian and the Danish, are outside drinking wine which looks really tempting. I would love a cold, crisp white wine right now. I go inside and order a salad and Aquarius. I need hydration, not alcohol.

This is a very Spanish café; lots of locals come in, which I absolutely love. I take my shoes off and slowly enjoy my salad, watching the Spanish people coming and going, and rest. It's been quite a day.

It's a big commitment moving on. I have to walk a further 10 kilometres as there's no accommodation before that. But it's not too late in the day, I feel OK and it's not too hot out either. So, I think it's doable. At 1.15 pm there's plenty of time, I don't need to rush. But I understand that there is a severe hill to climb.

The salad tastes good, just what I needed. I step back onto the pretty streets, very conscious that I don't have a bed for tonight. But in Itero de Vega there are four albergues. As I leave the village, there's a second huge church and then open countryside. The path snakes up to the top of a huge hill where I am heading. One boy is in front but he disappears fast with his long legs and youth. Then I psyche myself up and get on with the steep hill that's in front of me. It's tough but I do feel fitter and, to be honest, I climb it fairly easily. I am panting and do have to stop but not that much. I am almost enjoying it.

Yes, I think I did enjoy climbing that hill. That's never happened to me before. I have never been technically fit and it's not something that I ever considered I would enjoy. The views are phenomenal back over the pretty hilltop village of **Castrojeriz** and vast countryside everywhere. This is incredibly rural. I love the Meseta and take lots of photos.

Further on, I sit at the alto on my own. No one is on the path below, no tiny dots coming from the village that I have just been to, and no one is in front. This is so special. How often can you sit at the top of a hill like this and know there is no one else around for miles? I sit and enjoy it for a while, taking in the views and the stillness. It's so quiet, with no noise at all. The solitude is wonderful. I love it and can feel my soul being nourished.

I walk across the top of the hill and down the steep path. In front is the Meseta, miles and miles of countryside, all hay coloured, with the path that I will be taking running through the middle. I see two people on bikes but no one else.

I have my eye on a particular hostel, called San Nicolas, which is a *donavito*. Payment is by donations, no fixed price, and it doesn't have any electricity. I saw it in the Brierley book and I want to experience that, if there is room.

It just appears in front of me, I recognise it from the photo. I could easily have walked past, as it's a stone building in the middle of nowhere. I wasn't expecting to simply come across it. Brilliant. Let's hope there's a bed. If not, I am 1.7 kilometres from **Itero**.

I step inside through the big, arched door in the middle of the building and find a huge, long table almost the length of the room, a small church altar to the left, and bunk beds to my right. I ask the man sitting at the desk, if there are any beds but I don't understand his reply. I am also distracted by his face, he looks like he has a big birthmark on his nose and forehead. He asks if I am French. Someone translates and says that I can have a mattress up at the altar.

Yes, why not? Let's do this.

I say yes, a mattress is good. I can stay, this day just keeps getting better and better. I can't believe how lucky I am. This really was on my wish list but I didn't think I would be here early enough to get a bed.

I put my bag down on a bench and turn around to see four bunk beds with people sleeping. I don't really know what's happening but I see that they have run out of beds. Apparently, a mattress will be put on the floor by the altar later. Dinner is at 7.00 pm, then a ceremony. Oh dear, what have I done?

The toilet and shower are in a building out the back where there is electricity to charge my phone. There's no electricity in this church-hostel room. I sit down, that's all I care about, taking the weight off my feet. I stop my app, I have walked 19 miles today. That's insane and some of it was over that big hill. I must be getting stronger.

When my feet feel more rested, I take a walk around the building. It's all pretty chilled here. It's too late to wash any clothes as they won't dry and I have clean clothes for tomorrow. I shower and then write my journal. I sit on the bench next to the arched front door, and a French lady talks to me. She doesn't know any English and I drag out my school French so we manage to talk about something.

It's an hour till dinner. I don't know what's happening now. It's all donation, no set charge. I get told that the money from yesterday in the donation box feeds us today and our money will feed tomorrow's pilgrims. What a lovely idea.

I am a bit nervous about dinner, I am not going to lie. I wanted a different experience and here it is. We are all hanging around watching the table get set. A man has a job of pitting olives from a big jar. And then cutting them into four. There are lots of Italians. This is a very crazy time. The cooking is happening in this building, which surprises me and the church end has a tiny window letting some light in. The long table down the centre of the building has been laid with plates, wine and water. Behind a curtain appears a tiny kitchen area , an Italian man who looks remarkably like Marco Pierre White who is cooking pasta. I think I might be in Italy today. Italian accents everywhere and now Italian food. I am not complaining though.

But I can't deny, it's all a bit strange.

The Italians must have different watches on, as dinner is finally ready at 8.00 pm. One poor man kept looking at his watch leading up to the meal, he looked like he might faint with hunger. I am not a huge pasta fan and there is talk of sardines. I also don't like olives, so I'm not sure, but I am starving. I told them I don't eat meat when I signed in and they asked if I eat fish so I said yes as I didn't want to be difficult. I didn't think the whole meal would be fish.

But I didn't know what to expect anyway. I am in a church. I didn't even see the kitchen hiding behind the curtain and the sink is the font, which has been adapted, but it's definitely a font. This is very different.

They ring a big bell on the wall for dinner but, first, a ceremony.

Oh dear.

We all go up the few steps to the altar, a little nervous, and three people put robes on with shells hanging off and we all sit down on the chairs in a semicircle. They read a prayer in Italian, English and French, saying a different prayer to each of us, as a man goes round and washes our feet.

It's all a little surreal but he washes our feet with such love. The man with the broken face, it turns out, does not have a birthmark, he fell off the step yesterday and cut his face up. He speaks English and French as well as Italian, so I am not sure why he didn't understand me when I arrived. He has remembered every one of our names and nationality, without hesitation, and reads us the prayer as we have our feet washed and blessed which is a symbol of getting to Santiago.

We eat by candlelight. The pasta is amazing, it has so much flavour, with a seasoning made from old bread and spices instead of parmesan. Everyone here is a new face except for René, the German girl who was at the hostel dinner yesterday. She is also veggie but eating fish if she has to. We eat salad for the second course which I don't really need as I'm full, but it's very good. And melon with cinnamon to finish.

I love my new set of friends. A lot of Italians, a big man with a great sense of humour, two German boys – one who was ahead of me before the hill – a French lady, an English lady who speaks Spanish and French, and a Portuguese man. The conversation flows easily. I actually feel relaxed at the table. Over dinner, we discuss what time to get up in the morning. Everyone wants a different time, 6.00, 6.30, 7.00, 7.30, because we all have different schedules and there are lots of laughs.

After dinner, we all go and wash up in the building out the back, using torches to get there in the dark. We are told to wash five dishes and get to the back of the queue, it's a lot of fun. There are laughs out the back as we wander around in the dark getting between both buildings.

It's now 9.30 pm. I am shattered. I got up early after a bad sleep and I am usually in bed by now. But the lady has suggested some singing before bed.

None of us want to sing. Me most of all, but you have to go with the flow and the singing takes place by the altar in my bedroom, so I can't go to sleep until it's over. I am nervous but try to relax. The lady is a great singer and starts humming, prompting us to join in. In the dark candlelit church, it seems fitting. She sings hallelujah and we join her. It's actually a very unique experience that probably only comes once in a lifetime. The gentle noises that we have collectively created hum round the stone church and it's very spiritual. She doesn't overdo it and then it's bedtime.

I thought we were on mattresses but it's a camp bed which I don't like, as I get stuck in them. But I am very grateful to be here. There are three of us on the altar, two German boys and me. It's all a bit odd. What would everyone think at home, if they could see me now? We stay in our clothes in case it gets cold, as there's no heating, and we get into our sleeping bags.

This has been by far one of the best days I have ever had. Possibly in my life and most definitely the best day on the Camino. It's a day that has met all my needs: nature, good food, good tea, music, tranquillity, fitness and friendships. A perfect day which will stay with me for the rest of my life.

Day 18 Saturday 24th September

Itero de la Vega to Villalcazar de Sirga
19.89 miles

It's morning and we are woken to the sound of Italian church music which is a first for me and quite beautiful. It's the first time I have woken up in a church, let alone to Italian music. I look up at the ceiling from my camp bed and study it, because I am still trying to take every detail in. For such a plain building on the outside, it has a very pretty dome ceiling indoors.

I can smell coffee and the candles have been re-lit. The church looks really homely, with just a few candles on the table and one on the wall. It's almost dark again with a hint of warmth, bringing a glow to the room. I get such a feeling of history here and this is probably as close as I am ever going to get to feeling what pilgrims from hundreds of years ago felt. The hostels that I have been in are a modern version of the Camino, even if they are in old buildings. In this hostel, I can sense what it might have been like.

We chat easily over breakfast, the candles illuminating people's faces. There's such a lovely energy and atmosphere here, I don't really want to leave this special place but we have to. As we are about to go the fourth lady, who hasn't said much but ate with us last night and again this morning, reads a prayer to us outside in front of the large, arched front door. They wear their capes again with the scallop shells. The prayers are in Italian, so I don't understand the words but I know they are blessings for us on our way to Santiago.

As I walk away from the hostel at 8.00 am, I feel like I am on a pilgrimage to Santiago. I knew that, obviously, but now, I really feel it. I have been blessed, stayed in a 'real' pilgrim hostel, and now I am walking to Santiago.

The last 24 hours are going to stay with me forever.

I walk over a bridge; I have not seen so much water under a bridge in ages which has made the fields a lush green. Luckily, I don't need my torch as I couldn't find it yesterday. I must have lost it, which is a shame. I am surprised that I don't lose more of my things. There are so many stops and unpacking my bag every day. I have slept in 18 different beds so far and visited different locations, benches, walls and cafés. I am surprised I have anything left.

I quickly arrive in **Itero de la Vega** where there is a stunning mural on the wall. I stop to take a few photos. It's a great piece of art. It's now 8.5 kilometres to **Boadilla del Camino.** The next village has a lot of orange painted houses and feels very broken, there are lots of houses which need major work. And a smell of animal slurry which is very pungent. There's not a soul about.

As I leave the village, the sun shines on the hay fields, making them glow. There's a very long, straight path ahead of me which gives me time to think about last night. It's difficult to comprehend what happened. I had a beautiful day walking across the Meseta; had tea and cake at that wonderful albergue with the music, my fitness kicking in at last; the view and peace at the top of that hill, and one of the best night's accommodation I have ever had. I have stayed in some lovely hotels over the years, but last night wasn't about luxury, it was about being enveloped in something, I am not quite sure what. I was surprised how quickly a collection of strangers could mould together to become one authentic group of people, enjoying each other's company. I feel grateful that I was able to experience it.

The long open tracks across flat countryside are very peaceful. The only sound is my feet on the gravel. I stop so that I can hear nothing, and cherish it.

Then two lads run past me with backpacks on. Not huge ones, but big enough. How crazy is that?

I grumble in my head about how painful the stones are underfoot and hope the path is not like this for five miles. No wonder people sprain their ankles a lot here. Joan, the lady from Viana who rescued me from the bulls, has messaged me to say that she sprained her ankle and has gone home. It can happen to any of us.

Just as I am getting quite weary with the long stony road, I see a small, beautifully painted stone sitting on a marker. It's holding down a piece of laminated card that says, 'Take me to Santiago,' and a website to tell me what to do. It's just what I need to brighten my mood. Such a lot of care has gone into painting the stone and it's a lovely idea.

At last, I arrive at **Boadilla del Camino**, where a huge church dominates the village. I go into a café, where I order tea and it comes in the tiniest teapot which a lot of cafés have here. It's a teacup sized pot but it's tea, plus any bigger and I would need a wee. Just as I look for a seat, I see the lads who ran by me and talk to them. They live in Newquay, not far from me, so we have a little chat. They only have two weeks off work so they are running 50 kilometres a day. I do hope they make it, maybe they will come back and walk it one day. Then the two Canadian ladies turn up from last night. A German lady invites me to sit with her. She overheard my conversation with the boys.

She is called Sandra and we walk together to Fromista. It's a pretty walk along a canal, a very different feel to anything I have seen in Spain. We could be in England. We talk about books as she said in the café that she liked Raynor Winn's book and I tell her about mine, sitting next to hers on the shelf in a bookshop in

Mevagissey. Or at least it was when I put it there and cheekily took a photo.

I tell her that I found a stone and she admits that she was the lady who left it. She brought a kilo of painted stones with her and has been placing them along the Camino. Now she only has about 300 grams left. She says it's not working out how she planned it because people are keeping them as souvenirs as they are so nice. I promise to carry mine for a while and replace it.

We talk about all the different ways people are doing the Camino. She knows of someone who brought a broom and a football with him. And so many people we've both heard of have walked from afar, like Belgium, Germany, or Holland before getting to St Jean. It's the same walk but everyone is doing it their own way.

Fromista is a working town. We go over the canal which is impressive with the bridges and locks. The centre has lots of roads, it's a much bigger place than the previous few. I don't fancy eating here, so I walk out of town. I do need a break before I continue so I sit on a bench and take my shoes off to eat some sunflower seeds and nuts that I still have from England. The man I spoke to briefly in the café just now passes and I offer him some sunflower seeds. We chat for a bit while we eat them. This is his second time doing this Camino.

I have walked ten miles and I need to do another seven if I want to get to **Villalcazar de Sirga**. René and the other lady from last night walk by, heading for the same place as me.

I am so hungry. I hope the next town has a nice café and I can get some lunch.

I walk to the next village, **Poblacion de Campos**, with a lovely German guy that slept at the altar with me. He lives in Berlin and I went in spring 1990 just after the wall came down. He tells me how different it still is between the east and west, different pay, accommodation, etc. He was born after the wall came down but still the east and west are very different places, although it is blending.

I stop in the village by the fountain to rest my feet. There's a tiny supermarket but, unfortunately, it's shut. There's no food here, although I did smell something lovely but it came from someone's house, something with onions. I should have eaten in Fromista, that was silly not to. It's four kilometres to the next place. Will I make it on two thin slices of baguette from 7.30 am this morning and a few nuts?

I am going to try. It's 1.00 pm.

As I come out of the village, there are two choices of paths, one by road and one more scenic. I see the sign for the scenic route and go that way but it feels like I am going back into the village. Unfortunately, I will have to stop and look at my book. I am so tired and hungry.

I sit on a wall and take my bag off to get Brierley out so that I can see where I went wrong. I think I have worked it out. I put my bag back on and a man approaches me, just as I am clicking the strap shut. He walks up to me and stands in front of me with a black bucket, it looks like he has been to his allotment. He has a few different things in the bottom.

He picks out a tomato and offers it to me. I am a bit confused. Is he trying to sell me one? This doesn't normally happen to me.

It's huge so I say, '*Este grande*.'

He replies, '*No entiendo*.'

I bravely say, '*Más pequeño*,' and he rummages in his bucket and finds a smaller one. I say, '*Si*.' He hands it to me and I reach for my money but he says, '*Buen Camino*,' and walks off.

I say, '*Muchas gracias*.'

I am shocked. What just happened? I walk back the way I came to correct myself and a flood of emotion washes over me and tears appear. I let them flow. I feel vulnerable and loved all at the same time and overwhelmed with what just happened. It feels like an angel appeared just when I needed it. A total stranger has offered me some of his daily trip to the allotment. It was for his family and he gave some to me, showing such kindness. I wipe my tears away.

I am so hungry that the timing is perfect. I take a bite and it's juicy and full of flavour, intense and home grown. I want him to know how hungry I am and how kind he was, but he's gone.

I eat it slowly, devouring every mouthful. It could not have come at a better time. I am now on a very long, straight road but I feel happier.

The sky is black but I can't walk any faster. The German lady said it was going to rain about 2.00 pm but last time I rushed somewhere because of the rain it never did. And the time it did rain it was almost nothing and over before it even got started.

I can see the town but it's still a way off, this is a tough bit. I walk through the village, **Villovieco**, hoping for a café but it's dead. There's no one about, no café, no people at all, just lots of agricultural machinery lying around. It was a big error not eating at Fromista. I know there's a packet of biscuits in the depths of my bag from breakfast in Burgos so I sit on a wall and find them, five little biscuits which will keep me going. I could do with a wee but there's nowhere to go. Then it starts to rain. I get my poncho on, this is a nuisance.

I have 6.5 kilometres to do and the heavens are about to open. I put ibuprofen gel on my feet as they are aching. I see the path and start walking. A man on a bike whizzes by and says, '*Buen Camino*,' and points to the bar and shouts, 'Bar!' at me.

How annoying, I didn't know there was a bar at the edge of the village. It would have been in Brierley but I didn't look. I have just had biscuits which has taken the edge off my appetite but I just want to get to the next town, so I ignore the bar and carry on up the path by the river.

The rain is bad. Even though I have my poncho on, it's still not covering my bag properly. My sleeping bag feels a bit damp which is not good. I have to go back to the bar and stay there until it clears. I get wet walking there but then I am in the dry. I want chips but the lady hasn't got any, so I have *patatas bravas* without the sauce, so basically small potatoes in the fryer. They hit the spot and I am not hungry anymore. The rain clears and I get going.

The mud is now like clay, clinging to my feet, actually a little dangerous. It's dry, and then it's slippery and I really don't want to fall over. I have to wear my poncho as it's soaked and I don't know what else to do with it.

I eventually arrive at **Villalcazar de Sirga**, which is another traditional Spanish village dominated by a huge church. It has a square pedestrian area.

I can't find the *municipal* until a boy cycles over and asks if I am looking for a hostel. I feel a bit uncomfortable, like I am being 'rounded up'. The Spanish boy has an unusual dangly earring, which reminds me of a scene in *Breaking Bad* that didn't end well. I think it's the way he is cycling, in big sweeping circles and there is no one else around. I follow him to the hostel, which looks more like someone's house, although there is a sign by the door saying albergue. I step through the fly screen into a dark reception that has a desk and a hippy, who says hello. I feel a little uneasy, then another pilgrim arrives, a man, and I feel better. We both sign in, and he tells us it's a donativo. That's what I was in last night, but this is more like an albergue.

The bedroom is perfect, everything is clean, there's a good kitchen and the upstairs is much brighter than the reception area. The room has six bunk beds for 12 people and there's only me and this man at the moment. He's not chatty, which is OK with me.

I shower first. I have to put €1.00 in to make the shower work, but that's fair enough in a *donavito*. My sore feet feel every bobble in the bottom of the shower tray, they have walked another 19 miles today which is crazy.

After my shower, I go over to look at the church. It's not the prettiest from the outside, very square, and nothing ornate about it. But inside is very different. It has huge stone pillars with lots of arches, and it feels very cathedral-like. The altar is very modest compared to some of the very intense, gold blingy ones that I have seen. To enhance the whole experience, there is music playing. I sit down with lots of other people and listen. I realise it's a man singing and playing some unusual instruments discreetly in the corner. The singing is almost spiritual, he has a high-pitched voice and is chanting a song with words I can't understand, but it's beautiful and mesmerising while the acoustics in the church capture it. I could sit here all evening and listen to him.

I spend some more time wandering around the church, listening to the man singing and playing the instruments. The ceilings are like flower petals and there are lovely round windows with a floral pattern. It's quite beautiful.

After a good look around, I drag myself away and go to the miniature supermarket for bread, hummus, tomato, cheese and orange Fanta, and go back to the kitchen to plate up my food and chill on my bed, eating it. I can see the church from the bedroom window, it's a lovely spot here. I pack my bag ready for tomorrow, as we have to leave at 7.00 am, and rest.

Day 19 Sunday 25th September

Villalcazar de Sirga to Terradillos de los Templarios
19.69 miles

At 7.20 am, I am on the road. It's dark but I manage as I am in the residential area.

There are no pilgrims or anyone about. I don't think many pilgrims stayed in this village last night. It's a long, straight path by the road to the next village and the sunrise turns the sky pink. My hands are freezing, I have my walking poles under my arms so that I can put my hands in my pockets. I am going to need to buy some gloves.

Carrion de los Condes looks interesting. Emma stayed here last night and messaged me to say it would be good to catch up. She must be a couple of hours in front of me. I want to sit down and eat my picnic but I am too cold. It's a busy town with a few shops and a good atmosphere.

I plod out of town, feeling like a tortoise that needs sunshine to get it moving. I come to a road junction with no cars again. All these roads and intersections and no cars. I sit on a wall in a sunny spot, and I take my bag off. I make a picnic of bread and hummus which is delicious. A few people pass me but no familiar faces. Where are they all? I wash it down with half a bottle of orange Fanta from yesterday. Then I change my shoes from sandals to lace ups. It's usually the other way around but I want the comfort of lace ups today.

Emma messages me back with a list of her next four accommodations. I will see if I can catch up with her soon. I feel refreshed. Sometimes you just need to stop to go faster.

That worked. I have a spring in my step now. The paths are good and by the road, almost like sand, very easy to walk on. I walk with a man from Italy for a little way, he has a strong Italian accent and is a nurse in Sicily. He goes on as he is walking faster.

The road goes on and on and on. I need to sit down but there are no seats at all. I stop at the food truck and order a toastie and fresh orange juice, which they juice in front of me. It's just what I need. There's 7.5 kilometres to the next village, so it's a good idea to stop now.

I message the hostel that Emma is staying at. If they have a space I will go for it, if not I hope to get a spot in either albergues in the next place, **Calzadilla de la Cueza**, at the end of this 7.5 kilometres stage. I put my socks back on and get going.

I am marching now, enjoying myself, overtaking people and getting some mileage done. The orange juice and toastie were good fuel. It's very warm with no shelter at all, so I stop at the only shaded rest area. I have walked three miles in an hour. I think that's the fastest I have walked so far, pretty good with a backpack on. I receive an email back and I am booked in Emma's hostel. I decide to leave it as a surprise, rather than messaging her.

The next section is a bit tougher as I am tired. The path just reaches out in front for miles. The albergue at **Calzadilla de la Cueza** has a café. So, I use the loo and get a cold lemonade which is very refreshing after that long open walk. I should really change socks but I have no idea where they are in the bag and I'm not unpacking it.

It's still 9.5 kilometres to go which is a long way. I hope this is not a mistake, it's 2.00 pm, but I am booked in. The path is full of stones again, nasty ones, just when my feet are sore and sensitive.

At **Ledigos** I talk to a Spanish lady in the village. She has a happy, smiley personality and is very chatty. She doesn't speak any English, so we talk in Spanish – well, she talks, but amazingly, I understand her. This is the first time that I have had a conversation, albeit a small one, with someone totally in Spanish and I feel really chuffed. She asks me if I am staying in this village or going to the next one. I tell her the name and she smiles and says she is helping out later in the kitchen in that albergue. I can't believe that I understood all of that.

The last three kilometres feel like ten, it's so tough. I ache all over and every step hurts. The albergue, Jacques de Molay, is buzzing with people enjoying the outdoor area, painted orange, with a Mediterranean feel again. There are tables everywhere and a few familiar faces. I spot Emma, she is talking to the man that I shared my sunflower seeds with earlier. When she sees me, she jumps out of her chair and hugs me. It's good to see her again. I have been on my own, walking for three days now, which I have enjoyed but it's nice to be with familiar faces again.

My room has three single beds, no bunks and one man's stuff is already there. I have walked 19 miles again, that's three days in a row. My feet know it, but apart from that, I am OK. I shower and join Emma outside but the flies are annoying, so we go into the bar and have a good catch up. Emma gets a piece of vegan *empenada* and I have hot water on my tea leaves with a small cake. Nessa is here, so she joins us, and there are people on the next table that Emma knows, including Liz who is really nice. It's a lovely hostel with a happy atmosphere. I get a second cup of water on top of my tea leaves, and buy a bag of non-branded crisps, which I haven't seen in years. It's just a see-through bag with no writing on it. I go back to my room to eat them with the rest of the hummus from yesterday. There is food in the bar but they don't know what is being cooked, which is strange.

I go back down to join Emma and she is talking to Karen who I met walking into Belorado when her son had gone to look for accommodation. Her son is here too, Ieuan, a Welsh lad. We talk about how to pronounce his name, which sounds more like Yian. It's a lovely evening, Ieuan has done the Camino twice on his own and is now enjoying walking with his mum. He says everyone should walk the Camino every few years. I say that I am never doing it again. I am glad I am doing it now, but have absolutely no intention of ever walking it again.

Pierre, the French man who was on the bunk over me in Hotel Abdad, is on another table, and we chat to him. He started in St Puy, France with Ieuan so they will both have done over 1000 kilometres when they get to Santiago. It's been a brilliant, chilled social evening.

I return to my room at 9.00 pm and both men are in bed with the lights out. Thank goodness I made my bed before I went back down.

It's a very small room, and I have no idea what my roommates look like. This is my new normal and it's very odd.

Day 20 Monday 26th September

Terradillos de los Templarios to Sahagun
9.02 miles

Unfortunately, I didn't sleep well and I have no idea why because I was tired, there was no snoring, and the bed was comfy. It might have been a bit too weird not knowing what these men look like. I got woken at 3.39 am by cockerels – two of them. One did a cock-a-doodle-doo and the other did a cocka-oo-oo. It was like a bad alarm clock that I couldn't switch off.

The man in the bed next to me got up and went about 6.30 am, no bother. The other man faffed for half an hour or more while I hid under my covers. It was too late to say hello. I do know he was English because he was talking in his sleep about percentages. I just hid under the covers until he had gone and then packed my bag.

I have a headache and I feel a bit odd. I can't walk 19 miles on a pot of hummus, bread and crisps, it's silly. I am booked into a monastery today which is only 12 kilometres away, so there should be plenty of time to find some food.

It's cold out, so I put on both my trousers, two tops and two cardigans. It's late by the time I leave so the sun is up but there is a chill in the air. Liz is on the stairs getting ready. I chat with her for a bit while I lace up my shoes. And off I go at a very slow pace. I realise that I have not had a meal since the Italians' pasta. I stop and get out my nuts and sunflower seeds and put a big handful in my pocket to eat as I walk.

I stop at the next village, **Moratinos**, which has wine cellars built into a hill that are possibly 500 years old. I stop and take that in for a moment. There's a sign that says, 'No, hobbits don't live here!' and tells you all about the 'bodegas' which were used to store food and wine. They are built into the hills and have little doors with stone decorations at the entrance. They do look like little hobbit houses.

It's quiet again on the footpath next to the road, a contrast to the chatter and friendship of last night.

When I get to Sahagun, I will be halfway to Santiago. I thought that would make me happy, but it means I have to walk it all again, the same distance, the same pain, which seems daunting. It's actually more daunting than starting and having 500 miles to walk. I know what is needed now, I know how deep I have to dig to keep moving forwards.

We were talking last night with Ieuan and Karen about walking holidays, like Hadrian's wall and the Peak District, but I have no plans to go on a walking holiday. Some people I have met love walking holidays but, actually, I don't. That's such a stupid thing to say halfway through a 500-mile walk. But this doesn't feel like a walking holiday.

This is the Camino, it's blisters and bunk beds. It's day after day of walking, often on my own. I wouldn't call it a holiday. When I picture the Peak District holiday, I imagine walking across beautiful countryside, going back to a lovely guest house, having a bath with a big fluffy towel, then eating a fantastic hearty meal over a glass of wine.

This is not that.

This is wearing the same clothes for days, sleeping on plastic mattresses with paper sheets, sharing bedrooms with strangers who snore and walk around in their underwear. It's not knowing what you will eat next, or where, and dealing with blisters, and definitely no bath and no fluffy towel. I feel morose this morning. I am physically a little bit off, my tummy is not good, it's probably empty. I feel weak mentally, a little fragile. My feet are hurting already so thank goodness it's a small walk today.

I am really not feeling this anymore and I want to go home. I think maybe three 19-mile days on very little food was not a good idea. I have had so many great moments; the day across the Meseta, staying in the church, the company last night, but at the end of the day, you have to keep walking whether you are in pain or not. Every day I have to walk and I am not sure I want to anymore.

I plod along, feeling a bit low.

I can see Sahagun in the distance, it's not too far to go. This usually spurs me on but not today. I sit on a concrete wall by the side of the path and road. This whole trip is insane.

I need water but my water bladder is empty, I forgot to fill it. And I just can't take my bag off now. I sit and listen to the birds and chill for a moment and watch people walk by, all at different paces.

I feel like Forrest Gump who doesn't want to run any more. I don't even want to walk into Sahagun and I am almost there. I really need some water, so I am going to push myself into Sahagun to get a cup of tea or water.

It's very commercial on the edge of the town, and it doesn't really get any better. In Sahagun, there's a huge piece of an old historic building, just the end of it, which looks strange surrounded by roads and newer buildings. It feels like they don't want to knock it down but they don't want to keep it either. I take a photo of a pilgrim statue which I really like and a map of the Camino on a brass plaque that shows I am halfway.

It's time to find my accommodation. Monasterio de Santa Cruz. It's not open yet, so I go to the supermarket just over the road. Buying food always cheers me up. I get a litre of the most expensive fruit juice on the shelf, hoping that it has more vitamins and tastes amazing, as well as some cakes, a tin of white beans, fizzy orange, fizzy lemon, a tomato, bread and a bag of frozen peas to put in some soup. Emma said she made dinner with frozen vegetables and now I am craving frozen peas.

I am like a kid in a sweet shop, I haven't been in a proper supermarket with aisles for ages. As I walk out, I see Emma and Nessa. They are just going into the supermarket. They see my big bag of goodies and laugh.

I walk over to the monastery which doesn't look very impressive or old from the outside. When I get in, I see it's quite modern. It has a spacious hallway with a tiled floor and oval windows, letting in a lot of light. The friendly staff show me to my room which is small with two bunk beds and a bathroom, so it's very luxurious. I get the bottom bunk as I am so early. It's only 1.00 pm.

I get my washing in the machine straight away and hang it out on the line, in the hope that it dries. They have a kettle in the kitchen which is great news. The man who showed me to my room is Irish, so of course there is going to be a kettle. Afterwards, I chill in the courtyard with a cup of tea and cake. I still feel fragile and it's a little chilly so I go to my room and relax.

I am not doing the 'share your story over coffee', I did want to do one of those, but not today. Though I will do the Mass at 6.30 pm.

After a rest, my empty tummy takes me back to the kitchen and I make pea and bean soup and take it out into the courtyard to eat. I ring my daughter, Ciara, as it's her birthday. I wouldn't have seen her today, even if I was in England, as she is in Greece working as a mermaid, entertaining holiday makers in the hotels. Then I make another tea. I am full and content now. Surprisingly, my mood has lifted. I wonder if it's food related.

After all that chilling, it's time for Mass, and I am very nervous. I asked if I could still attend as a non-religious person and got told it was OK. I have seen so many of these churches decorated with lots of shiny gold and now I am sitting in one, to do what you are supposed to do, and it feels weird.

I am sure I am going to stick out like a sore thumb, but oh well. The huge gold wall in front of me will keep me entertained while I wait. Nothing seems to be happening very fast.

The huge gold backdrop to the altar is floor to ceiling with a domed top surrounded by a stone frame. It's a 3D work of art, with figurines, cherubs, figures, grapes and even pillars. Everything is sprayed gold. It's a bit over the top and probably has a story attached to it. I don't suppose all these figures are random.

It's only 40 minutes, I can do this. I have been to enough catholic weddings and christenings to know you need to be ready to stand up and sit down, or kneel really fast so that no one catches you out. The priest arrives, if that's what he is, and there are nuns as well who all look so old. The congregation is a mix of pilgrims, some I recognise, while some are local people.

At the end, we all have to stand in a semi-circle and be blessed by the priest and a tiny nun who has piercing eyes. The overall feeling is discomfort, boredom and misunderstanding. I won't be doing that again.

I go back to my room and carry on chilling until it's time to go to bed. My roommate turns up, I say hello from my bed, and she ignores me. OK then.

Day 21 Tuesday 27th September

Sahagun to Reliegos
19.61 miles

Eleven hours later, I wake up after a deep and comfortable sleep. So, I must have been exhausted and it was a good decision to stop walking at 1.00 pm yesterday.

I consider breakfast but it looks like last night's dinner which I didn't attend, and I am quite grateful now. It was a communal dinner and everyone was asked to bring food from the supermarket. I like a buffet very much but I had a feeling it would be pastry and more pastry. Another day I might have attended, but I wasn't feeling very social yesterday.

I have half a litre of juice to drink and a tomato, so I decide to miss breakfast and get on the road at 8.00 am. I drink my juice as I go and carry my poles. I am walking at a good speed and feel so much better today.

No one said that this walk was going to be easy. I have to remember to be kind to myself and take breaks when I need to and eat better. Otherwise, I am not going to get to the end. I still have 250 miles to go.

I left my phone on loud after my Duolingo lesson yesterday and it tells me that I just walked three miles in an hour which is good. René from Germany, who was at the hostel last night and the Italian church, is behind me. No one is in front.

My juice is finished but I can't find a bin, which means I can't use my poles. It's a long straight road again but the path is OK. There are benches as well. I don't need them right now but it's good they are here. When I do stop at a bench, I have walked 5.18 miles. I can throw the bottle away now as there's a bin, meaning I can walk with the poles.

I stop for tea at an albergue, more because I need a wee but also so that I stop a little bit more. It's a big hostel on the edge of town with an open, spacious grassy area at the front. It's good to stop and chill for a bit. I don't want to walk a 19-mile day again. I have proved to myself that I can, now I need to slow it down, but that means the next half will take longer. I don't know, I'll just listen to my body and see what it says. As I walk on, I find a spot to return the painted stone that I found, so someone else will enjoy picking it up.

The next village, **Bercianos del Real Camino**, has a lot of straw houses. They look like normal houses but if you look closely you can see the straw. I touch the wall and it's rock solid with tiny bits of hay. They are very rustic looking. Some are being renovated, so the village has a mixture of very old, almost falling down houses next to new brick houses. The new houses change the whole look of the street but obviously makes the village seem like it's moving on and keeps families in the area. What I find comforting is no one wants a bigger house, they just replace the old one with new materials.

Sheila, who is originally English but has been living in Australia for many years, walks with me into **El Burgo Ranero**. I walk through the village, even though it looks like the sort of place I might like to stop. I have 12 kilometres to go and Sheila is stopping here.

As I'm leaving, I see trees that have crochet wraps on their trunks, all different colours. Then I pass the village cemetery, which is so well looked after, before continuing on a very straight, flat path for a while and take a break on a bench for a little picnic of crisps and orange Fanta. I have walked nine miles.

I take my socks off and notice blood. My feet don't hurt, only ache, and there's no specific pain. I look closely and my toenail has cut into the next toe's skin. I was thinking of cutting my toenails as I have been away for three weeks now, but my scissors broke.

A huge dog or wolf is about a quarter of a mile ahead on the path. Being scared of dogs, I stop and go down towards the deep ditch by the side of the road, and up again onto the road. There are no cars, there rarely are. The dog seems to be staring at me. Then, thankfully, it walks into the field. I stay in the road until I realise it's a sheep dog, not a normal type. This one is a big hairy thing. I get back on the path. It's still looking at me, probably being protective of his sheep; there are a lot of them in the field. A few minutes later, the farmer appears so I relax and walk past him.

Villamarco is in the Brierley book, but it's not a village. There's nothing here, just as the book suggests. There is a little sheltered area though and I stop. It's a milestone, this non place. It comes towards the end of a very long stretch. I take my shoes and socks off and open my second can of Fanta. It's chilly and my cake wrapper keeps almost blowing away. So, it's time to put my shoes and backpack on and get moving. It's about five kilometres to go until I can rest for the night.

The Russian girl that I have stayed in a couple of hostels with walks beside me for the last couple of miles. We have a nice chat and a laugh, she's lovely and it helps to pass the time till I get to **Reliegos**. We go our separate ways as she has a reservation and I don't. I walk through town looking for the *municipal* but when I find it, it looks horrible, really small with washing drying on airers in the street. There's a La Parada hostel advert on the next street on an A board, so I browse on gronze.com quickly to check it looks OK.

I go in. It looks nice but there's no one at reception, so I go to the bar and Mr Grumpy comes out to help. I pay and he reluctantly walks me upstairs – 'Boots here, shower there, room there' – before he goes back down. Three people are resting on the three bunk beds and therefore I am on the top. I am disappointed for sure but I will be OK.

I am not going to cry today, I am getting used to being on the top and I try to mentally prepare myself that I might be. I am more in control of my expectations. I sit on the floor and do my stretches. I can't believe I walked 19 miles again today. I wasn't going to do that again.

After my shower, I sit in the courtyard area which has a few tables and it's sunny so I make a tea with the microwave and read Brierley.

I haven't eaten a proper meal for a while but I don't have the energy to go round the village looking. I make another miso soup, that's what I brought it for, and I can use the thawed frozen peas that I have from yesterday and eat the crisps from the other day too. I eat it in the garden and then brush my teeth and climb onto my top bunk.

Day 22 Wednesday 28th September

Reliegos to Leon
16.30 miles

Despite being on the top bunk and everyone snoring, I did get a good sleep.

The French people are awake at 6.15 am, while a man is walking round the room with his headtorch on. He actually talks to me at one point but I can't see a thing as he is blinding me until his wife tells him off. As everyone is awake, and because I want to get to Leon at a sensible time, I am out of the door by 6.50 am, carrying a tomato.

It's dark and I trip a few times on the gravel, so I walk in the road since it's safe with only one car every 15 minutes. The light from my own headtorch isn't very good, I might need a new battery already. I touch the button to see if there's a brighter setting and realise it's pointing up. Dippy. No wonder. After a while, a few more cars start to go past so I get back on the path. The sunrise is the best I have seen yet on the Camino. An entire 360 degrees of gold, orange and pink streaked across the sky.

Mansilla de las Mulas is an interesting old place, with a medieval wall going round the whole village. I am going to research this place a bit more. The wall is huge and decayed, so not complete like it would have been, but it's so prominent and historic. I walk through the gap and it feels like an alleyway as the walls are so tall. As I wander round, I can see a lot of the village is being renovated, from straw and mud to brick. It has a nice feel to it, very old, but unfortunately no cafés to stop at. I am too early and they are all shut.

So, I sit on a bench at the far end of the village and eat a piece of cake. It's 6.1 kilometres to the next town, **Puente Villarente**. I will have to just do it. It's 8.30 am and I have walked four miles already.

As I go over the big bridge, I see hills, the flatness has gone. It's also a little colder. I need to buy a coat and gloves in Leon.

Villarmoros has a long straight, wide path next to the road. I stop in **Puente Villarente** and go into a busy, bustling Spanish café on the main road, ordering a red tea. I have no idea what that is but they didn't have black. I also eat a tuna *empanada*. I have not had any *empanada* yet and promised myself that I would eat something this morning. The red tea has a strange harsh taste, but there's no milk in it which might have softened it but never mind. It's good to sit down and people watch. The café sells bread in one corner and posh cakes, while there's a deli which also sells chilled cakes. This feels like Spain: a community shop and café. A lot of places I stop at are for the pilgrims, but this is full of Spanish locals.

I message Emma to tell her where I am and by 10.30 am, I am back on the road. I really want to get to Leon because I have a vegan dinner date with her there. That should put a spring in my step. There are lots of shops on this stretch of road; normal shops, a pet shop, hardware, electrical. It reminds me of my childhood, in the old days before retail parks and supermarkets were invented, and the high street was full of independent shops.

I see the Russian and Danish lady sitting on a bench resting their feet and say hello. At 11.30 am, I sit down in a covered area in **Arcahueja**. It has a fountain and benches. Then I go uphill, I haven't done that in a while.

As I approach Leon, there are loads of industrial units, then car dealerships and garages for fixing cars. There's lots of traffic and juggernauts. The air is thick with petrol and diesel. I can see Leon in front of me. It's huge, much bigger than I expected.

I bump into Penny and Nick from **Atapuerca** and a new man from Alaska that they are walking with. It's great to catch up with them. It seems like ages to get to the cathedral, you can't see it, which makes it difficult to judge where you are. Then we walk into the old town and it feels like we are close now with the thin, tall streets.

I go to a market in a big square and I really want a peach. I ask for two that are ready to eat. The lady hands them to me and doesn't charge me which is so sweet.

I find my hostel, Globetrotter, and you can see the cathedral from the front door. Inside, it's very modern. The bedroom has 12 bunk beds with privacy curtains and a white towel. I have a shower and relax in my big white towel on my bed. I have walked 16 miles today, that's not much short of the 19 miles I wasn't going to walk again.

Once I am dressed, I start to message Emma and see where we should meet to go to dinner when she walks into the room. We burst out laughing. What are the chances of us ending up in the same hostel, let alone the same room? There are about 25 hostels in Leon, and it took me ages to decide which one to go to. Emma said she saw my odd poles in my locker as she came into the room and thought it must be me.

We walk past the huge cathedral and go off to eat at the vegan place with Nessa and her friend. The food is amazing, especially because I haven't eaten a meal in days. I have a vegan burger with chips, it's so good. Emma has pizza and Nessa and her friend have rice and pasta.

Sitting eating a meal with friends that I have made on the Camino wasn't something I ever thought would happen. I thought I was walking solo, so to have friends to go to dinner with is a bonus. We chat about our different experiences and it's good to hear what everyone else has been doing.

After lunch, I go into the cathedral. The stained glass windows are phenomenal, but the cathedral is not as intricate and detailed as Burgos. It was a waste of money, but you have to pay if you want to go in, and I did.

Pilgrims, at the very least, should get in free with their *credencial,* in my opinion.

With the need to buy a coat, I walk to Decathlon. The one I pick is hideous but there isn't much choice. I also get a pair of gloves, and I walk back with Nessa who has ended up here as well. I pop into the supermarket to get some orange juice. I am so thirsty that I drink it in the street. I also buy a lemon Fanta and a KitKat and then go home to the hostel. I make a much needed cup of tea with the kettle in the tiny kitchen and take it back to the room.

I chat with Emma. There's no one else in our room so we have it all to ourselves, for now. She has bought a new pair of trousers and some mascara. She isn't feeling like her true self. She brought with her some zip off walking trousers for the Camino which have been good but not what she would ever wear at home. After 20 days of Camino clothes, she wants to feel more like herself and that means wearing trousers that she likes, putting on a bit of mascara and donating her walking shorts at the next hostel.

We talk about Sarria. Both of us are reading our Brierley. He says that we mustn't get irritated by the new pilgrims who start in Sarria. I don't think it's going to affect me, since it will be new faces to talk to. I can't imagine getting annoyed by new people.

Emma is in a bit of pain and managed to buy some more painkillers to help with her back. She has also bought a bottle of delicious looking pink wine. She only wants one glass and offers me some. It's difficult to refuse as I would love a glass, it's exactly the one that I would buy if I was choosing a bottle of wine. But I am sticking to my no alcohol rule and she takes it to the fridge for someone else to drink.

I am not sure what to do tomorrow, how far to go or what time to leave. I will decide in the morning.

Day 23 Thursday 29th September

Leon to San Martin del Camino
14.75 miles

I woke at 8.30 am. I slept really well, it was cosy with the curtain and the cotton sheets. I make a cup of tea and casually pack my bag, which seems to really slow me down. It's the complete opposite of the usual quick, fast, efficient get out of here.

It might rain so I put my sleeping bag in a black sack to protect it. Now I have a raincoat as extra luggage but I think it was the perfect time to buy it.

Emma has left, we are walking solo today. I am going to slowly walk out of town and take photos of the places that I didn't see yesterday and it's all on the route out. I have poles under arms as I am carrying half a litre of orange juice. It's complicated leaving the city. There are so many roads and cars. Every few minutes, I am looking at the app to make sure I am going the right way. I am so glad Emma showed me how to use it.

I follow a tall girl with an orange backpack, hoping she is a pilgrim. I have to step up my pace to keep up with her as she is way ahead with longer legs than me. I eventually lose her but now I can see Camino signs on the road, so it's OK. It's busy roads for miles and, eventually, I turn right past some bodegas.

It's starting to spit with rain now which is annoying. I am not sure whether to put my poncho on. I walk through a big industrial area. I would have rather bypassed Leon. It was industrial walking in, and industrial walking out. I don't think the centre of the city was impressive enough to make up for the ugly entrance and exit.

I see Emma up ahead, chatting to people at a Camino stop point. I need the loo badly and, luckily, there is one. I shouldn't have drunk half a litre of orange juice. I buy a banana, while Emma carries on. I put my poncho on. I might as well do it calmly and with help than in a panic when the heavens open.

I catch Emma up, seeing her ahead in the drizzle. There's no point walking solo on this awful stretch. When it's a Meseta or lovely countryside, it's nice to be on your own but not so much now. So, we walk together. Sometimes we can't hear each other over the traffic. It's a dull path next to a main road with juggernauts going by. Luckily, the rain soon eases.

We come to a little café and sit down, both tired and in need of refreshments. I get a tortilla and a little packet of lemon biscuits, as strangely we were talking about lemon biscuits on the way here. The tea is good, although still black. Emma tastes the best tomato on toast she has had on the Camino so far, it's a good café. Meredith and Nick arrive as we are leaving; we chat for a bit and then move on.

We carry on to Emma's accommodation and she crosses the busy main road, while I plod on another five kilometres. I haven't taken any photos – it was the dullest walk, next to the main road.

I don't have a reservation but there is a bed for me at Santa Ana. I ask for a bottom bunk. When we get there, the eight bottom bunks are all taken. I am so disappointed. The photo I saw before showed a different room, unless I have gotten confused and I'm at the wrong hostel, which is possible.

The bunks don't even have a ladder. How on earth am I going to get up there?

I sit on the floor, on the cold hard tiles, and feel quite sad for myself. My favourite part of the day is doing my stretches and that has been taken from me. It's not easy chilling either, sitting outside the toilet on the floor. I find it difficult to relax, if I don't have a routine. At home, I drink tea and chill, on the Camino I can sometimes do that. When I sit quietly and drink my tea, it's not just about having a drink, it's the whole setting time aside to relax with a hot drink to unwind.

Now, on the Camino, I have this new stretching routine where I seem to relax for ten minutes. So now that I can't do it, I don't know how to relax. I need to physically do something. I feel fed up. It's been a difficult day walking by the side of the road. I am also hungry and this long, busy road is full of houses, no restaurants or shops. I didn't even ask what the menu was when I checked in.

So, what am I to do now?

I could get the mattress down and sleep on it. I could just sleep in my sleeping bag on the floor, or I could try and climb up on the bunk and stay still all night, so that I don't fall out, as there are no guards.

I just want this to end now. I want to get to Santiago and return to normal life. Big towels, beds without strangers, food when you want it, food of your own choice. A day without a backpack on.

I drink some Fanta that I have been carrying all day and the last piece of cake from the monastery. It's not been a good eating day, again, and I walked 14 miles. I look in Brierley and plan tomorrow how to get out of here, back on the road, and get to Santiago.

I phone Phil and have a moan. He is very supportive, saying how well I have done. I feel better when I get off the phone. We were talking about dates when I might end, which is actually exciting.

I message Emma, she says that her hostel is lovely, and she is happy there. She sends me a silly GIF of someone bouncing off a wall from a trampoline, trying to make light of my bunk bed dilemma, which makes me laugh. I think today was tough on a lot of levels. I try to reserve somewhere for tomorrow and hope they reply soon, so that I know what's happening.

I don't even want to shower today. I always shower after my stretches but today I don't want to. I don't want to get naked and cold, then dry with my hand towel. I just don't want to do it. It's getting really dark and it feels like bad weather is coming. I hope it's not going to rain tomorrow, that's not going to be a lot of fun.

I eat the lemon biscuits. I am not especially hungry now, so that's good. I will have a banana and a peach for breakfast and there will be lots of places to stop tomorrow. I like the days where there are lots of villages and cafés.

Almost everyone has gone to the pilgrim's meal now, which is strange as I didn't even get shown the menu. I clean my teeth and try to climb up to the top of the bunk while it's quiet. I manage to climb up going from the foot of the bed, but it isn't easy. I have no idea how I am getting down in the morning and I definitely can't go for a wee in the night.

I sleep in the clothes that I walked in. I have put my glasses in my knickers as I don't know what to do with them, and my phone which I need as a clock tomorrow in my trousers.

Goodnight from a miserable Paula.

Day 24 Friday 30th September

San Martin to Astorga
16.61 miles

I slept surprisingly well. Every time I turned over, I hung onto the edge of the mattress to reassure myself. I woke every time someone went to the loo as the light came on and illuminated the room. One man went for a wee and it sounded like an elephant. How could he hold that much liquid in his bladder?

By 6.20 am, people are gradually making soft noises, getting gadgets unplugged and starting to pack. The first person leaves at 6.30 am. I start to zip up my sleeping bag in the dark on the top bunk and get it back in its bag. Then I try to climb down off the bed, which isn't easy with my tiny legs. I get on my knees with my bum facing the door and try to do the reverse of what I did to get up here. I hurt myself a bit reaching down to find a foothold on the bottom bunk, since I can't see what I am doing, and have to hope that my foot will find something solid. I manage it and, once I'm stable on the wood of the bottom bunk, the rest is easy. I go to the loo and then get out of here.

I feel a bit grim and sticky after sleeping in my clothes. But the sooner I get going, the sooner I can get to a shower. I looked at my email before leaving and the accommodation that I wanted is full. So I will get to a breakfast spot and try to book the other one in the village.

I find a bench outside next to a streetlamp and put my new coat on. Wearing something new feels really strange. I have been wearing the same things now for three weeks. It feels luxurious and very comforting to have a new coat, even if it's a hideous style and colour.

At 6.50 am, I start walking. It's pitch black but not too cold. I am on the main road, I never left it, so it's obvious which way to go. There are lots of stars this morning. At 7.15 am, the sun is round the edge of the world, not visible yet but just taking the edge off the blackness. The sky is now a very dark blue. It's a shame that I don't have my torch. I forgot to get it out of my bag and I don't want to stop now.

I am using my phone torch but, if a car goes by, I use their headlights. The cars from behind are better, the ones facing me dazzle me. I put my phone away. I go slowly if there are no cars, or even stop in case I fall or trip on a stone that I can't see. Then I move faster when the path is illuminated. I must look very strange. At 7.50 am, it's light enough to see. The sun is just coming up and I have walked 2.68 miles already.

I arrive at **Hospital de Orbigo** village now, and I see a tall, striking water tower illuminated by the sun. It looks like just the sort of place I would have liked to stop at which is a terrible shame. But this walk is full of accommodation disappointments and then little gems. You honestly can't call it. It's determined by the location and I couldn't have walked any further yesterday.

I have walked six kilometres this morning. And if I had stopped here, I probably wouldn't be stopping in Astorga tonight as it would only be 13 kilometres further on. But it is a lovely traditional village, with a very long impressive stone bridge going over the river. There isn't any water flowing under it but there must have been once. It feels very historic and so pretty with the early sun shining on it.

I want some breakfast but I pass one café thinking there might be another and there isn't. So, I sit on a bench at the end of the village and eat my peach. I take my socks off; the floor is cold but I rest them on my bag. I have to air them at every opportunity. There's a choice of paths here and it's amusing watching the interaction between people as they choose which way to go. It's a busy section.

I open Brierley and I find my schedule which I wrote last night, so I know which way I am going. The countryside route.

It's wonderful to be in the countryside again after all those roads in and out of Leon. I walk through **Villares de Orbigo**, then rough terrain of red soil and stones which look a lot like potatoes.

I go up a steep hill. I am not hill-fit at the moment or maybe I am dehydrated. I struggled to have a wee at the hostel this morning, so I need to drink more today.

I arrive at another little village, **Santibanez de Valdeiglesia**. This is what I like, another Spanish village with the church bells ringing as I get close. I have missed this. The village is so quiet, the shutters on the houses are down. I am not sure if that's because people are asleep or not at home. There's no one around, just a couple of pilgrims. There's nothing to eat here which is a shame. I find a bench at the end of the village to rest my legs and feet.

I have a long, hard walk on stones, hungry and with too many clothes on. I am struggling a bit. There are no benches as I am out in the countryside, so I sit on the edge of a ditch on the rich, red dusty soil. It's difficult to walk into the ditch with the bag on but I do it and sit down. I take my bag and socks off and eat the banana that I have been carrying. It's 11.20 am and I have walked just over ten miles on a peach. No wonder I am flaking.

I climb back out of the ditch without toppling over and, feeling refreshed, I keep walking. The red soil is very striking against the bright blue sky and, as I get to the top of the hill, I see mountains in the distance. It's good because that means I am getting nearer to Santiago but scary as I have to climb some of those mountains.

I stop again and all I can hear are the birds. It's so peaceful. In front of me is a building just off the red track. As I approach, I see a few pilgrims and heart-shaped stone patterns in the grass. There is a round table with random bowls and plates of food. This seems to be a funky, hippy, self-service pit stop, full of love and hearts. It is very welcome after the last few miles and hills. I have a watermelon slice, a few crisps, homemade lemonade and sit down on a cushion under the canopy to enjoy the food and the atmosphere. I love these random places on the Camino, they always seem to be just as you need them. Before I leave, I throw some money onto the pile of coins in the middle of the table. It's all very informal.

Further on, the countryside is flat and I am now at the top of the hill. There is a steep man-made path with a stunning view across to **Astorga** through the tree lined path.

I learn from my mistakes and try not to be so indecisive about eating places, so walk straight into a Spanish bar in **San Justo de la Vega**, without weighing up the menu, the seating arrangement, the clientele. I need to sit down soon because I can feel a blister coming and my feet are on fire. I buy a tortilla and tea and take my socks off. A few people look at me – that's the problem if you go to 'normal' eateries, it's not normal to take your shoes off as soon as you sit down but I have to, or I won't be able to walk any further.

It's 1.00 pm and I have walked just over 13 miles. I am not sure what to do now. I wanted to get to **Murias de Rechivaldo**, the other side of Astorga but it's another 3.6 kilometres. It's doable, but I will see how I feel after a break.

My feet are really sore – there's definitely a blister coming, so that decides it. I haven't washed my socks in three days which is not good. But getting them dry is very difficult, and I only have one pair that I like. Plus, I feel awful not showering yesterday and sleeping in my clothes, so it's early enough in the day for me to get some washing done and dry.

It takes ages to get to the hostel. I can see the cathedral but I have to go over a complicated rail bridge that, from a distance, looks like a rollercoaster ride at a theme park.

Why have they made it that complicated? Then a big roundabout, then a left turn when it feels like it should be right.

Finally, I arrive in beautiful **Astorga**. I walk through a square with a stunning monument at one end, old and ornate, and there are lots of cafés with outside seating and lots of trees. I love it, and already want to come back for a longer trip and I haven't even seen it all yet. I walk past a Gaudi building that I have to stop and photograph. It has pale stone with intricate windows and details everywhere. Right next to it is the cathedral. I am in sensory overload and don't know where to look.

I haven't booked anywhere as I didn't know how far I was going and the one I wanted in the next town was full, but I walk into my first choice of hostel, San Javier, that I have already researched, thrilled to find they have a bed. It's right next to the cathedral and it's very old with a wooden ceiling, wooden stairs, a split level kitchen and dining area with lots of sunken comfy seats. There's a quaint courtyard with washing dangling off a line on the first floor. I have struck lucky here. I am taken up the creaky stairs to the top floor, where there are lots of single beds and a pitched roof.

My first job is to get some washing in the machine, every second counts to get it dry. I empty my bag, put on my blue dress, and everything else goes in the wash. I have no underwear on, which is not ideal, and I have to be careful moving about, especially on the stairs. I can't walk fast or even use both feet on the stairs so it's not looking that unusual. I shower and, while I wait for the washing, I make a cup of tea with a kettle in the kitchen, then sit in the squishy area, planning tomorrow's walk and accommodation.

I love it here, it has what you would call a good vibe. I hang my washing out on the pully drying lines up in the sky before going up to relax in my room.

As soon as some underwear is dry, I go and explore and, before I know it, I am climbing 125 steps, round and round the skinny stone staircase up to the top of the cathedral tower. I take photos of the view and meet a pilgrim who started the same day as me that I haven't met before.

Then I go inside the main part of the cathedral. Well, I stand outside for a while staring at an enormous door. Door doesn't describe it, it's more of a huge entrance with an amazing stone dome over the top, with detailed carvings showing scenes from the Bible, I guess. The intricacy and detail keep me fixed to it for a while until I go inside where it's quite traditional, with some beautiful ceilings and stained glass windows, but not worth the money it cost me to get in here.

Time for something to eat. I don't feel like eating in a restaurant. I have a tiny beach dress on, which doesn't seem right for a restaurant and it's a little chilly. So I buy a microwave pasta meal and take it back to the hostel kitchen to cook. I have to find someone to tell me what to do with it, as I can't read the instructions, but it's delicious, hot and comforting.

I get most of my washing in. Some items are still at the far end of the pully system and I would have to take about ten pieces of someone else's clothing off to reach mine. Hopefully I can reach it in the morning.

There are about 26 beds in the room so there's lots of hustle and bustle. And it's an open staircase so I can hear the kitchen and smell whatever it is that someone has just burnt, but it's all good.

Day 25 Saturday 1st October

Astorga to Foncebadon
16.53 miles

In all my 24 days on the road, I have never heard such a disrespectful bunch of noisy people.

One person left very early with a quick zip of their sleeping bag and off they went. The group of Italians opposite have been packing for about half an hour and talking constantly, about what I don't know. It's only 6.10 am. They are packing huge suitcases, one has already been bumped down the 13th century stairs noisily, and they are still finishing the other. They packed last night – well, that's what I thought they were doing – so what they have left to pack and why they need a deep conversation about it is a mystery.

One person is still snoring, lucky them. There were a few snorers, which is going to happen in a room this size. There's also another ten people rustling and packing bags. It's very busy this morning. I was going to have a lie in as it's only 13 miles to walk today, hilly, but not as long as yesterday. And my feet still hurt.

The muscles on the back of my ankles hurt. I keep trying to stretch them but it's not comfortable. Plus, the blister on the ball of my right foot and the blister on my left baby toe has dried and the skin is coming away. It's not painful but it keeps catching on the paper bedsheet and I am not sure what to do. I am worried I will get a blister in the same spot, on the tender new skin.

The Italians have gone down the creaky stairs but it seems that everyone is awake now. I might just lie here. I have to go and get my washing that I couldn't reach yesterday.

I am not in a hurry.

There's no email about my accommodation in Foncebadon, so I will have to rethink. Maybe stay in **Rabanal del Camino**. Tomorrow looks very hilly and challenging, so I was thinking about going a bit further today and getting ahead of myself. I might just see how my feet are.

It's an easy walk out of town and a lovely sunrise. Quite busy with pilgrims. I arrive at the town that I couldn't get a reservation for yesterday, **Murias de Rechivaldo**, which looks nice but I still enjoyed staying in the hostel near the cathedral in **Astorga**.

I think as I walk in the dark about what to do after Santiago. Finisterre or Muxia or both? I just can't decide. I googled them yesterday and didn't get a better idea. To be honest, I don't desperately want to go to either place. Finisterre was my goal when I got on the ferry to Santander, but I am not so sure now.

Drat, I missed my turning that my piece of paper says to take. I should have turned right by now but I didn't see any signs. I can't remember why I wanted to go that way but everyone is going this way so it can't be wrong.

Now, I can see the village to the right about half a mile away, and I remember why I wanted to go there. Oh well, it's done now. You can't see everything.

It's a very long track and busy with people, a few dogs, a farmer, and several goats and sheep that walk with us. Some sheep are just behind me walking patiently, they are so fat close up. Then they run away, over onto the grass, and into a field.

Eventually, I get to a little town called **Santa Catalina de Somoza** which only has one tiny street with three cafés on it. I stop for breakfast, determined not to make the same mistake as yesterday. I have a toastie in a small but busy café. My feet are a little sore so I put a Compeed on my left foot. Now my right heel is also a bit sore.

While waiting for the toastie, I take off my coat and socks and put my headtorch away. I message Emma to say that there is vegan food here, I think she is in **Astorga** as well. I left early so she might be behind me. It's 9.15 am and I have walked over five miles. If I go as far as **Rabanal**, then I'll only have eight miles left to **Foncebadon**, but I don't have any accommodation yet.

As I walk on further, I see mountains. Which one of those have I got to climb over?

I almost fly to **El Ganso**. I don't know what was in that tea but I have been overtaking people and walking for three hours.

Up ahead, a girl is sitting on a huge stone, nursing her feet and looking through a small bag. I ask her if she is OK. Her foot looks nasty. I give her a Compeed, as she has run out. It looked so raw that I am not sure a Compeed is the answer but it should get her moving to the next village. Then I see a French couple I have seen a few times; she never says a word and he talks non-stop.

I slow down now, the blister hotspot hurting and my energy gone. But I can see **Rabanal** at the foot of the mountains. It's a tough two kilometres to the village as the ground is stony and aggravating my feet.

The path leading into the village has stone decorations laid into it, making it feel loved. It's just one street and all the buildings are stone with lots of flowers. One of those stone buildings is a tiny shop. I buy a Diet Coke, the first one I have seen, and a bag of crisps and sit in a spacious outdoor garden area opposite. It's like a little oasis, sitting under a palm tree umbrella at a table, and I take my shoes off.

But I need to make a decision and quite quickly. I am not walking up the mountain without a reservation. There's still no email so I ring some places. I need to make a quick decision now or book somewhere here. Three hostels don't answer their phones. One is full but another, thankfully, takes my booking. It's still early so it's good timing. There's another five kilometres to go up the mountain, but there's no rush.

I have a new blister, drat, that's not good. I put my sandals on instead, it's been a bit warmer today and I think the warmth in my lace ups is what has been giving me blisters. It's 1.31 pm. Off I go, this is going to be tough.

My bag is digging into my back. Rammed full with my shoes in it, they are so bulky. But I am not unpacking it. Just keep moving. Leaving the village up a gentle incline on a tree lined path, it doesn't feel like climbing a mountain. Then it goes uphill much more steeply and I have sweat on my face again; salt is dripping in my eyes. I haven't been like this in a while.

I sit down on a post to get my heartrate back to normal, it's really thumping in my chest. I have to take this seriously, there is no one around to help if I get unwell. I take my time, letting my body recover, and have a drink. I also take off my cardigan, I have way too many clothes on.

But, on the plus side, it's so peaceful here, so high up surrounded by trees and views.

I get going and soon there are nasty diagonal stones. Please don't let the path be like this all the way to **Foncebadon**. I type the hostel into Google and it says it will be 46 minutes until I get there. But does Google know the terrain that I have to walk on? Does it know that I have walked 15 miles already today? Does Google know I am tired and there are stones everywhere and I have a ten kilo-plus bag on my back *and* two blisters?

Does Google know all that?

No.

I reach another seating area that I take advantage of. I still have 36 minutes to go but I need another break, so I stay and have a drink. I will go faster after the break. I really don't want a heart attack on the side of a mountain.

Eventually, I can see the town sat on the hill and it's very exciting. I can't believe I am going to stay here.

I walk past accommodation that looks perfect with views across the hills and keep walking, until Google says I have gone too far. I am staying at the hostel that I liked the look of, Convento de Foncebadon, and get really excited once I see it. It looks great and has a restaurant, so I can eat.

I check in at the bar area and I am taken to the room which is small with three bunks, and I get a bottom bed next to a window with a ledge to put some of my stuff, and there's a toilet and shower room just for us. I lie on my bed, stretch, and breathe out, very happy. I am spending the night on the mountain.

I take a shower, wash what I am wearing, and go and hang it on the line. The washing line, if it cared, has a great view of the mountains. I go back and get my camera as it's such an amazing spot.

A little later, I take all my paperwork to the bar, get some hot water for my tea from the coffee machine, and buy some cake to justify sitting here and getting free hot water. I sit and work out where to stop tomorrow and what hostel to stay in, then write my schedule and do my three words and mileage. I love this part of the day.

Emma messages me; she is in Foncebadon as well. She says she needs to rest as her blister is huge. She also says she isn't going to Finisterre now, which is uncanny as I had decided the same thing. I have been thinking since I left the Italian church that I am going to Santiago, that will be my final destination. It's still possible I will get the bus to Finisterre, but I am definitely not walking.

I go back to the room for a bit to syringe my blister and put Betadine on it. It's 5.30 pm, and I'm thinking about looking for some food. I don't see anyone eating in the bar and the menu doesn't inspire me. So, I go and check on my washing. The bar next door looks unique and I can smell good things, so I go to the front to see if there's a menu and I see Ieuan and Karen sitting on the wall at the front. I chat with them. They are going in to eat as Ieuan went in this restaurant to eat eight years ago and loved it. He has been looking forward to returning.

The bar opens in ten minutes. Before I know it, I have joined them for dinner at a table for three. I only went to check my washing. Luckily, I carry my purse around with me all the time in my nylon bag.

It's a very unique place, with stone walls, and wooden tables and chairs. There is absolutely nothing modern here. It is like stepping back in time, apparently medieval times. The staff are wearing long dresses in autumn colours. I love it and I can see why Ieuan wanted to come back here and share it with his mum. It also smells great, my tummy is rumbling in anticipation.

We get seated at a heavy wooden table next to a dresser that has drinking vessels which look like animal horns. It's not a place for vegetarians but I am going with the flow, sitting in a beautiful restaurant on the side of a mountain. The food is amazing, just as I knew it would be. I have sea bass and it's cooked to perfection. Two hours later, after a lovely meal and good company with Karen and Ieuan, we leave and I go and get my washing in.

Back to the room and it's full and loud, being so small. Then the Italian people return and pull all the shutters down without asking, which causes friction. One lady is wandering around in her knickers and they turn the light out when it suits them without asking.

Oh well. I am used to this random life now.

Day 26 Sunday 2nd October

Foncebadon to El Acebo
8 miles

I wake up to a lightshow of torches. I retrieve my phone from the tangle of phones and get back into bed. It's going to take me ages to pack as I have stuff everywhere. As they all seem to be in a hurry, I am going to let them all go, as usual.

I am not walking in the dark on a mountain for two reasons. Firstly, it's dangerous but I also want to see the views, especially in the morning. I want to get to Santiago but I'm not in a desperate hurry. Not today anyway, although that could change.

I also want to see how Emma is. She's having trouble with her blisters and might need some of my padding and tape. All the shutters in the bedroom are down, so I have no idea how light or dark it is outside.

Both of my trousers are still damp on the waistband. That's the first time that's happened and it was hot yesterday. I have also packed my lace ups so my bag is bulky now. I will wear my sandals because of the blister on the back of my foot.

I've found my gloves which I am happy about but they are sewn together by the washing instructions so I need scissors to separate them, and my tiny scissors are broken. I leave at 7.30 am and it's still dark outside which makes me happy as I really wanted to see the sunrise while on the mountain.

The sunrise is magical. I step out of the hostel and it's still very dark and everywhere is quiet. I still can't believe that I am on the side of a mountain. The sky is indigo blue with gold streaks across it. I walk back down the hill slightly to the open mountains and take a photo but it's nothing like the real vision in front of me. A deep line of gold and pink mixed together across the horizon. With nothing in the way to spoil it, just mountains.

Two pilgrims appear on the path. They must have walked up that track in the dark which is stupid. It's full of stones and dangerous in the daylight yet they have walked it in the dark, plus they have missed the views. What's the point of doing this walk in record time if you don't see any of it? I eat my banana, so that I can put my headtorch on and hold my poles to walk out of town. I keep stopping to look at the sunrise behind me, it's changing every time I glance back. I can see the glow of the sun on the footpath in front of me.

I really wanted to walk up here on the mountains to a sunrise and it's happening. I turn around again and take in the beauty of it, and I feel emotional with tears welling in my eyes. I suddenly feel really happy and content, totally at peace with myself and my surroundings. I got what I wanted, a sunrise on a beautiful mountain, and I feel so privileged. I don't always get what I want in life. Who does? But, today, I am not only lucky enough to be walking on a mountain, early in the morning and experiencing the silence and peace, but I get this beautiful sunrise. I let the tears fall, as I stare at the view and watch the colours change across the sky, a display of nature at its very best, just for me, as I see no one else around. It's good to feel emotional, it's good to be touched by something. I am in a really good, happy place. I appreciate how lucky I am to be here.

I hear the tinkle of cattle bells and that's all the noise that I can hear. It's simply beautiful and serene and so unlike normal life. It's a real treat. I can see tiny clusters of lights in tiny villages far away on the mountains. When I turn to carry on, I can feel the sun on my back, strong and warm like protection, warmth, and love. I can't describe it, it's almost spiritual.

Round the corner soon will be Cruz de Ferro. It's a highlight of the trip for some people as it's a place to lay a stone from home with all the others and take a moment. I don't know where this tower is but it's not far away. I was hoping to be there for the sunrise as it is a special place. But I am happy seeing the sunset on my own.

A few people walk past but no one chats. It's not a time to chat.

I walk on, following the path and I see the spike of **Cruz de Ferro**. It's on the other side of the mountain and so I am happy with my decision not to have rushed here and to just enjoy the sunrise as it happened. Everyone is little silhouettes next to the tall spike against the pale pink sky. There are lots of people here and the path is by a road, which is not what I was expecting at all.

I see Emma putting her stone down that she brought from England from her grandson and I stop for a moment. She has been carrying that stone, wanting to lay it here, the whole way from St Jean. I feel emotional for her.

By the time I get there, Emma has just got down from the stones and Ieuan and Karen are here as well. Emma takes a photo of me with the spike in the background and I quickly take my glasses off as 'I am vain'. We both laugh. I have my stripey trousers that get mistaken for pyjamas, my new teal coloured pac-a-mac coat, my flowery sun hat with a headtorch attached, and sandals – and I am 'so vain' that I want to take my glasses off.

Cruz de Ferro is not quite the place I thought it would be. But there's certainly a whole lot of love here. When I go up and take a look, there are millions of stones with messages on them. Lots of names, words, different languages, dates, some brightly coloured, some just stones. It's quite moving.

I walk with Emma and pass a random caravan serving drinks on the edge of the mountain but we move on. The scenery is stunning again. We are 1500 metres up and it's similar to the Pyrenees, although these mountains seem greener, as if they have been covered in a green fluffy blanket, and they feel closer to us, almost as if you could touch them. The Pyrenees felt bigger, taller and more mountainous. This feels softer.

We get to **Manjarin**. We both read in the Brierley book last night that this village has a population of one, and we see him. He has a unique ramshackle house and he calls out, '*Buen Camino*!' and rings his bell as we pass. What a character.

There are seriously nasty stones here that we have to deal with and must concentrate so we don't lose our footing, and we both have blisters. I am melting in my coat and we are both hungry, so we stop by a tree, sit on a stone and eat vegan cake the lady gave Emma at her hostel, and some biscuits that I had with me which, luckily, are vegan too.

I syringe my blister, squirt the liquid in the hedge and say, 'What has my life come to?' and we both laugh. I can't believe how much fluid is in it. I cover the blister in brown liquid, pack my coat away and we move on.

I am walking so slowly and Emma has a good pace going despite her blisters, and so she walks on. Now I don't have to worry about delaying her. Every so often, I just stop and take another photo and listen to the silence. Lots of people walk by and I have to keep moving to one side. Nick calls out to me from behind as he recognises my trousers which is funny. I see René as well. It's lovely to see so many familiar faces.

I plod on very, very slowly. Time is irrelevant now. A few days ago I was so anxious to get to Santiago to see how it feels to take my bag off for good, to stop walking and go home for a cuppa and real food. But today, even though I had a plan to take me to the other side of **Molinaseca**, I know I am not going to get there and that's OK. I am OK with doing this at a different pace. Suddenly, I am not in a hurry. I will get there when I get there. I have no idea what has shifted in me. My ferry home is not for three weeks, so I have as long as I need.

I feel happy, almost, about the blisters – not the pain, but the slowing down. I think part of me is walking slow because I don't want to leave the mountain. It's stunning up here, surrounded by beauty, and music, as two Italian lads walk by singing.

After about a kilometre of rough stones, which are hard on my feet and mind, I see a tiny village and I want to get to it. I sit on a stone plinth and take off my cardigan without taking off the backpack which is not an easy thing to do. Then I continue on the nasty stones. Ieuan and Karen go by, they are taking it steady too.

I am genuinely a bit scared now. It's much steeper than I would like and there are lots of loose rocks. I walk incredibly slowly, watching every single step. I don't want to twist or break an ankle.

Eventually, I can see the little hillside village which has black roofs. Emma is sitting on a bench overlooking the village chatting to people. I sit down for a bit and we decide, if there is a bed here, we will stop. Both of us are in pain and we need to sort our blisters out.

We walk the last little bit into this adorable little village. The street is thin and the houses are built of stone with wooden balconies. For some reason, it reminds me of a wild west film – I think it's the age and the wood. There are a lot of cafés and accommodation, it's quite busy for a tiny hilltop village that you can barely see until you are here.

We arrive at a hostel and both like the look of it: Meson El Acebo. It looks like all the other buildings in the street, stone walls and a wooden balcony on the first floor with flowers and, luckily, they have beds for us.

We are the first to arrive, meaning we can pick any bed we like in the big room. Emma picks a top bunk as she can see the mountains and that glorious view from the bed. I go for a bottom on the other side of the room, although I do consider a top bunk, briefly, as it is a good view.

I stretch and breathe out before dragging myself into the shower, where I drain my blisters again and cover them in brown stuff. Afterwards, I hang my washing out in the large back garden full of chairs, tables and umbrellas, and the most gorgeous view of the mountains. I get some hot water for my tea from the coffee machine. The member of staff working there isn't very amused, so I leave 50 cents on the counter which cheers him up slightly.

I go and settle myself in the garden with Brierley and sit looking at the mountains.

I am so happy that I got blisters because I have ended up here. It's lovely to spend another night on the side of the same mountain. The sun is shining so strongly that I have to move tables or I will burn. I would never have stopped here if it weren't for the pain. We only walked eight miles. I have been doing 15 or 20 miles a day.

I don't regret having walked some of the way very fast. Those 19-mile days were more than walking, they were pushing myself. At 57, to start pushing yourself physically is possibly stupid, but I only did it when I felt I could cope. I am proud of myself, walking 16 miles in one day, then three days in a row of 19 miles, and finally a day of eight miles today, so I did listen to my body and rested when I needed to.

I could have walked to the next village today, but why? This albergue is lovely, with the garden overlooking the mountains. I would never have visited this unique village, if it wasn't on the Camino, and I wouldn't have stayed here if it wasn't for the blisters. It's not every day that you get to stay in a mountainside village for €10.00 and, because we are here early, we can really unwind and make the most of it.

I don't even want to plan tomorrow's route. I will end up where I end up. The long schedule that I wrote a few days ago had me arriving in Santiago on Tuesday 11th. That's not going to happen now. But it's OK. I was in such a huge hurry to get this done. Now I am not in a hurry and I don't know why. I also don't want to go to Finisterre at all. My end goal now is Santiago. That's why my feet were washed and blessed, because I am walking to Santiago.

I do want that cup of tea out of my own cup, and my own bed and some English food, especially some vegetables. But I am also enjoying the weather and the new relaxed state. It's roughly ten days left now. I need to enjoy every one of them, as I am never doing this again. Ever.

It's hot in the garden, even in the shade, so I decide to go and explore the village, if my feet will allow me. It doesn't take long to walk around, it's very small and so photogenic. I take lots of pictures. It's quiet at the moment, with not many pilgrims walking through.

I wander up and down the street and nearly go for a drink with a lady pilgrim I met in the street but I want to get back. I sit in the garden with an ice cream and make some sort of plan for tomorrow. It's a vague plan depending on my feet. I drain them again and then go out to see Emma, who is talking to a friend on the seats in front of the hostel, in the tiny street. I recognise him and it takes a while for the penny to drop. He was in the church with the candlelit dinner. He is much quieter when he's not around Italians which is interesting. I often noticed when Italians get together, they get much louder.

We decide to eat at the albergue. There's not much choice for a vegetarian but, luckily, they have Emma's pizza as it's the only thing she wanted. I go for the pilgrim's meal, a bean soup, which is delicious, full of runner beans (which I love) and it feels very nutritious, before tucking into a vegetable stir fry, full of soggy asparagus and strange pickled mushrooms. It's interesting. I don't like the look of the dessert so I ask for a banana to take away. The waiter seems a little surprised but brings me one on a plate. I don't think he understood.

I go up to my room and I am ready for bed. I feel completely relaxed and tired. I drain the blister again and pack my bag. Out of the bedroom window is the most vivid sunset, streaks of red and gold across the sky behind the mountains. I have seen the sun rise and the sun set on this mountain today. What an absolute treat.

I have been seriously thinking about leaving my lace ups behind. I think they are what has caused my new set of blisters. It's a big decision and I will see how I feel about it in the morning.

Everyone is in bed by 8.30 pm and quiet. I am still on my phone but everyone else is asleep.

Day 27 Monday 3rd October

El Acebo to Ponferrada
10 miles

There was no major snoring or fuss and I slept well. I had a blanket over my sleeping bag so I was very snuggly. My blister has not completely re-filled so I am going to leave it alone. Every time I put the syringe in it, I risk getting an infection.

Shall I leave my shoes? I am feeling anxious about leaving them. We have such a small selection of clothes and belongings that leaving something behind seems out of balance. I am quite attached to them, but they have given me blisters and I was probably going to leave them at the end, which is about ten days away. I can wear socks with sandals.

Ooh, it's scary. Shall I? Shan't I?

It will make my bag lighter, not bulky with shoes. I think it's the right decision. I am not the first person to leave shoes behind. But, if it rains, I will need them. I take a photo of them and leave them on the tiled floor. They look so sad and abandoned. Gosh, it's just a pair of shoes. I walk away.

Emma and I are out walking by 8.00 am. We travel by road for the first bit which is so much easier than all those rocks. Not one car passes us. A little while later though, we're back onto walking over stones.

We arrive in **Riego de Ambros**, another tiny hilltop village and out comes the camera. A caravan appears on the left, selling vegan food. We haven't had any breakfast. We consider walking on as we aren't getting very far these days but it's just too tempting. We both order avocado on toast and I get a proper cup of tea, real tea leaves and oat milk in a mug. I am so happy. This mountain keeps surprising me. It has given me so much and made me slow down. Even this morning, I was considering a 30 kilometre day, mainly because accommodation is sketchy after Ponferrada, but I went with the flow and sat down for breakfast. Thinking about it, 30 kilometres was never actually going to happen leaving at 8.00 am with a blister, even if it's a well behaved blister.

We rest on the furniture made out of palettes with bright orange cushions. Everything about this place has such a great atmosphere. The man in the caravan is chilled even though he is cooking so many things and the coffee machine is not working. Lots of people come and go and the food is amazing. There are even donkeys to look at which are noisy as he needs to feed them.

Further on in the village, a Spanish man shows us a really old house with dates on it, then advises us to watch our feet and not the scenery as we walk down to the next bit. We have heard stories of broken ankles, so we will be careful.

On the walk down, I feel cheerful. Even the rocks aren't bothering me, they are part of the journey and they will end. When they do end, we are back down to normal level and off the mountain, so I am in no hurry. This is my favourite mountain ever. I have never had a favourite mountain before; I actually don't usually like mountains but I love this one.

I seem to have found a new calmness and feeling of fulfilment.

We are at the bottom of the hill now and have reached **Molinaseca**. There's another stone bridge to cross to get to the village. There are cafés along the edge of the river and it even has a tiny flow of water.

The village has one long, narrow street with the familiar looking balconies but it's slightly bigger and has lost the intimate feel of the last two hilltop villages. It has some very skinny alleyways leading to the next street. I can only just get through them with my backpack on. I didn't need to go through them but wanted to see if I fit. I wonder what their story is and why they are so skinny?

We stop for a drink in the main street. The man working here doesn't seem that bothered about serving us but that's OK, it's relaxed here. I drain my blister discreetly and squirt it under the table which is totally gross but I live in a parallel universe now where that feels totally acceptable. I put iodine on it and it stings.

Once we walk out of the village, the pain is really bad. Emma insists that I stop and put some wadding on and tape it. I do and it feels much more comfortable. The pain fades away. Then we walk on a long, straight modern road, a complete contrast to the last few days; modern houses that smell of money, a bit pretentious compared to all the humble, old buildings we have seen.

At the option whether to go through the town or the country, I sit down for a minute and sort my wadding out, as it has moved, and Emma gives me some longer bits of tape. The last bit into town is a struggle. We are both tired and hungry and Emma's feet are hurting as well. Mine aren't too bad at the moment, compared to what they were, but it would be good to sit down.

We reach the medieval bit of Ponferrada where the castle is huge and looks like a fairy tale drawing. We sit by the castle and think about what to do. It's 2.30 pm and I am so tempted to move on. There are three more towns at two kilometre intervals, but they don't have many beds. This is where I was going to stop at the *donavito*, San Nicolas de Flue, rather than staying on the mountain last night. I think it's too sketchy walking any further with my feet as they are. So, we both walk over to the hostel that I was going to stay in last night.

It's the right decision: a lovely hostel with a huge outdoor space with tables, grass and flowers. It has 174 beds and we are in a women's room of six. Emma very kindly lets me have the bottom bunk.

I work on my stretches. I usually shower straight away but there's a queue, so I make a cup of tea, happy to see that there's a kettle. Even Emma gets excited for me if she sees a kettle now. I take my green tea outside to the grass area and rest for a bit. I need to decide whether to go inside the castle or not. And what I am going to do for food.

I decide to walk into town, past the huge dominating castle and into the old town, which is very peaceful. There's no one about, as it's siesta time. I can't decide whether to go to the castle or not. I'm not that bothered, I am hungry mostly but several restaurants are shut. My feet are hurting again, the blister has filled up, so I decide to go to the supermarket that I passed. I catch a glimpse of the new, slimmer me in a shop window which makes me very happy. I have been the same weight for ages, and constantly trying to lose half a stone or more. My reflection tells me I am slimmer which is great.

The supermarket is quite sparse and I wander around trying to make a decision. I buy savoury biscuits, a tomato, banana, cheese, orange Fanta, Pot Noodle and a packet of chocolate wafers. Back at the hostel, I make some miso soup. I take the sachet out of the Pot Noodle though as I am not sure what flavour it is and add the soup instead. It's yummy, the noodles really hit the spot.

This is a lovely hostel with a nice atmosphere. In the big outdoor area, lots of people are chilling on the grass or benches, seats, and at tables. I spend some time out in the garden writing a new long range schedule, knowing I could finish the Camino in nine days. I also book tomorrow's hostel in **Villafranca del Bierzo**.

I might leave earlier tomorrow. I have not done an early start for a while and it's mainly roads leaving Ponferrada so it's safe. It would be good to have some free time in the next hostel to wander around.

Day 28 Tuesday 4th October

Ponferrada to Villafranca del Bierzo
16.90 miles

That was a terrible night's sleep. There are only six of us but one lady isn't well and should really be in a single room, and one French lady had no respect for any of her roommates. She came in at about 9.00 pm and noisily packed her bag. I chose to go to sleep early, so it's not her fault. But she whispered to her friend for about an hour. She was a foot away from me, so whispering wasn't going to make her any quieter, and took a plastic bag with paperwork inside up to her bunk, rustling for a bit. She must have put all the things back in the plastic bag under her pillow as it made a noise all night. She also ended up getting annoyed because she hadn't charged her phone; there were no sockets left. Not only that, but she went to the loo at some point in the night and unplugged our phones to put hers in which is OK, we all need our phones charged, but she just made a fuss about everything, noisily.

It was all too much, with the other lady blowing her nose loudly and coughing.

I was awake at 4.38 am and got up to reach my phone thinking it was morning. But it wasn't, so I tried to go back to sleep. At 6.10 am, the noisy French lady was rustling again.

I got up, looked at Emma, and said a bit too loudly, 'Unbelievable.' Her face said she agreed. So, I got up and left, taking all my stuff to the kitchen to sort there, not the bedroom. The kitchen was very busy.

I left, getting as far as the zebra crossing about five minutes away, before realising that I didn't have my walking poles, only a banana in one hand and my headtorch in the other, with my feet still hurting. I went back to the hostel and decided to repack my bag better, as things were digging into my back. I sat in the garden area and put my socks on with gauze in them. And started again.

Now, I follow a man through town. I know my way back to the castle, but then I am not sure. But he sits down at a bar that's just opening up, where it's still dark and they are putting chairs out. It's like a ghost town, dark and quiet.

There are lights on the buildings and castle though, illuminating it which is good to see, but there's still no one around. I look at the app and see that I am slightly off the yellow line so that's why. There are still things sticking in my back but I am not stopping.

I walk through a residential area with lots of signs, out into the countryside. There's no nice sunrise today, only cold and misty instead.

I stop after 5.63 miles at Taberna Mateo in **Fuentes Nuevas** at 9.00 am. I order tea and I'm happy to discover it's proper tea leaves in a glass thing with lots of water. I eat my chocolate wafer from my bag though, as there's not much food on offer that I want.

Refreshed, I walk on. I feel so much better sitting down. You wouldn't leave your house at 6.30 am with a huge backpack on, without breakfast, and walk five miles.

It's seven kilometres to **Cacabelos**, then nine kilometres to **Villafranca.** The mountains have lost the mist and look green now. It's beginning to warm up.

Camponaraya is a busy town with a main road going through it. On a bench, on the other side of the road, is a man with no shoes rummaging in his bag for something. Another man is drinking coffee barefoot on a chair outside a café. It doesn't seem strange when you do it yourself but it is odd to look at. I see Liz at a bus stop, she is getting a bus as her back hurts.

A lot of people get buses and there are opinions about that on the Camino, strong opinions. Some people have problems with their health and simply can't walk it all, others get an injury and then can't walk the rest of the way. Some have flights booked home and need to get to Santiago on a certain date. And I ask myself, is it better to try and do this, even if you have to get the odd bus, or should you just stay home and watch TV?

Personally, I will only get on a bus if I really have to. Even if that's painful and mentally challenging. I don't want to arrive in Santiago refreshed, having sent my bag on, and travelled on buses. I want to feel like I walked the whole way. I will crawl into that square if I have to.

Now, back in the countryside, I see grape vines again. It's a lovely rural route to **Cacabelos** and it has taken me nearly five hours to do ten miles. My feet are on fire and I am worried that new blisters are forming again.

I desperately need a wee, so I stop at a bar and go to the disabled toilet as I am not going to make it downstairs. Then I order tea. I had my heart set on a salad but, instead, I eat some more chocolate wafers from my bag and put a Compeed on the toe of my right foot.

Emma walks by and sits with me for a bit before I retape my gauze and get going. I have taken my socks off and walk a few steps but the pain is bad. Admitting defeat, I reach a bench and sit down. Emma carries on as we are walking solo today. After a while, I put my socks back on and the pain is bearable again.

Out of town, there's a tough hill. I keep walking between the stony path and the tarmac, then back to the path when a car comes – anything to save the stabbing feeling of stones under my tender feet.

There's a decision to make now: travelling by road is a bit quicker, but there's also a pretty way too. I choose pretty as I am only here once. It's a slow walk, and I squeal when I step on a stone wrong. I go through the strangest little village called **Valtuille de Arriba**. It's very rural with lots of old buildings, some falling down. But the views are amazing, with fields of young grape vines, not at all like the Rioja region where they are more established. This feels like a very long walk up and down hills with lots of stones. Maybe I should have gone the other way, but I can't resist pretty.

I can see the tip of a church tower before it's quickly gone again. The village must be in the valley. So close and yet so far. My feet are burning now and I just want to sit down or get there. Emma catches me up, telling me she stopped in the veggie place. It helps to chat to her, and distract me from my feet, but each step is a struggle.

Thankfully, it's all downhill into **Villafranca**, an unusual place with the familiar old, narrow streets that we are used to, along with some shops and a river. And some big important castles and buildings.

Eventually, I get to my hostel. It's perfect and the staff make me a cup of tea while they deal with another pilgrim. I am just glad to sit down, it's 3.00 pm now. I walked almost 17 miles. The tea is very welcome. The receptionist talks to me in Spanish and asks me if I speak the language. I tell him I am trying to learn. He asks if we should continue talking in Spanish and I say yes, it's the only way I am going to learn. I understand all about the breakfast, the pay and the time to leave. But I can't actually speak back, so I really need to work on that.

The hostel is called Albergue de la Piedra, which means rock, and there is a huge piece of rock in the reception and on the landing. The building has been built with it as a feature.

The room is bright and spacious in the loft, with high ceilings, and only has seven single beds up here. I am a bit disappointed to see the lady from last night with the cough and her whispery friend but there's no sign of the noisy lady. It's a great room, with a view of the mountains out of the window.

I have a very much needed shower and wash a few clothes, but the line is full and I don't think they will dry. Instead, I chill on my bed for an hour, sorting out a possible schedule for the next day, and rest. It's going to be tough getting to **O'Cebreiro** tomorrow. I am not going to book, just see how far I get. It should all be flat before a huge hill.

After a nice rest, I go out as I want to take some photos, look around a bit and find some food. Most of the places to eat are shut and open again about 7.00 pm, so I end up back at the supermarket and buy some delicious looking bread, similar to what we had the other day with the avocado. Plus, some guacamole, cheese, a salad bowl, Fanta and apple cake before going back to the hostel kitchen. I make myself a feast. I feel full and happy and have loads left for tomorrow. I hope it's not too heavy.

I make tea in the reception with the kettle, take it all the way back to the loft, and sit on my bed under my sleeping bag and eat my apple cake. This has been a snuggly hostel. I feel very rested.

It's only 7.30 pm but I am ready for bed.

Day 29 Wednesday 5th October

Villafranca del Bierzo to O'Cebreiro
19.55 miles

The lady with the cough must be getting better. She slept much more peacefully. There was a little snoring, but I slept very well.

I wake up at 6.45 am and half the room has left already. I am nervous to see how my feet are. Ronan, who was in the bed next to me, is dressed and now chatting to me, which still, even after 28 days feels strange when I am still in bed. Life on the Camino has different boundaries and it still surprises me.

It won't be light till 8.00 am, so I go down and make a cup of tea to bring back upstairs and eat the other apple cake that I bought yesterday. I finish the crunchy tomato biscuits too, then refill my water bladder and pack my bag. I am carrying way too much food today, but at least I can stop whenever I want and have something to eat that won't be cake or tortilla. A little picnic to look forward to.

At 8.30 am, I step outside, feeling the cold on my face. I forgot to cut my gloves in half, so I still can't wear them. This is such a contrast to yesterday and my feet are cold in sandals with no socks. But I think they feel OK. I don't want to put socks on unless they get painful. I am not looking forward to the 600 metre climb, if I get that far. I guess it will be even colder up there.

There are mountains everywhere but no direct, obvious route. I walk two and a half miles on a smooth concrete floor, following the road through a mountain valley.

Pereje is a very old village, and lots of people still live here, with hanging flower baskets, outside the houses. But as I leave, there are some derelict houses, sweeping round in a curve with wooden balconies. The roofs are falling in and it all looks very sad. For some reason, these derelict houses pull at my heartstrings, and I can feel the energy of the past. I stop and look at them where, once, they would have been full of people, and now they are falling down.

I would love to step back in time and meet the community that used to live here and feel what this street was like. What did they wear? What did they look like? Where did they work? What happened and why has it all been abandoned? Surely someone owns it.

The next village is **Trabadelo**. The albergue is buzzing with people. There are cups and glasses in the bar area. I put my rucksack down outside by a chair and accidentally knock a bin lid off. I put it back but it falls off again. I grab a drink to sit outside, in the hopes of watching people going by. I did want to eat some food here but I can't really get my own bread out and spread guacamole over it. It's hardly discreet, so I eat a wafer thing instead before I get walking again. There's an awful lot of graffiti on the Camino signposts, which has annoyed me a bit. But this one says, 'Live for the moments you can't put into words.' I like this and think about that sentence as I walk. The Camino is an emotional journey which, as the writing says, you can't always put into words. It's very fitting.

A couple of miles on, I have to stop and put a plaster on.

I am wincing with pain now. I might not have put the plaster on the right spot. So, I put a sock on as it helped yesterday. If I had any style left at all, it's gone now. I am wearing sandals, with one sock on and one sock off.

It is helping a little bit but not enough, so I have to walk slowly.

I manage a pit stop in **La Portela de Valcarce** and eat bread and guacamole on a bench, next to a stone statue of a pilgrim that says Santiago is 190 miles away. I am sure the last signpost said we were closer than that.

At **Vega de Valcarce**, I visit a traditional church for a sit down. It's a very humble church with no bling and I like it. I also buy an ice cream as a treat to cool me down.

I sit on another bench to take the weight off my feet again a little further on and hear a voice I recognise; Emma is at the hostel opposite my bench. I can hear her talking to the lady who is showing her around her room. How spooky is that? She appears at her balcony, chuffed that she has a nice room and a vegan dinner later. We chat for a minute, me from the ground and her up on her balcony, and then I move on, smiling.

At **Las Herrerias**, I can't make a decision about whether to commit to going up the mountain or not, so I get a lemonade in a bar and take my socks off to have a think. I take the plaster off again and put it on differently, going up over the top of the toe. It feels much more comfortable and I decide that I am going up the mountain. It's 3.15 pm.

I see Karen and Ieuan as I pass through the village. They've had a rest day as Ieuan went up the alternative, challenging route yesterday. I follow the steep road, and go through a wooded area. It's tough and I have to keep stopping to rest. I buy a drink at **La Faba** and sit in a lovely outdoor area to drink it, really chuffed that I got this far. It took an hour and a quarter.

At 5.28 pm, I arrive at the next village, **Laguna de Castilla**, which has a smelly farm with cow pats everywhere. I keep walking uphill and eventually reach the top. I hear church bells and there are lots of people by the edge of a wall before a stunning view of the mountains. These people look like tourists, they don't look like they climbed a mountain, and then I understand. There are buses parked in a bus area. The views of the mountains are breath-taking, just rolling on and on into the distance. No wonder people come here by bus.

The village of **O'Cebreiro** is a little dream, full of round houses with slanted straw roofs that remind me of beehives. It's such a cute village and so random at the top of a mountain. But it's buzzing with people and chit chat. I try to find the *municipal.* It's 6.30 pm and I didn't make a reservation.

I can't find it. I walk around and around and ask two people. Then I see Mike from the Midlands, who I haven't seen since **Los Arcos**. I ask him where it is as I know he stays in the *municipals* and he takes me, he is going back anyway.

I am so grateful to see a friendly face and also get a room. O'Cebreiro Xunta. Without even showering, I eat some bread, sitting on my bunk bed before going out to take photos. My feet are sore and it's cobbled but I have a look round before it gets dark. I visit a shop down a steep set of steps, which has a square roof that looks like a cross between a thatched roof and an umbrella you can find on a Spanish beach. I buy some Fanta, two bananas and some biscuits, then go back to shower and climb into bed with a plan to work out what to do tomorrow. I walked nearly 20 miles again today, that's not slowing things down.

Day 30 Thursday 6th October

O'Cebreiro to Triacastela
13.91 miles

I didn't have a great sleep as the building is very cold, as you would expect on the side of a mountain, 1200 metres up.

The man who snored told me last night before he got into bed that I should push him if he snores. That's what his wife does and it works. Even with his permission, that was not something I was going to do. Can you imagine him waking up and seeing me shoving him? Although, it was kind of him to offer and I think he was genuine.

I know I live in a very strange world at the moment but that felt like a step too far. I am actually quite pleased that I do still understand some boundaries. They haven't all disappeared in St Jean, some are still intact.

Someone put medieval music through to our room but I ignore it all and try to sleep. Then the lights go on. I look at my phone and it's 8.00 am. I am supposed to be outside now. Oops. It won't take me long, just get dressed and clean my teeth.

I've decided not to go to Samos and stay in an amazing monastery, which I am slightly disappointed about because I was quite keen to go, but I have been to two monasteries now, although I wouldn't mind another one and I think Samos would be very special. It's more because it's a dangerous road, and the timings are not right. It would be a long day of walking, or two very short days, and I would arrive very late. So, I have decided to take the other route.

I am literally the last one to leave the hostel at 8.20 am. The boot shelf is empty, with just my odd walking poles left.

I stand outside, sorting myself out amongst the amazing view of fluffy clouds hovering below on the mountains. It's not as cold as I thought it would be out here, not warm but not bitter either.

The climb begins up and then steeply down, up again, down again. I am sweating already and need to stop and catch my breath. I eat a banana for energy.

I get to **Linares** where there is a huge statue of a pilgrim walking in the wind, bent over. I can't get a good photo as it's too misty but that doesn't matter. Every pilgrim passing stops to take a photo – some with more enthusiasm, climbing up so they can stand next to him.

I have walked 2.6 miles, and it's a good place to sit and eat my bread and guacamole, which is all I have eaten for a while. My last proper meal was two days ago in **El Acebo**. I need a hot meal soon. I might eat out from now on, and stop carrying food around with me. The man opposite me is spreading peanut butter from a jar onto crackers. This is obviously a good picnic spot.

I didn't make a schedule to follow today and I am missing it. I do like to know how far it is between the villages, even if I don't mind where I end up. I look on the map and nothing is more than three kilometres apart, so I relax. When I stand up to move on, my headtorch crashes to the ground in pieces. It was on the back of my bag and must have bumped off the stone wall when I sat down. That's annoying but it's my own fault.

Hospital de la Condesa is another smelly farming village with cow pats all over the ground. The path is by the road but it's beautiful countryside, with red leaves showing that autumn is on its way. A lot of time as passed and I wonder how different I will be when I get back home? I can see that I have physically changed. My trousers are almost hanging off me. Will I be different mentally too, and in what way?

I think I have realised that I can do anything. I can pull it out of the bag when I need to. I can climb that mountain, walk the last three kilometres to a hostel, even if it's slowly, I can do it. I can get to sleep in a noisy dormitory. I can walk alone for miles and miles and make lots of decisions. I am very proud of myself.

I was hoping for a café somewhere, but the next hamlet has five or so buildings and none of them are a café. Ahead is a very steep climb. I can see people up ahead and, ooh, that looks tough. I have walked five miles now and I need a proper break …

Gosh, that was so tough. It was quite short but very steep and, thankfully, there is a café at the top. I don't hesitate, just go straight in and sit down. I buy a tea and an apple cake. It's a very busy café, with plates and cups everywhere, and dirty tables. They are making some money here.

I look in Brierley and see I am at **Alto do Poio**. I start my schedule again and jot some numbers and places down. I feel refreshed and, when I am done, I take my coat off, put it away, and get going. It's warm outside with a light chill now which is perfect.

It's so peaceful up here that I sit on a stone and look at the view for a while. I will be home before I know it, so I need to keep stopping to take it all in. Mountains are not usually my thing. It's the driving on them that scares me, all those hair pin bends. I arrived up here on this mountain by walking, so it wasn't as scary.

The next village is yet another smelly one with cow pats everywhere again.

I am at **Fonfria** by 12.50 pm. I have walked 7.6 miles. There is a busy, buzzing albergue, where I am tempted to stop and get a drink, but it stinks of cows and I only had a pit stop three kilometres away. So, I walk on.

I pass a very old lady taking six chickens for a walk, guiding them with a long stick. They all seem happy.

I start the descent, happy to find it's gentle and the paths are OK. Eventually, I arrive at **Biduedo**. I was going to walk on into the village but I see a man in a café bringing out a bowl of soup. That's me sold, after eating bread and guacamole for days. When it arrives, the Galician soup is like leek and potato with white beans. It's absolutely delicious and exactly what I wanted. I enjoy every single mouthful. I will google that when I get home. It's 2.00 pm now and off I go. I have walked just over nine miles, with six kilometres left to **Triacastela**.

The descent is not especially steep, but it goes on and on and hurts my knees. My feet are pushed forward. Then I slip on a loose stone and save myself from falling with the walking poles, gosh, that was a little scary. It's so easily done. I sit on a large boulder under some trees to recover, and chill for a moment.

I feel empty of worry up here in the mountains – something changed in me in **Foncebadon**. I usually worry a lot about everything at home. My children, their lives, them driving, their work, their happiness, my car, my finances, what I eat. Now I feel distracted and don't worry about much at all. But I am also not worrying about Camino worries. I got to the hostel at 6.30 pm yesterday with no accommodation booked at the top of a mountain. I wasn't worried at all and it worked out OK.

At 3.00 pm, I am tempted to stay in an albergue in **Fillobal**. I sit on the bench next to the hostel and google it, finding it looks nice. But I really want to get to **Triacastela**. I would have to start tomorrow with this descent and I would rather get it done now.

At last, I see the village, even though it still looks so far away. It's a nice walk down though, protected by trees, so it's shaded and the ground is soft. I will be so glad when this is over.

I finally reach **Triacastela** and walk past a very busy café, where it looks like everyone has stopped for a beer. I walk on and get my accommodation list out. I have already marked a few that I liked. It's a small village and the albergues are all near each other. I will try the one I had in mind first.

I am lucky there's a bed at Albergue Complexo Xacobeo. It's on the main street and, inside the big doors, it's bright and spacious with a lot of wood and a slate floor. I go straight for a shower and when I get back to my room, five noisy Spanish people have arrived. They are sorting through their bags that they had transported but I am not judging. Much.

I go down and hang my washing out on the line in the little courtyard and make a cup of tea. Unfortunately, I break a glass in the process. If they had a kettle here, I wouldn't need to put a glass of water in the microwave.

I take my tea and packet of lemon biscuits, which are my new favourites, and sit down in the little courtyard where the washing is with all my paperwork to sort out tomorrow. I have walked almost 14 miles today. I was going to go straight through Sarria but the accommodation on the other side is a bit rural and two hostels are shut. So, I book the monastery. I have a vague plan for the rest of the Camino, meaning I should be in Santiago on the 12th October. I need to book a train to Santander but first check if I can move my ferry nearer.

Right now, I am going to look round the village, if my feet let me, and search for a meal. I find a restaurant three doors down which has the same name as the hostel. I try and sit outside but feel silly on my own. It's really busy and I feel like billy no mates , so I go back inside where there are a few people eating on their own.

I work on my Duolingo at the table but, ironically, I don't even try to speak Spanish to the waiter, they are really busy. There are piles of used plates on tables – I could give them a hand in the kitchen. I eat a proper meal of very overcooked, tough meat, chips, egg and salad. It does the trick.

Back at the hostel, I collect my washing from the courtyard and go back to my room. I manage to rearrange my ferry, bringing it a week earlier. I am not going to

Finisterre at all. My destination is Santiago and I am happy with that. I don't especially want to go to the beach and stay in a guest house, which is what I had planned. I live by the sea in Cornwall, so I would rather go home. Plus, I don't have anything to wear at the beach, I don't even have a towel. I'm happy to have brought the ferry forwards, it feels the right thing to do. It was always just a guestimate, trying to work out how long I needed.

The room is lovely and quiet until they all return, two couples and a man. The men come back first. I hear them before they arrive, chatting away. Then the ladies come back giggling, which is nice but it goes on till 10.00 pm. I have my small light on. My bed has its own light and socket. The women sit on the bed opposite me chatting, so I turn my light off as if to say it is after ten. So, they whisper for a bit instead before getting into their own beds. Not long after, the very noisy man falls asleep and starts snoring. His friend sings to try and wake him and they all laugh about his snoring. Giving it another try, he taps on the bed three times until the sleeping man wakes and stops snoring. But, as soon as the man is asleep, he starts again.

His friend falls asleep and snores as well.

Day 31 Friday 7th October

Triacastela to Sarria
12 miles

They were all up at 7.00 am, chatting away, and left at 7.35 am. I hid under covers. I can't go early as my torch is broken.

The room is quiet now that they have left. My knee is very sore, I am going to have to keep ibuprofen gel handy today. I leave my poncho behind. It's not as painful as leaving the shoes and that was the right decision, and I also throw the torch in the bin. Leaving the poncho is a gamble as it is due to rain on Tuesday but my bag will be lighter over the hills. I will have to deal with it. I have a spare day so I can hide from rain without putting dates out if I have to.

It's still dark at 8.00 am but the streetlights are on. The restaurant that I was in yesterday is open and overflowing with people drinking coffee. The tiny street widens and, at the end, the Spanish people from my room are standing in front of a sign having their photo taken. I need to look closely at the sign because it's a major junction: Somas one way, and where I am going the other.

I cross the road towards the countryside. It's very misty across the fields but not too cold. Right now, it feels like November. I step aside and let people pass by; they don't have bags so they will zoom away. My destination today is straight uphill and past the accommodation that I think Emma is staying in. The village, **Balsa**, only has about five buildings – and three are derelict – but the hostel looks nice and rural with a good vibe.

I come up against a really tough hill, stuck with the people from my room last night behind me. I can't get away from them. Chatter, chatter, chatter. These hills are brutal! I puff my way to the top and come out of woodland into an open area, finally able to see the mountains again.

My bag does feel lighter today. I don't think it's just the poncho. I hardly have any food now. Except half a pack of biscuits, sunflower seeds from Cornwall, and a plum that won't seem to ripen.

OK, I do have food. I am a squirrel and I can't help it.

Further on, I reach a flat concrete path. With the people all thinned out now, I can hear the birds, with clouds below us. A welcome bit of silence and nature again. A couple are sitting just before the path where it leads into the wooded area, rolling a joint. Quite a surprise. I smile and walk past. It's very steep downhill and I must be careful of the leaves and loose stones. In front of me, two women are hugging a tree. I think we have all gone a little loopy. I keep looking at the tiny acorn holders on the floor, thinking they look like fairy bowls, and wonder if any fairies have come out of the woods to pick some up. Maybe after 400 miles of walking day after day, you lose the plot.

I walk on.

But this isn't funny anymore, it's very steep on loose uneven ground, covered in leaves. It's also difficult walking at an angle downhill with a big backpack on. It throws you off balance and these bits are incredibly steep. I am a little scared, so take it very slowly. It's damp too and I am not enjoying this short but horrible part of my journey. Up here, I am still in the clouds, and it's misty. I feel a bit weak and wish I had a banana with me. My bag feels as though it's in a good position right now and I don't want to take it off to get my seeds.

Montan is another slightly smelly village with cow pats and old unused houses, some being modernised. It's here that I see a vending machine. It looks so out of place in this very old, traditional village amongst the farm buildings, tucked in an alcove at the end of a rendered building. Next to the vending machine is a beautiful Siamese cat sitting on a small bench. My first thought is it looks like a shopkeeper to me. I half expect it to say, 'Put your money in and take your drink.' Maybe I inhaled some of that wacky backy.

I buy a can of Kas from the cat and vending machine, which is perfect – very refreshing and sugary. Another hippy dippy food place appears just out of the village. I would go in and take a look, if I hadn't already bought a can of Kas. But it doesn't feel right, I don't know why. Maybe I have had enough joint rolling, tree hugging, hippy dippyness today.

Down again, and I can't see anything through the clouds. I don't even know where I am, as the names are not matching my schedule. I come across a gentle incline for a while, so silent and eerie. I wonder where everyone else has gone?

I go over a cute stream crossing on old stones, arriving at **Furela**. At last, a name that's on my schedule. It's still misty, I nearly missed a marker. I can't see more than 50 metres in front of me. The floor is really slippery from the mist and the cow pats. My sticks keep sliding too, which is dangerous. What a morning.

Here I am, at another dairy farm with sheep and chickens.

At last, I just about see a café in the mist. I go in and, before I know it, I have ordered meat *empanada*. Trying to stick to a vegetarian diet, that's not good. But it was either that or octopus and I am so hungry. I get a cup of black tea as well. I feel bad ordering meat, and the pastry is thick and tough, so it's not even that great. But it's food, I am hungry, and it will fill my tummy.

My tracker says I have been walking for over three hours so far. I eat up before getting back on the road. The farm smell hits me as I walk back out into fresh air.

Another village, and another dog asleep. They are not bothering me as much now, I know they are probably going to stay asleep, only their ears twitch as I walk by.

I follow a road leading into Sarria. The path is flat and I am moving at a good pace now. It's a typical busy town walking in. I stop at an old-looking mural of ancient pilgrims, pausing for a few minutes to study it. A lot of murals so far have been modern, and colourful. This one is sepia looking, not at all humorous, and it feels very real. The pilgrims are wearing capes and their faces look concerned and tired. I really like it, feeling it's a little moment to connect with the past.

I walk past Hotel Alfonso which looks so posh I bet they have fluffy white towels and ensuite bathrooms. Not to worry, I am off to spend the night in a cold monastery.

There are a few steps on the way to the hostel. I pass the huge Sarria sign and reach the monastery shortly after. Albergue Monasterio de la Magdalena is a long, humble stone building with a gorgeous stone mosaic floor leading up to the front door. The different coloured stones have created such a stunning design that it seems wrong to walk on it. After checking in, I cross an internal courtyard to a room with 17 bunk beds. Only about five people are here at the moment. I work on my stretches and shower, discovering on the way that every view from all the windows is scenic, even the bathroom, looking out across Sarria with the mountains in the background.

Afterwards, I head down to the kitchen to make tea with microwaved water and sit out at the front of the monastery on an old stone seat with lemon biscuits. It's hot outside and I need to put my sun hat on.

A little later, I wander around the town and grab some food in a vegan place. It turns out to be a health shop with a couple of tables but the food is good. I order a posh pot noodle, absolutely crammed with vitamins and flavour. Exactly what my body needs.

At 5.30 pm, I have explored everywhere that I wanted to and had dinner, so I walk back to the monastery. I get to the top of the hill and find Ieuan and Karen there, chatting to a friend. I have a quick chat with them before heading back to the monastery.

I don't need tea, so I sit in the lounge area for a while. I think I will get an early night. The dormitory has filled up, with at least ten people here now, but it's a big room, with 34 beds in total, so we are all spaced out well.

I fall asleep at 7.00 pm but get woken shortly after by church bells. The bed is uncomfortable, as the paper sheet won't stay in place, and the sleeping bag is slippery against the plastic mattress, the pillow hard, but I do get to sleep again eventually, and sleep well.

Day 32 Saturday 8th September

Sarria to Gonzar
19.44 miles

The church bells wake me in the morning and there are only three of us left. We are supposed to be out by 8.00 am, so it's panic stations to go. I put my phone on charge while I pack as I didn't want to leave my phone unattended last night.

Outside, it's like Piccadilly Circus. There are pilgrims everywhere, who must be the new batch. I am late again, as usual these days. It's been too long now getting up late in a flap with no breakfast or drink.

Everyone has tiny day bags and they all look fresh. I haven't washed my hair in days and I often forget my deodorant. I also have saggy old clothes from losing weight and toning up. But I feel proud of how far I have walked, even if I'm embarrassed by my appearance, and annoyed at the huge groups of people. It feels like I am part of a school trip. There is so much chatter that it's making me irritable.

We travel across a railway track with no barriers or anything, which doesn't seem right, but we all survive. The new people stop in huddles at the top of steep hills, so I overtake them as I have been walking for a month, now much fitter and faster, even with ten kilos on my back. I feel like I am army trained today, compared to these newbies.

I honestly didn't think I would be that bothered by new people. Brierley told us to be generous and not irritated. When I read that part in the book, I understood. But the reality is that I am tired from walking for a month.

It's also such a different atmosphere today. No one is saying, '*Buen Camino.*'

I can hear music coming from behind me. Who plays music that loudly in a wooded area? I need to sit down and let them pass. It's all too much. Every language is piercing through me, I just want silence. I want to start walking again but streams of people walk past. It's a struggle to find a gap to actually re-join the walk.

Later, I arrive at the village **Barbadelo**. The café is overflowing, with lots of people going in or leaving. The Camino shop is full of people buying new walking poles and all sorts. Just as I start to leave the edge of the village, there's a loud gunshot which makes us all jump. They must be shooting close by in the woods.

I walk for a while with a lady who says she didn't expect so many people today either. She started in St Jean as well. At least I am not alone thinking there are a lot of people. But this lady didn't do the Meseta, she got a bus which, in my opinion, is a terrible shame. I enjoyed those days, in fact the Meseta was a highlight of the trip – a unique experience to get away from regular life and be totally immersed in nature.

I have to sit down and take my coat off, as I am hot and sweaty again with too many clothes on. My bag keeps falling over, it won't stand up. I am hot and bothered and very irritated today. I need to change how I feel. I don't want to be this negative.

The next bar is packed inside and out. People are queued to get into the building, the garden full of people, and more are hanging around the entrance with *credenciales* in their hands, keen to get them stamped.

I keep going. I have walked just over three miles today. I get to a wooded area which is a little stony but has much less people here. They must have all stopped at the last bar.

I walk as fast as I can to get away from everyone. But a group of about ten have already caught up with me. They don't have big bags, so of course they were going to catch up. I let them pass to allow my blood pressure to drop. Kids, families … I hate it.

I walk with a lady from Tunbridge Wells for a while, called Jo. She is lovely and it's not her fault that I am irritated, she's just on her trip like I am. Talking to Jo actually puts me firmly in my place. These new people aren't horrible. They haven't set out to annoy me and everyone else. Individually, they are just people, enjoying their trip. It's only that they started yesterday and I started 30 days ago. I am tired and excited to fulfil the last tiny part and they are now starting a 100-kilometre walk. If I was at home, a 100-kilometre walk would be a huge challenge. But, in comparison to over 800 kilometres, it's relatively small. So, meeting Jo has put it all in perspective.

I see another café and get in a queue for the toilet, getting in everyone's way with my bag which seems huge as no one else has one this big, they all seem to have day bags. There is also a queue for food, so I will just have to walk on. Seven miles with no food is not good. It's 11.30 am now.

In the next village, **Morgade**, I see a traditional stone building with a black roof, and tables and chairs outside next to the quiet road. It looks more like the Camino pit stops, which makes me happy. I get a big cup of tea and an *empanada*. It's lovely to sit outside and chill with only the normal number of pilgrims. This café is more like it. I can relax here: eat, drink and recharge.

A lady on the next table is wearing nail polish which seems odd now. I wanted to bring mine, and now it seems utterly ludicrous. Another lady walks out of the bar with lipstick on, this is all too strange. It's the first lipstick and nail polish that I have seen since France, 30 days ago.

I realise I don't know what to do about accommodation. One man is on the phone, trying to find a bed and receives a no. I haven't booked anywhere and, if all these new people are stopping in **Portomarin**, then accommodation is going to be stretched.

After a wonderful break and a chat with an American lady, I move on, refreshed both mentally and physically. At 10.61 miles, I stop at a stone shelter to rest my feet for a moment and then get going again. The countryside is so green here and there are lots of trees lining the road. It's lovely walking with a view of **Portomarin** and all its white buildings.

I stop spontaneously at another café, ordering another delicious Kas and crisps. I am almost there but I need a cold drink and this café has a view over to **Portomarin** with a big garden. I need to savour the last of these cafés and stop when I want to, without talking myself out of it. The walk is nearly over.

It's three kilometres on the app to **Portomarin**. I find a phone number to ring about accommodation and call them as I am walking, but no one answers. **Portomarin** is the other side of a huge, white bridge. I thought the buildings would be by the river, but the edges of the river are not defined or accessible. There are lots of white buildings here that are slightly elevated.

Greeting me at the end of the bridge is a steep set of steps, about 40 in total. I climb to the top and look back at the road going over the river, it's quite impressive.

Portomarin is really quiet, most places are shut. I have a wander but there's not much happening. I sit on the wall and ring the number again. I think, if I can book accommodation in the next village then I will go for it. If I stay here, it's going to be just as busy in the morning, like it was leaving Sarria. If I get out of sync it will be much quieter. But the next village is nearly eight kilometres away and uphill. I have already walked 14 miles today. Finally, a lady answers and asks me to arrive before 5.00 pm. It's 3.15 pm now and I don't know if that's possible but I say that I will try.

The way out of **Portomarin** is unusual, going back over the river on a different bridge. By 4.10 pm, I am melting and still far away from **Gonzar**.

It's good to see some woods but it's a steep incline. It's tough but every step is one closer to Santiago, which is exciting. Eventually, I arrive at a lovely hostel: Albergue Casa Garcia. It's in a small farming village, but not like the ones I passed through yesterday with rendered buildings. This one has a small collection of traditional Galicia buildings instead. The hostel itself is charming, with round walls and a black slanted roof, and people sitting outside at tables. It's very welcoming. I am thrilled that I get to stay here in such a traditional building. I walk in through a big wooden door to a sort of interior courtyard with a mishmash slate floor and tubs of flowers, along with more tables and chairs. The walls are stone here, like the outside, and I can see the slanted roof from inside too. To my right is a small bar and the lady who I spoke to on the phone.

The bedroom is stunning. It looks like something from a design magazine with a beautiful stone wall, a tiny deep window, and another slate floor. But this is probably the original everything. The wooden bunk beds just finish off the look. I love it.

I get a bottom bunk with cotton sheets which are already on the bed and I don't have to make it. I do some stretches, then shower straight away as I have walked another 19 miles today. I can also sit on the bed without banging my head which is nice. My feet are crusty where all the blisters have been. I have to be careful not to tug on them and make them raw.

I need to do some washing; I haven't done any in the last two days as I keep arriving late at the hostels and the monastery never had a drying place.

Heading straight back to the courtyard, I keep going until I reach the dining room in hope of some food. There aren't any menus or prices but it was €10.00 to stay here, so I don't think it will be expensive. I am in the middle of nowhere and hungry, so I just have to go with it. A member of staff tells me the menu, standing there reading it off by heart, covering every option. She tells everyone the menu in this way, but it would be much more efficient to have one printed. I order salad, followed by tuna and a lemon Kas.

When my food arrives, it's a generous portion of salad that would have done me, to be honest. But out comes grilled tuna afterwards which is cooked to perfection, accompanied by soggy vegetables but that's not a surprise. The meal is finished with a piece of Santiago cake which the waitress kindly puts in tin foil for me, so that I can take it away. The meal costs €13.50, which is good value. The Wi-Fi signal is not very good here though, at the table or in the bedroom, which is frustrating.

I fall asleep at 8.00 pm and wake at 11.19 pm, thinking it's morning, so I'm very pleased that I can go back to sleep. The smell of cows here is quite strong, as if one is standing in the room. I don't know if it's real, or if I'm just imagining it. But my bed is warm and snuggly, the sheets are wonderful, so much better than my paper bed sheets last night.

Suddenly, there's a strange noise like a cow in distress which alarms me, but I soon discover it's someone snoring. Who snores like that? Thankfully, they're sleeping in the other room so they don't really disturb me anymore than that. Snoring is at a minimum in my room.

Day 33 Sunday 9th October

Gonzar to Melide
19.58 miles

At 7.30 am, the light goes on and, as usual, I let everyone leave before me. **Melide** is in mind as a destination today, but I'm not sure since it seems a bit far. Hopefully, there will be other accommodation on the way.

I slept with wet hair, so now I have a funky hairdo. Outside, it's still dark at 7.50 am, a complete contrast to yesterday and, when I start walking, there's hardly a soul about. It's just me through the woods in the dark, surrounded by a layer of clouds. My face is soon wet with sweat and it's not even 9.00 am.

I head across the top of a hill and down into a farming village. There's an impressive old piece of stone with a plaque and arrow, saying it's 78.1 kilometres to Santiago. This is getting really exciting now. I am nearly there. Every marker that I go past is literally a countdown. I look at every single one.

I pass through another farming village and watch the cattle there. A daddy bull is sorting his children out, running after them and nudging them. I stand and watch with amusement.

In **Ventas de Naron**, I visit a café in the spacious centre of the village, feeling it's time for a cup of tea and a sneaky bit of my cake from dinner last night. I order a drink and take it outside, choosing to sit at a table and discreetly open up the tin foil at the top of my bag to sneak some cake. But a huge Alsatian dog comes over and swiftly sticks his head in my bag, apparently adamant on taking it for himself. I don't know what to do – I don't understand dogs and I am scared. He is so big up close, I rarely get this close to a dog out of choice. Do I push him away? What if he bites me? Being brave, I stand up, lift the bag off the floor and put it on the chair. The dog is confused for a minute.

My heart is beating hard and I stand with my back against the café wall with my hands in the air, basically overreacting and making a fool of myself. The dog quickly gives up and starts bothering the people on the next table instead, ending up humping a man's leg. The man pushes the dog away, over and over, and I worry it might snap and bite him but it doesn't. The dog then follows a lady into the toilet. Doesn't he belong to anyone? The owner of the café comes out and shoos him away, but he only goes to the open space in the centre of the village before coming back.

I end up talking to the lady next to me who is with her husband and ask about the church here, called Capela da Magdalena, that's in Brierley. This is an important historic village and, apparently, the church has a nice stamp for our collection. But she says it's shut, which is disappointing. She tells me that she went in yesterday and there was a blind man in there, who she helped to get the right spot on his *credencial* for the stamp by steering his hand. I don't know what to say.

She isn't moving very fast, if she was here yesterday afternoon and still here in the village now. She says she was in Sarria three days ago. How can she have taken so long? She kindly gives me a couple of prayer cards that she got in the church, which I thank her for.

I get up and say, '*Buen Camino*,' to her and her husband before looking for the church. It's literally round the corner but the door is locked. It's very small, and there is a plaque on the wall saying the little chapel is made from some stones of the original 13th century hospital nearby.

By now, it's 9.30 am and I've only walked 3.5 miles so off I go, not really that chilled after my pit stop, but at least

I had a drink. I walk past some noisy kennels. A little way ahead, I hear someone say, '*Buen Camino*,' and look round to find it's Emma. I can't believe it, I thought she was about a day behind me. We talk for a little bit, but I can see she's on a mission to get some miles in – she wants to meet her nephew, Fraiser, in Santiago, which I totally understand. So, I say goodbye. It was lovely to see her though.

At the next farm village, I see people ahead, standing and looking at something. When I get there, I see it's a cow and a calf, just born, and still damp. I watch the calf try to suckle milk and it almost falls over, not quite having got its balance yet. The farmer is sitting on a stool in the doorway, simply watching too.

Further on, **Ligonde** is a tiny, quiet village and I am still in the clouds. I walk along a fairly easy path and pass Emma having coffee. She waves but I won't stop and chat, she looks tired and probably needs some 'me' time.

Another village and I can smell wood burners, then another village and I am flaking by now. I look at my app, and see it says that I am close.

I walk into **Palas de Rei** with the lad from Berlin that I slept next to at the altar. It's nice to see him again. I wish I could remember his name. He is saying he hasn't seen too many people that he knows, only two from the Italian church but they have gone on already.

At 12.45 pm. I sit down in **Palas de Rei** in an unusual area: a square with benches and a big stand-alone cover, it's quite dramatic and a little strange. This place doesn't seem to have a centre, unless this is it. There are lots of roads, making it seem like a busy working town, not a traditional one. I look at my map and app, which says I have walked 11 miles. I don't see anywhere that I want to stop and eat at which is really annoying. A lot of places are shut and one or two are right on a busy road, so I keep walking.

Eventually, at the other end of town on the way out, I find somewhere to stop – a big bakery but they only have tortilla or cake. I go for the cake, even though I already still have some in my bag. I also have a quick chat with Pat from **Roncesvalles** who I met at the pilgrim's meal. She is booking into the albergue here attached to the bakery.

I promised everyone at home that I would eat well on this trip and I haven't. I seem to stop at the wrong places where there aren't good food options. It's 15 kilometres to Melide, but there are lots of places with accommodation before if I don't want to go that far.

After my stop at the bakery, I walk through a lovely wooded area, taking it slow, enjoying the walk. Annoyingly, I pass another albergue and café with soup on the menu. I should have waited but you just don't know.

I can't see the two people who were in front of me now. Where did they go? I check my app and see that I have taken a wrong turn, probably from getting distracted taking photos in this cute village. There are these strange buildings everywhere, looking like skinny garden sheds on plinths, three feet or so off the ground. They must be for storage or something. Another café appears in front of me on the path a little further on, looking inviting. I go inside and order tomato on toast, since I know Emma eats a lot of it, and because I suddenly fancy something savoury. I pick up a Kas out of the fridge before seeing that they have freshly squeezed orange here too, so I put the Kas back. It's not cheap but I need some fruit.

I sit outside, watching the trees and the people who walk by. On the radio, Boney M. is playing 'Rivers of Babylon' in the middle of the Spanish countryside, which feels random as it pulls me straight back to England. I am lucky that I have any teeth left after the toast, but it was good and the orange juice was perfect.

I get going again and find the small road is framed with trees, and leaves scattered all over the ground. I see something in the middle of the road and, when I get closer, I see it's a baby squirrel, just sitting there looking confused. It's a dark, deep brown colour and shiny. It hops away into the hedge and up a tree.

Further still, I pass through a village that has been modernised and cross a small, old stone bridge. Then my sleeping bag falls out of its straps and swings against the back of my legs. I walk on for a while but, because of the sleeping bag, every single step is annoying.

I take the bag off and dump it on the grass, feeling miserable. I am so tired now, really tired. There aren't any seats to sit on and sort myself out here so I sit on the grass instead. My clock says it's 5.12 pm or 6.12 pm. It keeps jumping, but I think it's nearer six. I have walked 17.69 miles and I wish my hostel was just round the corner. But I haven't even booked anywhere for the night and my energy and enthusiasm have run out. I feel sad and exhausted, sitting on the grass, and nearly cave into tears. I have pushed myself too far today and haven't eaten well.

I look in Brierley at a hostel that has 150 beds in Melide, it's a *municipal*. They should have a bed which means I don't have to phone around. I type the hostel into Google Maps and it says I'm 38 minutes away. I am going to have to dig deep to walk another 38 minutes. Now I have to get my bag off the ground and back on my shoulders. This is tough. I have no choice but to keep going. It's a slow walk.

Furelos is a place with a big bridge and a small town. It's now 23 minutes to the hostel. At last, I walk through **Melide**. It's busy with roads and shops and lots of people. Eventually, I arrive at my destination, Albergue municipal Melide, completely exhausted. From the outside, it looks like an old school. The reception is unmanned until a woman turns up but she seems a bit put out. She tells me yes, there is a bed which is a relief. I pay and she gives me a receipt then gets on with her work. I ask her where to go and she says upstairs, which is really helpful.

Once I find the room, I walk around the big space rammed full of bunk beds with wooden partitions and pick a bottom one that is free. Everything is very close together and it feels claustrophobic. I do my stretches. I need to shower and eat too. But I walked another 19 miles today and can't physically walk back to the supermarket. The kitchen downstairs looked full and busy as I walked by as well. So, I stay on my bed and eat the remnants of cake that I saved from the dog and drink some water.

I don't feel right. I am so hungry and annoyed at myself. I didn't need to walk 19 miles today. Or get myself in this state. I am utterly exhausted, starving hungry, my feet hurt, and this hostel is horrible. I can't relax. And I can't shower. I definitely need one, but I can't face the wet floors. I just know how awful they will be, not to mention they are downstairs. I don't want to leave my bag unattended either. I don't want to do anything.

I eat the nuts that I bought ages ago, in that lovely hostel at the hotel on that beautiful sunny day. They are so hard that I can't eat them at all, unless I dissolve them in my mouth first to break the crunchy shell. But it's all I have.

I go to sleep in my t-shirt that I have been wearing all day, feeling awful, sweaty and miserable.

However, I wake up again at 2.15 am in the morning, not able to go back to sleep. I should never have come to this hostel. But at 6.30 pm with no reservation, it seemed the best option, even though there might have been beds in other hostels. Why didn't I ring them to find out? It would have taken me five minutes. But I didn't.

I thought I would get here, go to sleep and get going in the morning. That was the plan. I didn't anticipate not getting any sleep. There must be 80 beds in this room, squashed together. There are about ten snorers down this end of the room. But they don't all snore at the same time. They stop and start. There's the deep snore, the puffing out snorer, the almost whistly one. And it's all on and off.

Then there's everyone turning over on their plastic mattresses, rustling their sleeping bags, sometimes unzipping them. I use mine as a cover but it keeps slipping off and I have to keep getting it back. My pillow is plastic with too much air in it, so it's hard and uncomfortable.

My feet really hurt too – the balls of my feet and my toes. If I try and stretch them, they sting. I should have put some gel on for the pain. But I am not rummaging for it now. Then there's the light. Apparently, I picked the worst bed in the room, with the light from the hall shining directly onto my pillow. It switches on every time someone gets up and opens the door. With so many bladders, there's almost a continuous flow of people opening the huge sliding door and triggering it. I am also hungry and thirsty.

All in all, this has been a bad choice.

But the good news is my feet shouldn't hurt like this again, as I am doing two short walking days and a tiny walk into Santiago on Wednesday. So tomorrow, I will stop at every café that I want to and hopefully find a nice hostel for tomorrow night. And eat something good.

Day 34 Monday 10th October

Melide to A Calle
13.67 miles

That was a very bad sleep.

At 6.00 am, two Spanish men talk to each other at normal levels with no consideration. Everyone is awake now. Then bags and sleeping bags get zipped and there is rustling for the next hour. I try to go back to sleep.

I go for a wee at 7.30 am and, for some reason, there's no light on. They turned off in the room at ten, maybe by control, but haven't come back on since, only the landing light still glows.

I step outside at 8.10 am, ready to get going, only to find it's raining. That throws me. I wasn't expecting rain and I don't have my poncho anymore. I am wearing my new coat but I don't have anything to cover up my sleeping bag. So now what?

I turn back and head into the lit reception, as it's still dark outside. Lots of people are trying to put ponchos on before they step out into the rain. I take out a carrier bag and wrap my sleeping bag in it, moving my Brierley and journal to the inside of the bag. There's nothing more I can do. At least it's only 13 miles today.

I walk off into town feeling grubby, sweaty, dirty, and irritated at my bad choices. I am sad that it's raining too. I pictured these last few days sitting drinking tea in every café that I came across to make up for the ones that I walked past earlier, all because I was rushed. Now that it's raining I won't be sitting outdoors at all today.

I keep going. It's almost stopped raining now, just more misty rain here and there, but the ground is still very wet. I walk through a wooded area before the heavens open unexpectedly and, even though I am in the woods, I get soaked. But there's nothing I can do. I would get just as wet standing still as moving. My sandals are holding up though. This would be a lovely walk in the dry.

I find myself worrying about Emma; she said she was leaving early today and she will be out in this horrible weather, rushing. I hope she is OK.

Oh, my God. Oh, my God.

Oh no.

What am I going to do?

In front of me is a stream with four large rocks to cross over. It's too deep to walk through, the water would be up to my calves or higher. I would have to take my shoes off and I might cut my feet. I could cross over the rocks, but I am scared. A lad comes by and flies across – hop, hop, hop – and he's gone.

A few others take their time. I know I have to go over it, I can't stay here. What's the matter with me? I have walked almost 500 miles, over mountains and across the Meseta. I can't end my walk at a stream.

But how will I balance with this bag on my back?

The rocks are soaking wet. What if I fall? I might bang my head and crash and die. No, I don't know what to do.

But … I have to try. I need to just try.

There are four big stones and I tackle the first two carefully. They are flat-ish. Two done, but the other two are bobbly and uneven. I panic and freeze. A lovely French man comes back onto the rocks to help me, but I might drag him in too if I fall. I don't want to do that. He gives me his arm and I take it. I am still holding my walking poles too, which makes it even harder.

I reach the last stone and feel tears coming. I can't. I just can't. I let go of his arm but he doesn't leave. He holds his hand out again and I take it. I get to the other side and burst into tears of relief. Everyone is kind. One lady asks how long I have been on the Camino and I tell her 30-

something days. She understands and says, 'The way will always provide.'

I take a deep breath and sort myself out, trying to control the tears.

I say goodbye, thank the man, and walk up a path through the trees alone, still crying and feeling emotional. That was horrible and I am so glad that I got across. I didn't want to fail, and I didn't want to fall in. That took heaps of courage for me to walk across, heaps and heaps. My wet trousers are stuck to my legs, and I have no idea how my sleeping bag is doing. I have no choice but to keep walking.

The solitude helps me return to normal.

A café appears after a short while, thank goodness. I step inside to order a tea and they're very busy, obviously. I take a seat at an outdoor area with a roof, along with all the other soggy people. No one has escaped the wet.

I try to relax. It's not quite the rest I pictured, sitting outside in the sunshine, but we are all wet and it's not that bad. I message Emma to see how she is. She is literally about to take her shoes off and see if the TENA Lady pad in her shoe has held up. She had this mad idea that it would cushion her blisters and help her get to Santiago. And now, of course, it has rained. She sends a photo of her feet. It looks awful, like a bandage that has come unravelled. She assures me it's not painful, only that the TENA Lady absorbed all the water from the rain and then exploded. I can't help laughing at the photo of the burst pad and the insanity of it. She is very keen to get to Santiago and trying everything that she can think of.

I think the rain has eased now, so I will get going too. It was a good cup of tea.

I walk with Jenelle and her dad for a bit who I met in Burgos at the washing machine. They have had a tough walk but enjoyed it. The rain is still with us but very light, before it eases completely. I stop at a café in **Ribadiso** but it's the same old food, so move on. The next one, a little further on, has a better menu and I park myself in the corner where I see a plug. It's naughty but I need my phone charged, it's almost dead. I plug it in before joining the queue. One lady has ordered loads of food and takes ages to get served. It takes ages to order my food too but at least my phone is charging. The longer I stay here, the more charge I will have.

I talk to another lady in the queue who says she is in no hurry. She started in Sarria. There's a huge map on the wall of the Camino destinations and she looks genuinely shocked when I tell her I started in St Jean. She says she is staying in luxury accommodation. Last night, she stayed in a hotel with lounge areas and an ensuite. I don't know what to say. I can't remember what it feels like *not* to share a room with a bunch of strangers. Lost for words, I decide not to say much at all. Our Camino experiences couldn't be further apart.

Finally, I sit down with some lentil soup. It's perfect and very filling. I am not in a hurry, so I take my time to enjoy it. I didn't have a hot meal yesterday and this is delightfully warm and satisfying.

I put my sun hat back on. Unfortunately, it's soaking wet but I don't have anywhere to put a wet hat, so it might as well be on my head. The lady and her friend are watching me. They look at my bag as I hoick it up onto my back. I wonder, what they are thinking? Are they envious that I have walked almost 500 miles? Do they think I am crazy? Are they looking at my bag thinking, why didn't I just get it sent on and save all the fuss? Are they judging me for staying in hostels and not luxury accommodation with ensuites? I will never know.

Right now, I am super proud of myself. I look at that huge map on the wall of all the stops: Pamplona, Los Arcos, Logroño, Burgos, Sahagun, Astorga, and all the rest. I have a head full of memories. Lots and lots of memories because I walked all of that. I have faced all the challenges head-on. I got across that stream, I might have been a bit emotional but I did it. They will never know what it feels like to get offered a tomato and cry because it's the kindest thing that could have happened at that precise moment. They won't understand what it feels like to skip a shower when you really need one but you can't face going to look for it and having to use your hand towel to dry off.

They have not experienced what I have. They are doing a very different trip with their own stories and memories. But they can't possibly feel as proud as I do right now.

At 12.50 pm, I leave the café.

Arzua is a working town, with one busy road going through the centre. I walk straight through it and leave on a country path, just as the sun tries to come out. The floor is streaming wet, muddy and soggy. My feet are also soggy.

The woods here are lovely though, and I hear the birds singing. There's no one around either, I think they must have all stayed in the last town. I want to sit on a bench under a tree for a minute and soak it all in but, unfortunately, it's too wet. The markers are counting down: 38 kilometres to go now. It's difficult to process, they are such small numbers.

The lentils from my soup were great fuel, and I fly up the hill. It's very up and down which is tough. I am sweating again with my coat on but can't be bothered to take it off. I am still trying to decide where to stop. I'm pleased though – I wanted to get to the other side of Arzua, and I have.

An albergue called Haidi Place with good reviews appears on my left. A man I recognise from the last two hostels is sitting in the garden. He says he thinks there is one space left, so I knock on the door but the owner has already filled the last space. I am disappointed as I could have stopped walking now, if there was room, but when I see a dog there too, I am not that bothered.

Hopefully, I don't have to walk too far.

Eventually, I sit on a rock and get my Brierley book out to try and narrow down somewhere to ring. I need to know where I am heading as I am getting very tired now. A kind girl passing by with her friend asks how I am and I say I am OK, just looking for a bed. She says she thinks there must be space where they are both going which is 300 metres away. I had already just googled it and couldn't make up my mind, but now it seems like a great idea, plus I can follow her and her friend, meaning I can switch my brain off.

The hostel, Albergue A Ponte de Fereiros, does have a bed for me. What a result. And it has a friendly looking restaurant and a nice vibe to it. My new friends, Nathaly and Jeff, are in the same room. I am on the top bunk against the wall, with a soft, cotton sheet. I chill for a bit in my bed. I have walked 13 miles today. Afterwards, I take a shower and feel so much better, then I wash all my clothes, which is long overdue. I even get them all dried in the dryer. A lot were wet anyway from the rain.

After a bit of a rest, I go through to the restaurant at 6.00 pm to order food. There's the pilgrim's meal and it's only €10.00, but I don't want anything on it, since it's mainly chicken. I scan the QR code instead and I'm delighted to find there is a vegan burger and chips available. I can't believe it! When it comes out, it's amazing – a great burger, with lots of salad in the bun, and the best chips I have eaten in a long time.

I am very happy!

Day 35 Tuesday 11th October

A Calle to Lavacolla
13.41 miles

It's lovely to have clean clothes to start the day. It's a real boost to my mood.

I rang a hostel in Lavacolla this morning at 8.00 am and got a bed booked in exactly the place that I wanted to be, so I am very pleased. For the last stretch to Santiago, it's a choice out of a ten kilometre walk to **Pedrouzo** which is a very short day, leaving a 20 kilometre walk to Santiago, *or* what I have managed: a booking in **Lavacolla** which is perfect, as it's a longer day today, and leaves me settled for the night with ten kilometres left to reach Santiago tomorrow.

The lanes are very quiet with mist on the fields. Lots of birds are singing, which makes me even happier. I pass two nice looking eating places. One is open, and one shut. But I have only been walking for an hour so I continue.

There's a lovely smell of damp earth and trees as I tread through the woods with a spring in step. I am so close to Santiago now, closer to completing this challenge. I was always mentally up for this, but I was never sure if my 57-year-old body (that hardly does any formal exercise) would make it.

But now, I am very proud of my body. It feels as if it's separate to me. I can control my mind, or at least try. I can try and pick myself up and keep moving. I can make my body walk with pain from blisters. But my body is separate. If it collapsed, I wouldn't be able to stop it. It would do what it needed to do without my permission. If I got ill, caught a cold, had food poisoning, I couldn't have stopped that either. So, I am proud that I've kept walking without any problems.

I pass through **Salceda** and stop on a wall to change my socks because they feel scratchy. I am not sure why, but they are uncomfortable, maybe it's the washing powder. There are so many chestnuts on the ground here, there have been for ages now. I need to stop myself from picking them up. I could have filled a truckful over the last few days. I am surprised that they are not in any dishes at the cafés, chestnut soup would be delicious.

I stop at **Brea** at 9.50 am, and I have walked 3.64 miles. There's a rural eating place with umbrellas and tables out the front. I order the breakfast deal: tea, orange juice and tomato on toast. When they bring it out, it's unusual, the tomato is puréed, but it tastes good. This stop is a nice break and gives my feet a chance to air. Even bare, they still feel scratchy which I don't understand. I need to keep an eye on them. New blisters might be forming but I don't have far to go now, I can cope with anything for the last bit. After a good rest, I get some paper from the toilet and wedge it into my sandals so my feet are padded and a bit more comfy. Emma would be proud. And off I go at 10.20 am.

I walk with a man who is looking forward to celebrating his birthday in Finisterre. He walks a lot faster than me so I let him walk on. I pass a stunning mural of a shell and a pilgrim, complete with a lovely blue sky.

I arrive in **Pedrouzo**. It's not looking too exciting, simply a modern working town which seems like it could be anywhere in the world. I help a man find the *municipal,* since his phone doesn't seem to be working. I look it up online and point him in the right direction. The Camino doesn't go into this town but I want to find somewhere to eat, so I go exploring. There isn't really a centre, just a street with a few shops, opticians, a fruit shop, etc. There are no cafés that I can see either, which is a shame as I was hoping to have lunch here. Instead, I pop into a fruit shop and buy a banana, plum and satsuma. The fruit is displayed so differently to our English shops, piled high in crates, like a Mediterranean market. Happy with my little selection, I thank the shopkeeper and leave.

It's 12.00 pm and I have walked over seven miles. The markers are really important now; I catch myself looking at each one in awe, the numbers so small compared to before. I remember the one at **Roncesvalles** that said 790 kilometres to go. Now they say 18 kilometres. It's difficult to comprehend.

I talk to an Australian couple who started the same day as me, but I have never seen them before. The man says we could have been 100 metres from each other the whole time. In **Amenal**, I see a bar that looks inviting but it only sells pizza. I hesitate, not having eaten pizza in ages. But a staff member says there's another bar only 50 metres away, over the road or under the tunnel.

When I get there though, it's all a bit quiet and there's not much choice of food here either. There is a menu but it doesn't feel right so I just order a pink Schweppes, which I've never tried before, and tomato crisps. It's 1.00 pm now and I have walked 9.36 miles. I am slightly disappointed that this place is not one of the cute rural ones I have walked past already on my travels. But we are not very rural in this area anymore. I might have missed some lovely spots but I can't get too upset about it now. Emma sends me a photo of herself with Fraiser in Santiago. I am so happy to see it, happy she has got there OK and that she now has a photo of them together.

Onwards, it's a lovely walk uphill through woodland, the sun shining brilliantly through the trees. I suddenly hear a plane take off and remember that we are near an airport. I turn a corner out of woods, discovering I am right next to a major road. It feels very much like the outskirts of a city, which I find so exciting.

A lady calls out to me and points out that I have a toilet roll hanging off my foot. I look down to see the shredded paper hanging off my shoe and explain to her why it is there, as it must look very odd, and thank her. It's good to remove it and stop people staring.

Further on, **San pol** is a sweet little village with two bars. It's tempting to stop as this is probably the last cute Spanish village but I only have two kilometres to go.

I walk with a Spanish lady. Her English is worse than my Spanish but we seem to have an amusing conversation. I can tell she is frustrated. She rattles on and I understand her a little. I am so keen to learn properly now. It turns out we are booked into the same hostel, Albergue Lavacolla, a big building that looks like a large, white house with enough parking out the front for a couple of buses. The room is well spaced, with lots of nicely arranged beds, and I get a bottom bunk in the corner which is great. The shower is also wonderful. I get some washing done and hung on the line in the big garden afterwards.

Feeling refreshed, I nip over the main road to the small supermarket for a banana as my breakfast, as well as another can of Kas, bread, cheese, a tomato, crisps and cakes. All the normal things. I would love to buy something English.

And now it's time to chill. I can't believe tomorrow I'll finally be in Santiago. It doesn't feel real. I won't have to think about how far to go tomorrow, wonder how many miles, or where to sleep because I am booked into a hostel. All I have to do is walk ten kilometres and my epic 500-mile walk will come to an end.

Simple.

Well, it's not been that simple. It's been a huge challenge.

I also have more new blisters forming. I am not sure whether to stick a Compeed on the soles of both feet or just get on with it. It would give me some padding at least. I have washed my socks but they are not going to be dry. Nathaly and Jeff are in the bunks next to me and I ask if they have a photo of the stream that I struggled on. They do and send it to me.

There's an air of calm in this hostel, with lots of people chilling on their beds. I guess everyone is getting up early tomorrow. We are so close that we might as well take advantage of that and get in the queue for *Compostela* and get to Mass.

I want to experience Mass, it will be a celebration of what we have all achieved. Unlike other people, I didn't find any religion on this journey. I didn't expect to. But I am not sure why that happens to some people and not others. What I have found on this Camino is kindness: the man with the tomato, the market girl with the peaches, kindness in hostels, sharing blister plasters, advice. People are keen to help each other. The man who helped me over the rocks wanted me to get to the other side and was patient with me. It's been humbling to see such kindness in a world where we don't always get the chance. I think that's what is wrong with our society today. People do want to help each other, but it's difficult. We all move around too fast, we don't always get to know our neighbours. We don't have communities anymore.

I have mixed feelings about religion, but it is a community. If you go to a service every Sunday you are going to know your community, and you help each other out. That part of our history is disappearing. I think that people want to help out their neighbours but it's not so easy to do anymore. We throw obstacles in the way, talk ourselves out of knocking on someone's door and asking if they are OK, or simply need a pint of milk from the shop.

This Camino feels like a community. We are all doing the same walk, in our own time. But we are all pilgrims, and we help each other out where we can. We are grateful for the opportunity to help others. Here, it is easy. I think, as human beings, we are programmed to be part of a community and, here, we are given that opportunity and we embrace it.

I was going to try and be social today. I have a little, but now I am back on my bunk bed hibernating. I have packed, except for my wet clothes that I have hung round the top of my bunk. I have a carrier bag to shove them in tomorrow. So, I just brush my teeth and go to bed. It feels kind of strange. All I am doing is ten kilometres tomorrow but it feels very important. No more walking after tomorrow. I think my feet will be grateful for the rest but I am not sure how I will feel.

How is it going to feel to end, to stop walking? What will I do with all the time? I won't have any structure anymore. After 36 days of walking, it doesn't seem possible to stop.

Day 36 Wednesday 12th October

Lavacolla to Santiago
10 miles

At 6.10 am, I wake and start moving all my things to reception. There are lots of people walking about quietly in the dark. I am ready by 6.45 am, but no one has left yet. I don't have a torch, so I was hoping to follow someone.

I have a bag full of wet washing. It's a shame it didn't dry, as I will have to wash it all again. But I don't need to worry about that. I am going to **Santiago.**

I can't believe it.

I press start on my walking app for the last time.

I follow two people out of the hostel across the road onto the path. They sprint ahead but, thankfully, there are streetlights to illuminate the way. A silhouette of headtorches overtake me before quickly disappearing. I am now on my own with the cockerels and the misty villages, lit occasionally by streetlights.

I am not in a rush. I am happy to have stayed where I did last night. I want to savour it all, this is such a short distance. An important walk.

But I can't see the numbers on the markers now, it's way too dark, before I plummet into an even darker section.

Oh no. It's pitch-black and I'm walking through a wooded area. There's a small road that I am walking beside so it's easy underfoot but it's very, very dark. I wouldn't want Ciara to do this, so why am I doing it?

I switch my torch on from my phone. This was such a stupid idea.

Up ahead, I see a single torch light heading my way. Oh dear. I am so vulnerable. I have potentially put myself in danger when I am so close to the end. I unclip my camera case on the front of my strap and feel for my alarm. I haven't even thought about needing it until now, but it's been within reach the whole time.

The torch light passes me, and I breathe out. Then I feel rain. I didn't even consider that it might rain today. My sleeping bag is going to get wet again.

I see a light in the village about half a mile away, which is just enough to guide me. It's not raining now, it must have only been water from the trees earlier on.

There are no stars out, it's just very misty and cloudy. I feel safe now that I have a streetlight near me. I'm not in a village but an industrial area with a few lights. It's 7.40 am and, by now, I have walked 1.8 miles. There are a few more spits of rain and another pitch-black road coming up. A car comes by and illuminates it for me. Why isn't the sun coming up yet?

I reach another industrial area and a shop setting up for the day. At 8.00 am, I have walked three miles and not seen any pilgrims in almost an hour. I accidentally go the wrong way, ending up at a road, and use the app to get back on track. I have missed a marker in the dark and see two pilgrims at the junction where I turned wrong. They go the right way, but immediately stop in a café, so I am on my own again. At 8.15 am, I finally see a sign that I can read, as it's getting light now.

Five kilometres to go. Ooooh, gosh, I am nearly there.

I leave the tree lined path as the sky turns light grey and misty. Ahead, I see heavy traffic. It's strange to think I won't be walking out of the city, but going by public transport instead.

At 9.00 am, the mist is clearing a little but I don't think I will see the cathedral any time soon so I don't know how close I am. It's a nice walk into the city, clean with gorgeous buildings. As I get nearer, there is a steady stream of pilgrims now, tap-tap with their walking poles, some seem deep in thought, others chatting. It's a huge day for everyone.

By now, I need a wee badly and don't want to be thinking about toilets when I get to the cathedral, so I ask in an albergue if I can use the loo and they say yes. When I come out, I find a bench, take my coat off and pack it away, and have a drink. And dither. Why am I dithering? I thought I would be in a desperate hurry.

What am I putting off?

The end?

Why?

Why aren't I running?

I think I am collecting myself, preparing for the end. Probably delaying it as well. After a few minutes, I am ready to walk in properly. I am ready to walk to **Santiago** cathedral.

I see the top of the spire, high in the sky, through the narrow streets, and get choked up. Tears are forming but I swallow them away. I don't want to lose it before I get there. I feel really emotional. Because here it is, 500 miles later.

Life has allowed me to do this walk. No one at home had an emergency. No one needed me. I wasn't called back. I was able to spare six weeks to do this walk and I am so grateful.

I follow a girl with a backpack on but she goes into a shop, drat. I look at my app and get back on the path. I walk past lots of shops along the narrow streets, all selling Camino knick-knacks. I turn a corner and see Emma sitting on a wall. We didn't plan to meet and she didn't know what time I would be here. As soon as she sees me, she gets choked up too. But she sits back down without talking to me. She knows that I have to walk through the arch on my own. But it's so lovely to see her.

I have tears now, falling gently down my cheeks, as I walk through the archway into the cathedral square. I use my walking poles out of habit. I could carry them but I need to do the last bit as a pilgrim, with the poles, like I did most of the walk. I am a pilgrim and I have walked 500 miles. These are the last few footsteps.

I come out of the arch and walk into the square, a little confused for a moment. Am I here? Do I need to go down the slope in front of me? Then I turn to my left and there is the cathedral, huge and majestic, dominating the square. I am overwhelmed. Choked up, crying and emotional.

Because I did it, I got here. I walked and walked until I made it.

I take a minute to pause, acknowledge the accomplishment, and feel the emotion. I stare at the magnificent cathedral which has been my goal for over a month. It looks so solid and real. I really am here. Emma comes over, tears in her eyes as well, and hugs me. It's so good to share the moment with someone, especially Emma. It feels right. We are so proud of each other; it wasn't easy, but we fought through the difficult days and we got here.

The square is full of emotion, full of people, and so much love. I have never felt anything like this. Everywhere I look, people are staring at the cathedral as if in a daze, some in groups, some on their own. And there are lots of photos being taken. This is a crucial, important moment. You can physically feel it.

Emma takes loads of photos of me where I am beaming from ear to ear. Then she explains she has to go for a tattoo she's got booked and I try to find the Pilgrim's Office to get my *Compostela* certificate. I head down the slope, turning right into the street I need. There's a bit of confusion though. Apparently, I need to get a QR code and then a number to get in a queue. Not like they used to do it centuries ago.

Because of this, one lady loses the plot a little. She doesn't know what to do, or can't work the QR code, and tries to force her way through the security. They don't let her in. I feel for her. I hate QR codes and if you thought you would just get in a line to be given a certificate only to be faced with a system you don't like, it must a bit overwhelming. For me though, I find it's an easy, well organised system. I get to the desk, where a man fills out my certificate, and buy a cute bracelet and a tube for my certificate to go into. I head to the locker room to store my bag till I can get to my hostel. I put all my stuff in the generous locker with a €2.00 coin and walk away.

Instinctively, I look for my poles. Where are they? Oh no ... I didn't really want to keep the short pole but my son, Aidan, bought me the other one and I want to keep it. To cut a very long story short, after walking around, changing money into Euro coins, twice, then trying three times to lock the locker, and losing €8.00, I end up having to find a man for help. I eventually find my poles and lock the locker back up again.

But, oh my, that was a very stressful half hour.

I make my way to the cathedral, it's almost time for Mass.

I stand outside, confused. I thought pilgrim's Mass was for pilgrims. And, without seeming rude, some of the people in the queue don't look like pilgrims. They are all ages, shapes, and wearing normal clothes. Definitely not pilgrims.

When I get into the cathedral, it's full to bursting with people, with hardly any room to walk along the aisles. Mass is taking place right in the middle and every chair is sat on. Some people are even sitting on the columns. I suddenly feel claustrophobic and have to leave.

I message Emma to say that I am going to find a cup of tea. I am really hungry, so I go to the café by the Pilgrim's Office, so that I can watch people go by. I get my cup of tea and a tortilla. But then see a face I recognise.

Quickly, I jump off my chair, leave my bag and food, to go over to the French man that I met on the mountain below **Foncebadon**. That day, he had started walking but changed his mind and gone back to a small village because he was shattered. We had walked some distance together but separately because of the language barrier. I saw him the next morning looking refreshed again. He is on his own now and looks a bit overwhelmed. He was always on his own when I saw him and I didn't want him to walk up this street, a very important street, with his certificate in his hand and not have anyone say well done to him. I am genuinely happy to see him and to know that he has completed his walk.

I stand in front of him and say hello. I want to hug him for some reason, maybe because that's what people do when they reach Santiago. Plus, we both struggled that day on the mountain – we shared something. But, due to language barriers, we have barely said anything to each other, so a hug might be a bit too much.

'Finish!' he says proudly with a huge smile. I say well done and touch his arm. He pats me gently back and, with nothing more we can say to each other, he walks on. But I am glad that I saw him.

I return to my chair and finish my drink.

Emma joins me after her tattoo and we walk to the square together to soak up the atmosphere. We sit on the slate floor to just watch and take it all in.

It's so lovely being here in the sunshine with the beautiful blue sky. Every so often, one of us stands up to take photos for people who have just arrived. A large group sings a song and we all cheer. It's an amazing atmosphere. We see a few people we know, like Mike from the Midlands who it's great to see again, and people that Emma knows too. And, of course, even people we don't know. We watch them all, feeling their tears and emotions. It's the perfect way to spend some time.

After a while, we get hungry so find a restaurant next to the one I had my cup of tea at, and where Emma ate yesterday. We both choose the same vegan lunch: vegan burger, chips, salad and a cold glass of crisp, white wine. After not drinking for the whole walk, and not since Phil and I went out for a meal in Truro six weeks ago, it's divine. We drink the whole bottle between us, getting slightly squiffy and chatting about everything and nothing. Meeting Emma has been a blessing. We see more people we know walk by, mainly people Emma knows as she is more chatty than me. It's a perfect lunch.

Full and satisfied, we go back to the square. It's the only place we want to be and we know Karen and Ieuan are due in today too. When they arrive, we jump up to go and greet them, giving them both a hug and sit with them for a while in the middle of the square. Then it's time to go and get my bag to go to the hostel.

Sadly, it's hugely disappointing. I am on the top bunk. There's no key for the locker, and there's no kitchen as it's out of order, so I can't even make a cup of tea which I was looking forward to. I feel a little deflated. I find my lock that I brought and haven't needed yet, snap my locker shut and go for a stroll around Santiago. On the way back to my room, I cancel tomorrow night's stay here and book two nights where Emma is instead. It's slightly further out of town but she has a room to herself, and it looks like an interesting place. Plus, a room to myself sounds great, I would like my own little space.

It's strange how I suddenly don't want to be in a shared room anymore. It's like the walk is done now, and so it's behind me, almost as if I have been hanging on. In the zone while I was walking, the dorms were part of it. Now, 36 days later with the walk finished, I want some privacy.

The rest of my stay in Santiago

Thursday 13th October

I meet Emma in the square the next day. I have my rucksack with me as I am between accommodations. She kindly looks after it while I go and get a tattoo.

I walk out in slight pain. Wow. Did I really just get a tattoo at age 57?

I proudly show Emma the *Buen Camino* written on my foot, which seems very fitting, and I love it. A permanent reminder of my walk. We go for a drink with a friend of hers and eat exactly the same food in the same restaurant as yesterday. Afterwards, we sit in the square again before walking back to the hostel for the night.

Friday 14th October

It's my third, and last full day, in Santiago. I won't see Emma again, unless we catch up back in England at some point. She has been the perfect companion. We seemed to instinctively understand each other and where the boundaries were. We walked together and we walked apart, so that we both got the best out of the Camino. We laughed a lot, shared some meals and rooms, and she was great company on this long walk.

I go on a walking tour, which is good, because it gives me a real sense of Santiago and I learn some more history. Then I go into the cathedral to see the *botafumeiro*.

I am an hour early to get a good seat and take in the atmosphere here. The cathedral fills up quickly and soon it is packed, like it was the other day. But, right now, I am chilled and in a different mental space. I have had a day to unwind and got here early specifically to carry on unwinding. Jo, who I met after Sarria, is sitting behind me with her husband. It's good to see a familiar face.

Someone squeezes in next to me, so we really are packed in like sardines. It's a beautiful cathedral to look at while I wait. I am in awe of all the work that goes into a cathedral or church, especially when you consider how long ago they were built, without today's modern machinery.

I am not sure I am going to enjoy Mass, but that's not why I am here. It's the conclusion to my Camino. It feels even more important after my walking tour where the guide gave us more background information. Hundreds of years ago, the old pilgrims didn't go and get a certificate with a QR code, they came straight to the cathedral after walking for months, sometimes years. Some of them didn't make it at all and died on the way.

This service is important.

I deserve to be here. I walked 500 miles and I qualify for this seat. It's also time for some personal reflection and a beautiful place to think.

What have I just done?

What have I achieved?

How do I feel?

What am I going home to?

How will I feel about home?

Will life feel different after this Camino?

All those questions, and I am not sure of the answers.

The service begins, and it's all in Spanish so I can't understand a word. But I can feel what he is saying, the intention of his words. The importance of it.

I feel a bit of a fraud not being Catholic. It's obvious here who is and who isn't. But I am a pilgrim and I deserve to be here. I watch people go up for communion and I wish I got this. This thing called religion. It means such a lot to some people. It goes back to my thoughts about being part of a community. My own opinion about the Catholic faith aside, as it's not a positive one, I imagine that belonging to a faith must feel good. To be part of something, just like I have been part of the Camino family for the last 36 days.

The atmosphere changes and there's excitement and anticipation as men in red robes get into position and a huge one-and-a-half-metre shiny incense burner is lifted into the air. The sound of choir songs echo as this huge incense swings over our heads, at some speed, from the rope attached to the dome ceiling of this beautiful building. The smell is intense. It's quite emotional.

I watch it swing back and forth, spreading incense over us, and think back to all the pilgrims who have been here before me, for hundreds and hundreds of years. The fact that the incense was used to disguise the smell of the pilgrims' bodies is difficult to process. I almost wish I could step back in time and be here 800 years ago, meet the people who had walked without decent shoes, who had arrived in such poor health and hygiene that they needed this incense to disperse around the cathedral. What was their experience, how did they feel? I really wish that I could talk to them. I wouldn't care about the smell, I would just like to meet them.

I can feel the difference between myself and the ancient pilgrims. Me, in 2022, with a modern backpack and ECCO walking sandals, with three adjustable straps for comfort. Compeed for my blisters and syringes. Hot showers and washing machines in modern hostels and a phone to navigate my way, to book accommodation and keep in touch with people. And, while my life on the Camino is different to my life at home, it's nothing compared to what ancient pilgrims endured, the pain and the illness they suffered, sometimes death. In some ways, it's insulting to even compare what I have just done to how the pilgrims over hundreds of years suffered. The mural on the wall at Sarria comes back to me, the sepia one of 'real' pilgrims.

I am grateful for the Camino, the markers helping me find Santiago, the good health that I had before and during the Camino. But the privilege of my modern-day experience is not lost on me.

The pilgrimage in ancient times was often seen as a test of faith. It showed your devotion. Some believed they would be cleansed of their sins. This pilgrimage tested them and their faith. This is why they started their journey and why they didn't give up. It gave them the drive to get to Santiago.

I have just completed this journey without any faith. Does that mean I relied on other forces when I struggled? What were those other incentives that kept me walking? Should I be more proud of myself, as I didn't have a faith pushing me forwards? Is it more impressive that I did it without a religious incentive? Or is religion and incentive the same thing? Is it the Camino itself, the community, that's the drive?

So many questions, that is what I have got from the Camino, some I can answer and some I can't.

Before I leave the cathedral, there's one more thing to do: get in the queue to pay my respects to the grave of St James. I walk down a few steps in the centre of the cathedral, look at the coffin, take a few minutes and walk back up.

I also walk back to the Seminario Menor for the last time – a huge, majestic building overlooking Santiago with the history of teaching religion. The Santiago lanes are beginning to look familiar to me. I almost know the way back now: turn left at the vegetable shop, across the main road, down by the school and back up the steep hill to the Seminario. I feel so sad, and emotional at every turning point. I walk past a shop I recognise, for the last time. I don't want to leave Santiago, it's a very special place.

I was so adamant that I would never do the Camino again. I am too old at 57 to be repeating experiences. I have limited time to do the bucket list that I have. But the love and emotion that I have felt here has been unexpected. I now totally understand why people do the Camino again and again.

I would maybe do it differently, stopping at a few more cafés, but then that would take weeks. In all, I have loved pushing myself physically.

It's very sad to think it's all over.

Journey home

I got to the ferry terminal in Santander way too early.

It's strange seeing people getting off the ferry just as I had done six weeks ago. Six weeks, is that all? It feels like a lifetime. I can barely remember how I felt when I left England.

I definitely feel a sense of patience since starting the Camino. Sometimes I walked ten hours a day, placing one foot in front of the other, and got where I needed to go. It never felt like ten hours. It felt like I understood time, that I could tolerate time, and time would move at the rate it has always moved, and I would end up in the village that I needed to be in. Time was a comfort, a stable, secure permanent and yet fluid. Time was all I had, today, tomorrow, and yesterday. It was all time.

I spent 36 days walking and walking and walking, feeling part of something, being in nature, soaking up the sun on my skin, the sweat dripping down my back, the hunger in my tummy and the pain in my feet. All the time, the days slipped away and I arrived at a hostel. The passing of time was my constant companion. I didn't fear it, I didn't hate it, it just was. And now I feel the same. I will sleep on the ferry. I will wake up, and time will pass, and the ferry will dock.

I have spent so much time with myself, long days with only '*Buen Camino*'s as greetings, ordering tea, and little to no conversation. Many hours walking across the Meseta, the open countryside, with all my belongings on my back. A tiny dot in a huge landscape, smaller than a grain of sand, putting one foot in front of the other and getting to my destination, with just me.

On the train journey back across the Spanish countryside, I get the strangest feelings looking out of the window. I can see the exact pieces of landscapes that I have crossed on foot, on my blistered feet. I think to myself, there are people walking out there now and you can't see them from the train window, they are much too tiny. I feel, in this moment, that my life is also very tiny. I am a tiny, minuscule speck that can't be seen. And yet, my life is important. When I return to England, to my family and friends, I won't be that tiny speck of human, walking across a huge vista, I will be important.

I like that I am both.

I have found solitude on the Camino, a place of comfort, inside my soul, a place that feels like home where I can be comfortable and at peace. Not once in the whole six weeks was I ever bored. And, if I felt alone, I challenged it, embraced it. I found my soul and sat with it, walked with it, felt comfortable, admired it and loved it.

Inwardly, I felt a peace that I have never felt before and my eyes were constantly looking at my surroundings. The vistas, the views, the landscapes, the clouds, the sunrises. Hay coloured fields to grape vines, and mountaintops to tiny Spanish villages and large cities. So many experiences and yet an inner peace. I cried over being given a tomato, I cried with frustration and sadness over being given a top bunk.

My emotions were available to feel and to experience.

I have felt such awe at myself, my own body, for walking 19 miles in a day. I felt pain. I stood in the hostel queues, with my feet feeling like great lumps of hot heavy coal, hopping from one foot to another like a bird, to relieve the pain in one foot for just five seconds. I always knew that, the next day, I would be rested, the pain would evaporate overnight, and I could start again.

I feel I need to thank and respect my body, treat it well for the rest of its life. Our life. We are one: me, my thoughts and my body. I need to fill it with nutrition, listen to it and be proud.

I am incredibly proud of myself.

I understand myself better.

Would I do it all again?

I think I might.

One week later

I am still waking up and panicking that I have overslept, and then wondering where am I walking today, or am I late? I am surprised that I still dream about the Camino, and I still walk in my dreams, to new destinations, to a new village. I suppose, after having the same routine for 36 days, it's probably not unusual.

I have forgotten how precious a cup of tea is. I thought I would treasure every cup but I have slipped back so easily and forgotten how I was always so desperate for a decent cup of tea.

I love my dressing gown, I do still appreciate that.

I have lost half a stone in weight, and I am more toned, especially in my legs, as you would expect after a 500-mile walk. Right now, my work trousers are much looser than they have ever been.

My life is indoors now. I have only been on one walk, which is such a contrast. The walk was a bit dull, if I am honest, because I knew where I was going – off to the Bissoe bike café for a cup of tea. That shows that the Camino was more than walking, it was about going somewhere new. I nearly said, '*Buen Camino*,' to someone on my walk, which felt very strange. It's different, the people on the walk are friendly, they say hello, and there were lots of families taking their kids out on their bikes. It's nice, but it's not the Camino. It's not a new path, a new destination, a new challenge.

It's not Spanish.

I went back to work and felt very detached, like my body was there but I wasn't. I walked into the kitchen where I usually cook or bake cakes, and there was a card waiting for me – welcome back – which was lovely. The kitchen and the routines were familiar but I felt one step removed. By midday, that feeling had dissolved.

I struggled to explain my trip to everyone. It wasn't a holiday, holidays are where you stay in hotels, go to the beach or go out exploring. This was a walk, an adventure and it's still difficult describing it to people now. My friends at work didn't know what questions to ask me, and I didn't know how to get across what I had experienced.

All I do know is I feel very grateful that I was able to do it.

My advice and tips

- Take John Brierley's book, *A Pilgrim's Guide to the Camino de Santiago*, with you. It's your support, your maps, your information, your distances, your hills.

- Get a good bag with lots of options for altering so that it fits well. In mine, there was a zip above my head that I learnt to put a snack, my passport and *credencial* in, meaning I could get some food without having to take my bag off. When you get to a hostel, you can also reach your passport and *credencial* without taking your bag off.

- Keep your passport and credencial in a plastic bag in case it rains, or something spills in your bag. I used the one they gave me in the Pilgrim's Office.

- Take three pairs of shoes, two for walking so you change depending where your blisters are, and flip-flops for the evening. Your feet are your priority. Without them, you can't walk.

- Get the right socks. One of mine, whilst being very expensive, was slightly too big and gave me blisters. Test them out and think about what time of year you are going.

- Take walking poles, even if you don't use them at home. I couldn't have managed without mine.

- Install the Buen Camino app and work out how to use it. It would have helped me if I had figured out how to use it beforehand.

- Don't try to do the Camino other people's way. Do it your own way.

- Stop at a café if you like the look of it and don't stress about the timings, within reason. A half hour break isn't going to throw your schedule out much.

- Use a water bladder. You are not going to want to take your bag off every time you need a drink, and you are not going to be able to reach a bottle unless your arms move differently to mine. Drinking little and often from a bladder is better. You don't have to fill it right up, you can just refill it whenever you do take your bag off.

- Make sure you have something completely different to wear in the evenings after your shower, when everything else is in the wash.

- As soon as you feel a hot spot of pain in your feet, stop. Have a look. Maybe put a bit of tape on, or a Compeed, or change your socks. If you ignore it, you will pay for it later.

- Don't take cheap blister plasters. They are OK at home but not for this level of walking.

- Air your feet at every single opportunity. Take your shoes and socks off before you get in queues for food and drink. Your feet will last longer. Also, change your socks as often as you can. Don't worry about fashion, socks and sandals are fine on the Camino. Even one sock on and one sock off is OK. Trust me :)

- Ringing to book accommodation sometimes works better at 8.00 am, once everyone has left the hostels. The albergue owners are going to be busy in the evenings.

- Gronze.com is useful to look in more detail at accommodation. Even if you are standing outside.

- Eat. Just sit down and eat.

- Once you get to the cathedral, enjoy it. Don't rush off to the Pilgrim's Office. It's only a bit of paper and you can get it later. Enjoy that special moment for as long as you want.

What I packed

(I travelled in September and October)

Osprey Tempest 30 Women's **backpack** in purple – brilliant.
Flip-flops – I was very happy to put these on at the end of each day.
ECCO **sandals** – brilliant.
Poncho – I wouldn't take a poncho again but I would take a rain cover for my bag. It was hot and I only needed to cover my bag whenever it rained.
Shorts – I wore them a lot during evenings.
Two different **tops** to wear with shorts – one would have been enough but they were incredibly light so it didn't matter.
Beach **dress** – I used my beach dress a lot to walk to the showers, when my clothes were in the wash, and to nip to the loo in the night.
Black and white **trousers** with pockets – I would take these again.
Blue stripey **trousers** – I would take these again.
Three black **tops** – I lost one of the three but, yes, I would take again.
Two pairs of **socks** – one pair was better than the other but I used both. I would probably take a third pair if I went again.
Miso **soup** – a great idea.
Selfie stick – I wouldn't take this again.
Tiny pair of **trainer socks** – I wouldn't take these again.
Black zipped **cardigan** – I didn't use this as much as I thought I would. I used my fleecy one more. I left the black one in Santander.
Two **bras** – perfect.
Three pairs of **knickers** – perfect.

Sun **hat** – I used both as a sun hat and cold weather hat. I would advise to get a non-flowery hat if wearing it in the morning with a head torch as it does look silly.
Notebook – absolutely yes. I wrote lots!
Two **pens** – I had to buy a third right at the end.
A Pilgrim's Guide to the Camino de Santiago by John Brierley – my 'bible' which I read and referred to all the time.
Thin nylon **bag** – this broke, unfortunately. It wasn't up for the job, so I would recommend taking a stronger one, but still make sure it's thin. Very useful when popping to the shops or the shower.
Water bladder – brilliant.
Two 500 ml Sistema **bottles** – I only needed one because I had the water bladder.
Pillow slip sleeping bag – I threw this away early on, as everywhere was clean and I got fresh ones every day.
Small **towel** – I would take this again.
Business cards – it might be vain but you've got to promote yourself wherever you can.
Sunglasses – of course, I would take again.
Two pairs of my regular **glasses** – I'd definitely take again.
Diary – not needed, I have no idea why I took this.
Bamboo **cup** – I used this a lot. I drink a lot of tea.
Green tea – I used as often as I could.

Packing cube:

Impulse **spray** – not really needed.
Two **masks** – I needed occasionally.
Painkillers (paracetamol, ibuprofen, naproxen) – I took way too many. I did use painkillers for my foot pain, but I didn't need to take so much.
Eye mask – I didn't need this personally, but a lot of other people used them.
Ibuprofen 10% gel – definitely recommend, I used it a lot.

Imodium – I didn't need them but I would take them again.
Two **pegs** – I did need them but then lost them so I managed without.
Multivitamins – I would take them again, although I didn't use them all.
Glasses chain – this broke but, luckily, I hung onto my glasses.

Pink nylon zip bag:

Small pouch with **earphones** – I would take again.
Camera charger – this broke and I replaced it.
Phone charger – I definitely needed this.
Adapter – I got a new two-pin one.

Wash bag (drawstring style, essential for hanging on shower doors so my toiletries didn't get wet):

Deodorant stick – it worked well.
Hand cream – I would definitely recommend.
Tiny **scissors** – these broke so I needed a stronger pair. I needed these for plaster tape and clipping toenails.
Tweezers – I would take these again.
Earbuds – handy for tickly ears and putting iodine on.
Hairbrush – of course, I would take again.
Shampoo, 35 ml – perfect.
Conditioner, 35 ml – mine broke so I managed without.
Soap in a tiny soap bag which my mum knitted me, and spare soap – perfect.
Sachet **shampoo** – I used this first.
Dental floss – definitely needed.
Carmex – I used this a lot.
Padlock – I used this once.
Nailfile – I would take this again.
Two tiny **emery boards** – perfect.
Tiny **mouthwash** – I would take this again.
Razor – I would take this again.

Eyeliner – I didn't use much but glad to have it.

Packing cube:

Toothpaste in a tiny pot with tiny toothbrush – perfect.
Day cream in a tiny pot – perfect.
Sun cream in a tiny pot – I didn't use much because I was mostly covered, but I did use this for the back of my neck.
Hair claw – I used this when I washed my hair.
Hairclips – I didn't use these but might have done.
Tiny **bulldog clips** – a daft idea.
Paperclips – what was I thinking?
Small **safety pins** – I didn't use these but they didn't take up much space.
Two **flannels** – I lost one but I was using them as cloths to wipe my face when it was hot.
Empty clip **pot** for food – I didn't use this as much as I thought I would, so I'm not sure I would take again.
Spork – very useful.
Compeed – yes, I would take again, and bought more.
Cheap **blister plasters** – useless, only take Compeed.
Normal **plasters** – no, useless.

On the outside of the bag:

Camera that could slide onto the waist strap of my bag – I would take this again.
New **zipper bag** with money and credit cards – brilliant.
Money belt with passport and money – I didn't use.
Two **walking poles** – absolutely, even odd ones are fine.
Alarm in a new front bag – comforting.

En route, I bought:

Iodine, tape and wadding. I was given a needle and syringe.

Headtorch but I broke it – I would definitely still take one, but wouldn't hang it on the outside then sit down on a stone wall. It will smash! :)
Gloves – I never used these because my scissors broke.

What I spent

The whole trip cost €1802.76.

In Spain
Accommodation – €402.50
Food in cafés, restaurants and supermarkets – €513.63
Extras (washing machines, Compeed, coat, entry to cathedrals, etc.) – €125.23
Total: €1041.36

Travel
Ferry from Plymouth to Santander – £400 (€450)
Moving ferry date – €100
San Sebastian Downtown River Hostel – £32.00 (€36.00)
Bus to San Sebastian – €8.00
Bus to Bayonne – €8.00
Bus to SJPP – €10.50
Train to Santander – €60.90
Two nights' accommodation in Santander – €92.00
Total: €761.40

St Jean Pied de Port
Accommodation – €25.00
Nutella waffle – €4.00
Supermarket shopping (long life salad, sandwich and banana) – €7.80

Day 1
Hostel **Roncesvalles**, including bed, dinner and breakfast – €31.00
Tortilla at Orisson – €5.00
Walked 16.56 miles.

Day 2
Hostel **Zubiri** – €9.00
Lemonade at the food truck – €2.00

Food and drink at the café €9.50
Walked 14.44 miles

Day 3
House accommodation at **Cizur Minor** – €23.00
Tea and cake at café – €3.50
Peach – €1.17
Walked 18.6 miles.

Day 4
Albergue Maralotz in **Cirauqui** with bed, dinner and breakfast – €31.00
Lemonade – €1.50
Salad and drink – €7.50
Walked 15.11 miles.

Day 5
Albergue Municipal San Cipriano, **Ayegui** – €11.00
Gazpacho soup – €4.00
Lunch – €10.45
Fruit – €2.67
Compeed – €18.50
Walked 12.17 miles.

Day 6
Hostel Isaac Santiago, **Los Arcos** – €8.00
Vegan cake – €3.50
Supermarket shopping (bread, cheese, tomato) – €2.60
Pharmacy – €5.35
Walked 13.13 miles.

Day 7
Hostel Andres Munoz, **Viana** – €9.50
Three lots of tapas and drinks – €18.40
Dryer – €2.00
KitKat – €1.10
Guitarist – €1.00
Walked 10.31 miles.

Day 8
Hostel La Bilbaina, **Logroño** – €15.00
Breakfast roll and tea – €2.80
Vegan lunch – €11.20
Supermarket shopping – €6.41
Walked 6.5 miles.

Day 9
Hostel Puerta de Najera, **Najera** – €15.00
Salad lunch – €6.50
Washing machine – €1.50
Supermarket shopping – €5.64
Walked 18.81 miles.

Day 10
Hostel Confradia de Santo, **Santo Domingo** – €13.00
Tea and muffin at golf course – €2.50
Tortilla – €2.00
Gazpacho – €4.00
Supermarket shopping – €5.64
Walked 14 miles.

Day 11
Hostel A Santiago, **Belorado** – €10.00
Ice cream – €1.00
Dinner – €12.00
Walked 14 miles.

Day 12
Hostel San Anton Abad, **Villafranca Montes de Oca** – €15.00
Chips – €2.50
Supermarket shopping (fruit, smoothie, risotto, cake, Kas, ice cream, Compeed, and bananas) – €15.75
Walked 8.5 miles.

Day 13
Hostel Peregrino Atapuerca, **Atpuerca** – €11.00
Tortilla and drink – €4.50
Supermarket shopping – €5.87
Walked 12 miles.

Day 14
Hostel Catedral de Burgos, **Burgos** – €23.00
Lead for camera – €12.90
Supermarket shopping – €4.91
Lemonade at bar – €2.30
Walked 13.40 miles.

Day 15 (rest day)
Hostel Catedral de Burgos, **Burgos** – €23.00
Breakfast – €3.50
Museum – €4.00
Supermarket shopping – €3.50
Cathedral – €5.00
Washer and dryer – €9.00
No official walking today.

Day 16
Hostel Alfar de Hornillos, **Hornillos** – €12.00
Dinner – €11.00
Walked 15.83 miles.

Day 17
Hostel San Nicolas, **Ermita de san Nicolas** – €15.00
Tea and cake – €4.50
Salad and drink – €6.50
Walked 19.17 miles.

Day 18
Hostel Villalcazar, **Villalcazar de Sirga** – €8.00
Tea – €1.30
Church – €1.00
Supermarket shopping – €8.30

Walked 19.89 miles.

Day 19
Hostel J de Molay, **Terradillos de Los Templarios** – €12.00
Food truck toastie and orange – €7.00
Lemonade – €2.00
Cake and crisps – €2.40
Walked 19.67 miles.

Day 20
Hostel Monasterio de Santa cruz, **Sahagun** – €6.00
Washing clothes – €3.00
Supermarket shopping – €9.24
Walked 9.02 miles.

Day 21
Hostel La Parada, **Reliegos** – €12.00
Tea – €1.30
Walked 19.61 miles.

Day 22
Hostel Globetrotter **Leon** – €16.00
Tea and *empanada* – €1.50
Vegan meal – €15.00
Cathedral – €6.00
New coat and gloves – €32.98
Supermarket shopping – €3.85
Walked 16.30 miles.

Day 23
Hostel Santa Ana, **San Martin del Camino** – €7.00
Snack at café – €4.30
Walked 14.75 miles.

Day 24
Hostel San Javier, **Astorga** – €12.00
Hippy food – €2.50

Tortilla and tea – €3.40
Washing machine – €4.00
Cathedral – €7.50
Supermarket shopping (microwave meal, chocolate, tomato, biscuits, juice, and a banana) – €8.45
Walked 16.61 miles.

Day 25
Hostel Convento de Foncebadon, **Foncebadon** – €12.00
Tea and toastie – €4.00
Crisps and coke – €3.00
Cake – €1.50
Dinner – €20.00
Walked 16.53 miles.

Day 26
Hostel Meson El Acebo, **El Acebo** – €10.00
Ice cream – €2.30
Fizzy orange – €1.80
Pilgrim meal – €12.00
Walked 8 miles.

Day 27
Hostel San Nicolas de Flue, **Ponferrada** – €7.00
Avocado toast and tea – €6.00
Supermarket shopping – €5.95
Walked 10 miles.

Day 28
Hostel Albergue de la Pierda, **Villafranca del Bierzo** – €12.00
Tea – €1.30
Tea – €1.50
Supermarket – €11.60
Walked 16.90 miles.

Day 29
Hostel O'Cebreiro Xunta, **O'Cebreiro** – €10.00

Orange juice – €1.80
Lemon Kas – €2.20
Tea – €1.30
Tienda straw shop – €3.80
Walked 19.88 miles.

Day 30
Hostel Complexo Xacobeo, **Triacastela** – €11.00
Tea and cake – €3.50
Galicia soup – €5.00
Dinner – €11.00
Walked 13.91 miles.

Day 31
Hostel Monasterio de la Magdalena, **Sarria** – €12.00
Empanada and tea – €3.70
Kas – €1.50
Vegan lunch – €14.90
Walked 12 miles.

Day 32
Hostel Casa Garcia, **Gonzar** – €10.00
Empanada and tea – €3.70
Kas and crisps – €3.50
Dinner – €13.50
Walked 19.44 miles.

Day 33
Hostel Melide Xunta, **Melide** – €8.00
Tea and cake – €3.20
Toast and orange juice – €5.40
Walked 19.88 miles.

Day 34
Hostel A Ponte de Ferreiros, **A Calle** – €15.00
Lentil soup – €5.00
Fanta – €1.90
Wash and dry – €6.50

Burger and chips – €6.50
Fanta – €1.90
Walked 13.67 miles.

Day 35
Hostel Lavacolla, **Lavacolla** – €13.00
Fruit – 75 cents.
Breakfast – €4.50
Schweppes and crisps – €3.50
Supermarket shopping – €7.50
Walked 13.41 miles.

Day 36
Hostel O Fogar De Teodormiro, **Santiago** – €19.50
Tea and tortilla – €6.70
Lunch – €12.00

Day 37
Hostel Seminario Menor, **Santiago** – €22.00
Tattoo – €50.00
Lunch – €12.00
Burger King – €7.55
Drink – €2.50

Day 38
Hostel Seminario – €22.00
Breakfast – €4.50
Knick-knacks – €26.50
Supermarket shopping (fluffy cakes, crisps, and a microwave pasta meal) – €5.00
Walking tour – €5.00

Printed in Great Britain
by Amazon

41578161R00158